# MATCH
# WITS
### WITH
# MENSA

# MATCH WITS WITH MENSA

## THE COMPLETE QUIZ BOOK

INTRODUCTION BY ISAAC ASIMOV

*Marvin Grosswirth, Dr. Abbie F. Salny, Alan Stillson, and the Members of American Mensa, Ltd.*

PERSEUS BOOKS

*Cambridge, Massachusetts*

# C O N T E N T S

❖

## THE MENSA GENIUS QUIZ BOOK   1

◆

## THE MENSA GENIUS QUIZ BOOK 2  127

◆

# THE MENSA GENIUS QUIZ-A-DAY BOOK 277

◆

# THE MENSA GENIUS A-B-C QUIZ BOOK 467

# The Fun of Answering
## by Isaac Asimov

This book contains questions—a large number of all kinds of questions.

If you just sit down and read them one after the other, I don't see how you can possibly enjoy the task. It would be as dull as reading the telephone book and would present you with fewer laughs.

No. The fun comes in trying to answer the questions on your own. The more difficult the question is to answer, the more fun it is, *provided you get the answer in the end*. (And I don't mean in the end of the book.)

In my case, however, I know that if I don't see the answer at once I am not likely to see it at all. I therefore tend to give up quickly. In so doing I know, with considerable sadness, that I have deprived myself of enormous quantities of pleasure.

For instance, I once made up a small puzzle that, I am quite confident, would stump almost anybody. It is this: "Name a common English word that contains somewhere in it, at the beginning, end, or middle, the three letters U-F-A in that order."

There is only *one* common English word (with its grammatical variations) that will answer the question. For some reason I have found that people don't get it and are forced to resign.

I asked it of a group numbering about a dozen and eleven of them gave up after five or ten minutes. They had clearly sucked the joy out of the question and were getting the bitter after-pressings of frustration. One person in the group refused to give up and was quite savage in rejecting my offer to answer the question. I had to whisper the answer to each of the other eleven, one at a time. The evening ended with my hold-out still holding out and I forgot about it. That was Friday.

Sunday morning, quite early, the telephone rang. It was my hold-out friend. He said, in a controlled and almost indifferent manner, "The word, Isaac, is 'manufacture.' "

I said, surprised, "Gee, that's right."

And, with an almost unbearably intense surge of triumph, he said, "You thought I wouldn't get it, didn't you?"

He still talks about it to this day.

I am under the impression he spent a sleepless night, a restless day, and then another sleepless night; that he puzzled and worried over that letter combination continually, that he grew drawn and haggard and faced the possibility of a miserable and lingering death through mental indigestion and then, in the end, by gnawing at the bone long enough, he found the answer and, with it, enough joy and ecstasy to make it all worthwhile.

Heavens, how I wish I were like that.

That's the kind of person this book is aimed for. There may be other kinds of joy for those of you who read this book, but surely there can be no pleasure as intense, as long-lasting, and as utterly without adverse side-effects.

What's more, let me introduce you to an allied joy, that of making up questions intended to stump your listeners. You have no idea how sweet it is to hear those magic words, "I give up." And there is the added jumping-up-and-down joy of giving them the answer and watching their faces fall. It's much better than beating them in tennis or handball, and you don't have to raise a sweat to do it.

You already have my U-F-A puzzle. Here's another. What word in the English language changes its pronunciation when it is capitalized? I won't keep you wondering in this case: Try "polish."

Here's one more. The United States contains a number of cities whose names begin with F. Which is the largest? (If you say Filadelphia, you will be shot at sunrise.) The answer is Fort Worth, Texas. If you think you would have got it, try G. I'll let you hang on that one.

Or suppose you spell out the numbers: one, two, three and so on. What is the smallest number that contains the letter "a"? You will spend some time being surprised when it turns out that the smallest number with an "a" in it is 1,000, which is one thousand. I hope you haven't answered 101 in the fallacious belief that that number is one hundred *and* one. Properly, that number is one hundred one.

Well, then, what's the smallest number that contains a "b"? The answer is 1,000,000,000, or one billion. Did you get that, too? Then try "c" and I'll let you hang on that one.

One last puzzle. There are four standard English

words that end in "dous." Two are favorable: "tremendous" and "stupendous." Two are unfavorable and the first of these is "horrendous." What is the other? No, I won't tell you.

If there's anything that heightens the fun of answering, it is the sense of competition that might be involved. In this book, you have a large series of quizzes that were given to (and answered by) a random group of Mensans. These are members of Mensa, an organization of high-IQ individuals. For some mysterious reason I am one of the two Honorary Vice-Presidents.

Compare your score with those achieved by the Mensans and show them up. (Those wise-guys think they're smart, huh?) If you do indeed beat them out, as you may well do, you might consider joining Mensa yourself.

If you fall short a bit, you might be interested in what Marvin Grosswirth has to say on how to boost your genius for puzzles. He is the very epitome of Mensan intelligence and virtue (in my opinion) and he has surveyed Mensa members to learn how they go about sharpening their wits and expanding their mental horizons.

So pass on to the book and have tons and kilotons of joy.

# This Thing Called Mensa

In 1945, two British barristers, Roland Berrill and Dr. L. L. Ware, thought it would be an interesting experiment to gather together people of exceptionally high intelligence. Mensa was founded in London that same year, and membership was—and still is—open to anyone whose score on any one of a number of recognized standard IQ tests is in the upper 2 percent of the general population. By 1961, when American Mensa was founded, the organization had already expanded to several other countries. There are now about 70,000 members worldwide, about 48,000 of whom belong to American Mensa.

*Mensa* is Latin for "table," and the name was chosen because the organization was founded as and continues to be a round-table society. The symbol suggests the coming together of equals. Because of its membership requirement, however, Mensa is often accused of elitism. In fact, it's no more "elite" than any other organization that has a requirement for membership, whether it's the American Legion, the Daughters of the American Revolution, the Actors Guild, the Authors League, or the plumbers' union. In America, there are more than 120 chapters of Mensa (called local groups), which engage in a wide variety of activities, from parties and open houses to speakers' meetings and museum trips. It is at these functions that the notion of elitism is laid to rest. As we mentioned in the introduction, Mensans come from virtually every trade, occupation, business, and profession. "If we're elitist," a national chairman once commented, "we're the most democratic elitist organization that ever existed!"

Mostly, Mensa provides an opportunity for intelligent people to meet and exchange ideas, opinions, prejudices, fears, jokes, or recipes in an atmosphere of unrestrained mindwork. The organization has a gifted children's program, a scholarship program, and the Mensa Educational and Research Foundation. There's a national magazine, local-group newsletters, and about 200 "SIGs"—Special Interest Groups—for Mensans who want to get together, by mail or in person, to share common interests.

In a sense, it's difficult to explain Mensa. At its heart, Mensa is more of a *feeling* than anything else. It's not easy to put into words. We just know that we wouldn't want to be without it.

# How to Take a Test-Any Test

If test taking makes you a little nervous, you're probably in luck. Studies have shown that a little anxiety is actually helpful. If you go into a test situation calm and completely assured, you probably won't do as well as when you are slightly concerned. Too much anxiety, on the other hand, can slow you down and interfere with your thinking.

Try to find out in advance what sort of test you're going to be taking. If it requires factual, multiple-choice answers, the best technique is a review of facts. If the test will include essay questions, you'll need to marshal your facts, organize them into a coherent whole, and practice expressing your ideas in good, clear language and in an appropriate sequence.

Also, you should determine how the test will be scored. If it's a multiple-choice test or a true-or-false test, or a mixture of the two types, and if it is scored on the basis of number of right answers only, then try guessing whenever you don't know the answer. Chances are your subconscious will be at work and will frequently offer a "hunch" about the correct answer. Even if it doesn't, what have you got to lose?

If, however, the test is scored so that you'll lose points for wrong answers, then first answer only those questions you're sure of. Then, if time permits, go over the ones you've skipped. Whether you answer any of the skipped ones depends largely on your gambling instincts.

If you're taking a test in which you're given a limited time in which to finish, first tackle the questions you can answer immediately, without taking time to think. After you've done that, go over the ones you skipped and answer those that require a brief moment of thought. Finally, do the ones you really have to ponder over.

Always review your work. People often find a careless error or two that can be immediately corrected. You may also find that you missed an important direction or instruction, for which you may be penalized.

And above all, remember to come to any test fresh, rested, and in as cheerful a mood as circumstances will allow. That alone can add 10 percent to your score.

# A Word about IQ and What It Is and Is Not

There is probably no psychological concept more used and abused than IQ. A very brief history will indicate why this is so.

Close to 100 years ago, Alfred Binet devised a series of tests to help the French government select children for classes for the retarded. He set up a series of tests, found out what ages they matched, and devised a scale based on this. If a four-year-old, for example, passed the four-year tests, he had an Intelligence Quotient of 100. This was obtained by dividing his Mental Age (M.A.) by his chronological age (C.A.). Because it was calculated MA/CA = (moving the decimal point two places to the right), the result was called a quotient.

This plan worked for a good many years, but it was obvious, even from the beginning, that there were many problems. A three-year-old, for example, who passes the six-year tests, and would thus have an IQ of 200, really cannot do what a six-year-old can. And when you reach the upper teens, the results cannot be computed this way. Why? Because it is difficult to measure intellectual growth in adulthood. Most people seem to reach a plateau in reasoning and many other processes. (Some claim it occurs at 13 or 14, which is why you often hear that certain films, books, etc. are geared to the average 13-year-old: That is a misinterpretation of this very fact.)

Rationally, you can't compare an 18-year-old and a 36-year-old on this sort of scale, so testers came up with another concept: Deviation IQ. This simply means that you—your wits, knowledge, intelligence—are matched against others in your own age group. If you're a 70-year-old, for example, you are matched against others over 65, and not with 30-year-olds. You are marked on a relative standing in your own group.

So what do IQ's mean? Nothing in themselves. As a relative measure, Intelligence Quotient is no longer an accurate description, but a rusty, misleading cliché. Your "percentile rank" is the more preferred score. A percentile rank means "the number below": For example, the percentile rank required for Mensa is the 98th. That means that ninety-eight out of every hundred people would score lower on the particular type of test taken.

But even here one important caution is in order: Even the concept of intelligence and how to measure it, is under severe criticism right now. Does pure intelligence exist? And if so, do intelligence tests measure it fairly?

Long-term studies of several hundred children—identified as "genius level" about 50 years ago—indicate that scoring well on an IQ test does predict school success. The children, now older adults, who have been studied continuously, achieved academic successes far above expectancy. They also tended to be far above average in most other measures as well, physical health, and financial success among them. However, not all of these high scorers did equally well. The reason is clear. An IQ test does not measure drive, persistence, creativity, or any of the myriad other skills that often count for more in achieving success out of school. A low score on an IQ test does not mean probable failure in life. All it means is that the person taking the test did poorly on that particular test. Most of us do not spend our lives in situations that can be measured by paper and pencil tests. Since this is so, scores obtained on such tests should be viewed with some restraint if they are very high and with some scepticism if they are low. They measure only one aspect of a total life pattern.

# THE MENSA GENIUS QUIZ BOOK

*Marvin Grosswirth, Abbie F. Salny, and
the Members of Mensa*

# Acknowledgments

Just so you'll know whom to blame, all of the quizzes and data referring to IQ tests and testing in general were supplied by Mensa psychologist Dr. Abbie Salny. The ancillary material was prepared by Mensa public relations officer Marvin Grosswirth (with the exception of the introduction, which is a joint effort, and Isaac Asimov's contribution, of course).

And just so you'll know whom to thank, we want to express our profound gratitude to the hundred or so Mensans who took time off from their Annual Gathering activities to participate in the quizzes. Special thanks go to those who pointed out small inconsistencies (which have been changed), and indicated one totally ambiguous question that has been replaced. Thanks, too, to those Mensans who took the new question for standardization purposes.

Throughout this book, you'll find contributions from Mensa members, all of whom are identified. We are grateful for their efforts, as we are to the many whose responses to our request for input had to be set aside. They were all interesting and useful, but there is just so much space.

Each local group of Mensa is headed by a Local Secretary (many of these terms are holdovers from our British origins) and almost every group publishes its own newsletter. We are indebted to the Local Secretaries and the editors of the newsletters for publicizing the fact that this book was in progress and that we needed information from members on how they polish their intellects.

This book would not have been possible without the cooperation of the American Mensa Committee (Mensa's board of directors) and its chairman, Gabriel Werba. We are also grateful to the small, harried, and overworked staff at the Mensa office, under the guidance of Executive Director Margot Seitelman, for their assistance and cooperation.

Most of all, however, we want to express our thanks and—at the risk of sounding maudlin—our love to all the members of Mensa—the shy and the brash, the young and young-at-heart, the geniuses and the kooks, the doctors and the janitors, the cops and the felons, the priests and the tycoons, the teachers and the students, the psychologists and the writers (yes, even those!)—all of you who have more than contributed to this book. You have, by your being, and by your being in Mensa, expanded our lives and our horizons.

It is a small recompense, we admit, but we'll try to repay a portion, at least, of our indebtedness: All net royalties from this book go to the Mensa Scholarship Fund. And this book is dedicated to you.

MARVIN GROSSWIRTH
ABBIE F. SALNY

*July, 1981*

# Are You a Secret Super Brain? (and don't even know it?)

What is the *real* puzzle in this unique book? It may be somewhere beyond what you think you see in the mind-expanding, brain-sizzling, devilishly entertaining questions that fill these pages.

Actually, the real puzzle here lies in finding a clue or two to your own IQ. THE MENSA GENIUS QUIZ BOOK solves that puzzle by pitting you against people with IQs in the top two percent of the general population.

Could you in fact be a super brain?

Carolina Varga Dinicu, a Middle Eastern dancer, is. So are Isaac Asimov, Theodore Bikel, R. Buckminster Fuller, Leslie Charteris (author of "The Saint" mystery stories), Donald Petersen (president of Ford Motor Company), and tens of thousands of other people, from high-school students to carpenters to physicists. Maybe you are, too.

The idea for this book began with the inclination to

make it fun and also simple (as distinguished from easy).

The quizzes here were developed and adapted to measure aptitudes similar to those measured by many IQ tests. The stumpers include *Vocabulary,* which is probably the single best predictor of intelligence; *Analogies,* which measures your ability to see relationships; *Mathemathics, Reasoning, and Logic,* which measure your ability to think logically and use the facts you know; and two sections that are mostly for fun but have considerable value as indicators of intelligence: *Trivia* and *Classics. Trivia* questions are a way of judging your store of general information. A lot of reading helps on this one. The *Classics* are problems that have been around for untold years. We included them not only because they're devilish fun at parties, but also to see how many you remember. More important, we included them because even the ones you don't know can be figured out logically through careful reading and a little open-mindedness.

To avoid any gnashing of teeth, we've divided each group of quizzes into two parts: The first part is a kind of practice quiz, called "Warm-Ups," to try at your own speed. When you've finished, mark yourself and see how well you did. (However, there is nothing to prevent you from plunging right in without doing the practice quizzes.)

After the "Warm-Ups," you'll find a short discussion on some of the philosophical aspects of intelligence and intelligence testing, along with what we hope will be useful suggestions, from members of

Mensa, on how they develop and improve their mental agility.

The second half of each group consists entirely of questions that were given to Mensa members at the organization's Annual Gathering in Louisville, Kentucky, in June, 1981. Over one hundred members took one or more of these quizzes, and more than twenty took all of them.

You can match wits with Mensa by tackling the second part—there is one set of questions for each section. Remember to keep track of your time.

These quizzes lay no claim to being a standardized intelligence test. However, if you compare your scores on each quiz with those obtained by Mensa members, you will be able to estimate whether you are as bright as the average Mensan. The sole requirement for membership in Mensa is a score on a standard IQ test in the top two percent as measured against the general population. This works out to 132 minimum on the Stanford-Binet and to 130 minimum on the most current Wechsler scales, the two major sets of intelligence tests.

When you take these quizzes, keep a record of your answers. When you have your scores and have compared them with those of Mensa members, note how you did. If you do as well as, or better than, the group of Mensans who took each quiz, you owe it to yourself to try to join Mensa, because you probably qualify. If you do nearly as well, you should also try.

If you don't do as well, don't worry about it. Some people don't do well on quizzes but do very well indeed in real life. The main thing to remember is that these are not scientifically designed IQ tests (although most of the questions are similar to the kind you'll find on many such tests), but quizzes for fun and information.

Despite our best efforts, it is entirely possible that we may have missed an alternative right answer. If you find such an answer, check it out carefully and if you are correct, give yourself a double score on that question for your ingenuity.

Incidentally, if you do better on the untimed sections than on the timed ones, you may be one of those people who does better without time pressure. That's worth knowing about yourself for future reference.

1

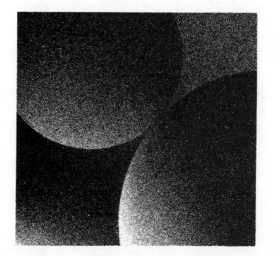

# TRIVIA

# Warm-Ups

 To do well on Trivia, you need a mind that is not only well-furnished, but a little overstuffed. Trivia buffs go around finding new trivia, just to stump other trivia buffs. It does happen to be a favorite pastime of many Mensa members.

1. Domenikos Theotocopoulus is better known as who?
2. Where would you be if your restaurant check was in forints?
3. In the novel by Jules Verne, who went around the world in eighty days?
4. If you heard people talking about ullage and botrytis, what would they be discussing?
5. Queensland, Victoria, and New South Wales are in what country?
6. Which one does not belong: George Sand, George Eliot, George Orwell?

7. What's so unusual about St. Michael's Mount and Mt. St. Michel?
8. Where are the islands of St. Pierre and Miquelon?
9. What were the occupations of the three men in a tub?
10. What is the name of the scale by which earthquakes are usually measured?
11. What species of living things has the greatest life expectancy?
12. What is the easternmost state in the United States?
13. What is the capital of Brazil?
14. What is the derivation of the word "boycott?"
15. Where did the United Nations meet, for almost five years, while the building in Manhattan was being finished?
16. If you commit uxoricide, whom have you killed?
17. Would you care to have your best friend become a lycanthrope? Why or why not?
18. What feast was Good King Wenceslaus celebrating?
19. Hemingway wrote a famous story about Mt. Kilimanjaro. In what country is the mountain located?
20. What's the astronomical name for the constellation usually called the Big Dipper?
21. She's known as Venus in Roman mythology. What was she called in Greece?
22. F. M. De Lesseps is most famous for what?
23. The Strait of Juan de Fuca lies between what two countries?

24. When it is 12 o'clock noon at the meridian in Greenwich, what time is it in New York (standard time for both)?
25. If you crossed Delaware Bay from south to north on the Lewes Ferry, where would you land?

# A Question of Relativity

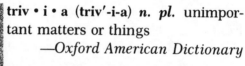

triv • i • a (**triv′-i-a**) *n. pl.* unimportant matters or things
—*Oxford American Dictionary*

If one accepts the dictionary definition of trivia, this question virtually begs to be asked: Why include "unimportant matters or things" in a set of questions designed to provide clues to one's intelligence? The answer is both simple and complex. First, the simple part.

A by-now tedious version of the chicken-and-egg question is whether some people like to take tests because they do well on them or whether they do well on tests because they like to take them. The point is that if you didn't think quizzes of this sort were a pleasure, you wouldn't be holding this book in your hands now (unless, of course, you're the unwilling victim of some tyrannical influence). So first of all, trivia questions are fun. They challenge the memory and probably no other type of question is so capable of evoking nostalgia: for schoolrooms long since cast into oblivion by events or even the wrecker's ball, for books once loved but now nearly forgotten, for youthful voyages and adventures, for past romances and childhood friends and acquaintances. Surely anything that can offer so much sheer joy and a bittersweet memory or two can hardly be regarded as "unimportant."

But whether trivia questions are unimportant *per se* is open to considerable discussion and here, the answer—or, more precisely, the answers—are far from simple. Among the many characteristics that go into defining intelligence is the ability to manipulate facts. This is not to suggest stretching or coloring the truth. It refers, rather, to the ability to examine a quantity of information and arrange the elements in such a way as to arrive at a conclusion, a decision, or a solution. Often, such manipulation is done in a way that we are barely conscious of. It's called *intuition*.

Intuition is not some mystic or mysterious force that belongs in the realm of psychic phenomena. It is real, definable, and, to a greater or lesser extent, present in all of us. Intuition is the accumulation of millions—perhaps even billions or trillions—of tiny, "trivial" bits of information that are stored in the recesses of our memories and that come together in an appropriate combination when the situation calls for it. For example, we have all experienced what current popular jargon calls "vibes." We meet someone for the first time, or even just watch a person enter a room, and instantly we experience a feeling, either positive or negative. When asked what creates that first impression, we are hard-pressed to offer specifics. But that human computer in our brains has received inputs—a facial expression, a mannerism, a way of walking, a style of dressing—and matched them up with past experiences with, and reactions to, those particular types of "trivial" information in the past. A kind of subconscious picture is drawn and in a fraction of a second, that picture is presented to the conscious mind as "good vibes" or "bad vibes."

The longer and more actively one lives, the keener the intuition. There are people who can look at a man dressed in a sport shirt, blazer, and jeans—in other words, a man who looks like a million other men—and declare "He's a cop" or "He's a schoolteacher." "How do you know?" "I don't know how I know; I just know. I can spot 'em a mile away." Invariably, the spotter is right. It is intuition, that enormous personal storehouse of seemingly trivial data.

If the accumulation of facts is so important to intuitive thinking, how much more important is it to conscious, active thinking? To think and behave intelligently requires two basic elements: the ability to accumulate facts—that is, to simply remember them—and the accumulation of facts that are useful. Remembering the fact that in the United States the standard width between railroad tracks is four feet, eight-and-a-half inches is a clear example of the first element, but it will probably prove to be a totally useless piece of information, except in trivia contests. However, that alone suggests the value of trivia quizzes: *They are a good indication of how well you remember; they can also provide an idea of the kinds of facts you remember.*

We are almost compelled, then, to conclude that the dictionary definition of trivia could use a little modification. It would be more accurate to describe trivia as *"relatively* unimportant matters or things." One person's triviality can be another's essentiality.

Consider, for example, the basic matter of the environment in which people think. Among the responses we received as to how Mensa members improve, enhance, or develop their intelligence, there were considerable details about what would seem, on the surface, to be trivialities. George J. Gore, a professor of management at the University of Cincinnati and president of a successful consulting firm, attacks a problem by making notes. "I use a legal-sized yellow pad and *always* a Scripto pencil," he writes, "the kind with thick lead and ready eraser." That may seem trivial to you, but to Professor Gore, they are essential to his thought mechanisms. So is his attitude. "I let myself feel under life-or-death pressure and reflect upon the social value of my undertaking . . . I think of how embarrassing it would be not to find a solution. I fume and seek wildly for alternatives." He writes down anything that comes to mind that could be of possible use to the particular project and then, he says, "with the problem on the front burner, I worry steadily until bedtime." The next morning, "I awaken with a fresh solution . . . I can count on my 'brownies' to solve the 'unsolvable' while I am sound asleep. 'I' do the easy part, i.e., lazy research and fretting." One gets a sense of freneticism, almost panic, in Prof. Gore's problem solving, but there is no doubt that part of his method is involved with seeming trivialities, such as the color of the writing paper and even the brand of pencil he uses.

There are others who would probably recoil in horror from Prof. Gore's method. "Meditation has been such a balancing force in all of my activities that it is nearly too obvious a technique to mention," writes Jeffrey Pickering of Spokane, Washington. "Buddhist meditation has accompanied significant changes in the way my mind/body works," he claims. "I find myself more capable of rote memorization of names and numbers, more insightful, more open to inspiration than I would have thought possible ten years ago." Thus, while Prof. Gore jams his brain with data, some of it at least seemingly trivial, Mr. Pickering clears his mind of irrelevancies to make way for the specific data he wants or needs. Lila M. Mallette, who is also known as Sri Lilananda and is the co-ordinator of Mensa's Human Potential Special Interest Group (SIG), points out that effective meditation requires attention to such seeming trivialities as the kind of clothing one wears, the room temperature, the amount of light, and even the surface on which one is lying.

If the cramming-the-head process or the total-clearing-of-the-brain process seems unsuited to your own style, you may want to consider an old but no less effective technique for remembering trivia. Irvin

K. Sasaki, a schoolteacher in Honolulu, finds mne-
monics (devices that aid the memory) useful in
teaching his students. His favorite type "is a sentence
made up of the beginning letters of the data to be
learned or remembered." It can be a nonsense sentence, of course, and even a humorous one, but the
key, according to Mr. Sasaki, is that "one should
make up his own sentence around a topic or situation
that interests him." By way of example, he relates
how he invited a group of fifth-graders to devise a
mnemonic that would help them remember the original thirteen American colonies, in order of settlement. Here is what they came up with: "Vicious
MonSters Hate Yukky Cooking. ManY Really Dig Pa-
payas 'N' Juicy Sweet Guavas." (Virginia, Mas-
Sachusetts, New Hampshire, New York, Connecti-
cut, MarYland, Rhode Island, Delaware, PennsYlvania,
North Carolina, New Jersey, South Carolina, Geor-
gia.) "Note," he notes, "the preoccupation of ten- and
eleven-year-olds with monsters and, also, the delicious tropical touch that flowed naturally from kids
living in Hawaii who have to learn about far-away
sister states."

Noted. Also noted is the fact that sometimes the
mnemonic is as difficult to remember as the data it is
supposed to help you remember. Perhaps, if I were a
ten-year-old Hawaiian. . . .

And now, if you are sufficiently impressed with the
notion that trivia isn't necessarily trivial, go on to the
next section. But don't take it *too* seriously. Just have
some fun, and maybe enjoy a few memories.

# Match Wits with Mensa

## TRIVIA TEST

Time started _____
Time elapsed _____

1. François Marie Arouet is better known as who?
2. If Cortez conquered Mexico, who conquered Peru?
3. Your friend gives you some nice Barsac. What do you have?
4. Where is Karl Marx buried?
5. Where would you be if your hotel bill was charged in markka?
6. What do dodo birds and kiwi birds have in common?
7. A distich is a rhyming couplet; what is a tryptich?
8. Which one of the following does not belong? Caravaggio, Corot, Copley, Cellini.

9. What does a dolorimeter measure?
10. If you had triskadekaphobia, what would you be afraid of?
11. Ferdinand and Isabella (of Columbus fame) had a daughter who became Queen of England. Who was her husband?
12. Samuel Clemens is better known as who?
13. What is the river, in mythology, that guards the Underworld?
14. What is the old Roman province of Lusitania called today?
15. Which American politician was known as "The Veep?"
16. Nobel gave funds for the Peace Prize. What did he help to invent or develop?
17. Name two of the Channel Islands that lie between England and France.
18. A new word, "serendipity," was coined from the title of a book, *The Three Princes of Serendip.* Where was Serendip?
19. Nock, fletching, and shaft. What sport uses these?
20. Argent, or, passant, rampant: To what do these terms refer?
21. If you order a restaurant dish that has Florentine in its name, what ingredient should you expect in the dish?
22. Gold is Au, Silver is Ag. What is Platinum?
23. If you went from New York to Rio de Janeiro, in what general direction would you be traveling?

24. To what country does Greenland belong?
25. If you crossed the Kill van Kull from north to south, where would you be?

Time finished _____

2

# VOCABULARY

# Warm-Ups

Try to choose the best definition of these words by yourself. Then try the second half—the Vocabulary test, which has been timed and normed against Mensa members. Good luck:

1. Paramount
   a) a range of hills in Paraguay
   b) top of a mountain
   c) above all others, superior
   d) semi-hilly
   e) beyond a particular range of hills
2. Pagan
   a) a variety of farm wagon
   b) a feast of certain Northwest tribes
   c) a form of payment in a barter system
   d) a heathen, one not believing in the true God
   e) an Indian home, round, with a hole in the top for smoke

3. Allay
   a) a former spelling of "alley"
   b) a French expression, meaning "Let's go!"
   c) to assuage; to temper or abate
   d) a form of soil, layered in types of earth
   e) a scoring term in hockey

4. Suppliant
   a) extremely limber and lithe
   b) folded in pleats, like a kilt
   c) of surpassing excellence
   d) a humble petitioner
   e) one who does not tell the truth

5. Dynastic
   a) pertaining to an explosive
   b) related to a Chinese type of antique
   c) pertaining to a succession of rulers from the same family or line
   d) pertaining to the state of being active or engaged in some activity
   e) related to the famous Dynas family of history

6. Feudal
   a) relating to antagonism between friends or relatives
   b) pertaining to the land-holding relationship between lord and vassal
   c) a particular type of shield used in heraldry to show historic descent
   d) pertaining to medieval songs and ballads
   e) pertaining to the clan warfare in Scotland in the early middle ages

7. Improvise

a) to be improvident and unthrifty; a spendthrift
b) to speak or perform on the spur of the moment; to act without previous plan
c) to act in a thrifty, forehanded, calculated manner
d) to lay in provisions
e) to require performance of a bond, as in a court of law

8. Metamorphosis
   a) a state of hypnotic sleepiness, medically induced
   b) the action or process of changing in shape or form
   c) a newly developed sleep-inducing drug
   d) a variety of vegetable preservative
   e) an extraordinarily large tropical moth

9. Paroxysm
   a) a fit (often figurative)
   b) a type of hairstyle adopted in Japan
   c) a bout of coughing
   d) an intellectual division between individuals
   e) a rift in a valley

10. Capricious
    a) relating to cooked goat or kid
    b) relating to an astrological sign
    c) unreasonable, arbitrary, stern
    d) fantastic, whimsical
    e) light and full of luminescence

11. Plebian
    a) poor, without money
    b) one of a group of soldiers

c) the electorate

d) one of, or pertaining to, the common people

e) one of, or pertaining to, the elite

12. Iniquity

a) unequal balances and scales in weighing

b) a new type of investment often called a Money Market fund

c) a gross injustice or public wrong; a sin

d) a climate that suffers from extremes of heat or cold

e) a legal term for an uneven distribution of assets in a bankruptcy

13. Pretentious

a) a pretense of someone who holds himself out as an elected officer, for example, or a doctor

b) showy, ostentatious, making claims (especially unwarranted) to great importance

c) a prevarication; a deliberate lie

d) fighting, angry, full of argumentative manners

e) very attentive and careful

14. Extant

a) a nautical measuring instrument

b) in existence, continuting to exist

c) a variety of insect, not found in North America

d) derived from a musical instrument

e) in addition to, above and beyond what is required

15. Perturbed

a) completely reversed in direction

b) pertaining to the building of large edifices

c) related to the inner part of cities

    d) greatly agitated, discomposed, disturbed greatly

    e) of, or pertaining to, through-traffic patterns

16. Usurp

    a) a style of noisy eating, especially liquids

    b) reverting back to an original state

    c) to appropriate wrongfully, especially for oneself

    d) old form of adjective relating to the U.S.

    e) above and beyond

17. Apparition

    a) a form of chemical instrumentation

    b) a form of biological instrumentation

    c) a ghost, phantom, immaterial object

    d) a camera originally developed to take pictures without film plates

    e) a particular style of clothing design

18. Circumlocution

    a) the surrounding walls of a city

    b) the moat surrounding a castle

    c) a walk around anything, or the outside of something

    d) a roundabout expression; the use of many words for few

    e) a complete trip around the world

19. Staunch

    a) strong, firm, resolute

    b) having a strong odor

    c) pertaining to a tree

    d) in chemistry, a term for noxious vapors

    e) improper, not moral, or ethical

20. Noisome

    a) appallingly loud

b) harmtul, bad smelling
c) noisy in a pleasant sense, like music
d) overly generous with praise
e) peculiar, highly eccentric

# In a Word . . .

 When confronted by a member attempting to explain and describe Mensa, people who have never before heard of it inevitably ask: "But what does Mensa do?" And just as inevitably, the answer comes back: "Well, it's mostly a social organization." This is often followed by a discussion of the need for intelligent people to communicate with each other and to meet people of diverse interests and backgrounds. It's not unusual, at a Mensa function, to find a group comprised of, say, a schoolteacher, a computer programmer, a bank teller, a carpenter, and a nuclear physicist locked in lively conversation. What Mensans do best is talk. Of course, it's not the only thing they do: While Mensa *is* a social organization, it is constitutionally committed to the fostering of human intelligence through various programs. But everything depends on communication. And obviously, the ability

to communicate—whether talking, writing, or listening—depends a great deal on the versatility of the
communicator. Conversation has been described as
an art. That may be overstating the case somewhat,
but for our purposes it offers a useful analogy. Let's
make a few comparisons.

The ability to paint or draw is a talent—a gift, if
you will. Many people believe that intelligence or,
more precisely, a high IQ is also a gift. If you give a
person with drawing talent a pencil and paper, he or
she will draw some very nice pictures, perhaps even
some great pictures. Similarly, if a person with a high
IQ is given a basic vocabulary, he or she will express
some interesting, perhaps even profound, ideas. But
give the drawer a variety of media—oils, pastels,
water colors, paper, canvas, wood, even a camera and
film—and teach their use, and both the artistic out-
put and its quality will be considerably greater.
Again, if a person with a high IQ is given a variety of
media—words, grammar, punctuation, other languages—he or she will be better able to produce
ideas.

Just as an artist with the need for self-expression
will somehow manage to acquire the media which
are best suited to that expression a person with a
high IQ is likely to acquire the words necessary for
his or her expression. Thus, we find ourselves in yet
another chicken-and-egg dilemma. Most experts agree
that a large and well-used vocabulary is an important—perhaps *the* most important—indicator of a
high IQ, but do intelligent people naturally add to

their store of words, or does the accumulation of words enhance a person's IQ? The answer to both is probably yes. To some extent, at least, intelligence is hereditary, but psychologists and others playing the IQ game tend to agree that environment, which includes both formal and informal education, has a profound effect on intelligence. (If you enjoy lively arguments in which the participants nearly come to blows, try to get two or three academicians to agree on the *extent* to which heredity and environment influence intelligence!)

It should come as no surprise, therefore, that of all the games, quizzes, and puzzles that abound, Mensans prefer those involving words and, as the following quiz indicates, those are the kind in which they do best. Of all the quizzes in this book, Mensans scored highest in this section. At almost every Regional or Annual Gathering you'll find a game room, and almost any time of the day or night, you'll find people there. To be sure, some will be playing bridge, or chess, or backgammon, or Dungeons and Dragons (a widely popular game in Mensa), but they are usually outnumbered by those playing Scrabble®, or Boggle®, or Perquacky®, or anagrams, or any of the other word games that abound. Even when they're alone, Mensans enjoy vocabulary challenges, as evidenced by those who responded to our request for tips and techniques of exercising and strengthening one's intelligence.

One favorite is Dictionary, a game that can be played solo or with others. Its rules are simple: The player simply flips open a reasonably large dictionary at random and the other player (if there is one) must define the first word (or, if you prefer, the last word) that appears on either page. Some people define the first word with more than two syllables. The variations are many, as are the methods of scoring. Feel free to make up your own.

Ed Oram of Atlanta was one of several members who offered an old, reliable technique for vocabulary stretching plus a mind-bending variation: anagrams. "I write a word, say *galleon*," he says, "then list as many words of four or more letters from the parent word, excluding proper names, plurals, and foreign words."

That was as far as I got in Ed's letter. I took another look at *galleon*, and in the margin jotted down *gall, gale, goal, gone, lone, angle, angel, legal, eagle, glen, gaol* (British for "jail"), *loge, ogle,* and *alone.* That took about three minutes and then I got stuck, so I forced myself to get back to work (i.e., writing this book). Why did I time myself? I have no idea; it just seemed the thing to do.

As though his little anagrammatic exercise did not cause enough trouble, Ed added the following:

> Whenever I really want to exercise my mind, I revert to an old problem I invented over twenty years ago, and have not yet solved: to create any 5 × 5 array of the letters of the alphabet (excluding Q), whereby all adjacent letters in the array can be linked by spelling out words:

```
Z – C – M   P – X
 \   |    \  |  /
S   A – R – E   Y
             |
W   T – H – G   D
     /       |
B   O   U   I – L
            |   |
J   F   V   N – K
```

Draw a line to link the letters in *knight, acme, expert, czar, ilk,* etc. There are 72 such links to be made altogether. My best score to date is 68. The letters may be rearranged at will; for example, in the above square, if R-H and G-D were interchanged, then *fjord* could be spelled out, but then H would be next to M, perhaps causing a problem there, unless O and T were interchanged to get *ohm,* but then J and T would create difficulties. . . .

This problem . . . can be tackled any time a pencil and paper are handy. Doubling of letters (e.g., *three*) or double use (e.g., *hedge*) are permitted . . . I'd love to see a solution to this problem before I die, but usually, F, V, and J are uncooperative. . . .

If you think you can solve the problem, you're certainly welcome to try. Send your solutions to *Mensa Book,* 1701 West Third St., Brooklyn, NY 11223. There are no prizes or awards, except the knowledge that you may help Ed Oram die a happy man.

Many word games and exercises seem silly and boring at first, but to a word lover, they frequently lay insidious traps. Case in point: a little exercise invented by Carlotta Follansbee of The Bronx, NY. "I have devised a game," she wrote, "to while away the time spent in the wrong traffic lane. Many license plates carry three letters. Very often these letters can be used in the same order (though not necessarily next to each other) in an English (or other) word." She then offers the following examples:

WKW – awkward
FCN  – confection
JTL  – judgmental
ABC  – abacus
HHD  – shepherd
AEK  – gaekwar
HRU  – thrust, through

"I try not to use the plural S, or to use I or N or G in *-ing* endings. Since so many New Jersey plates have a J, in my own game I allow myself to use it as a soft G—PJN can be *pigeon,* but not *pigpen*—I also use Q for O."

Nice try, I thought, but it's a boring game. I decided not to include it in this book. A day or two later, my wife, my son, and I were on our way to the neighborhood playground and Carlotta's game came to mind. I decided, in all fairness, to give it a try. That was a mistake: All conversation ceased as I began peering at the license plates of the passing cars, getting more and more hooked on the game. I found that the longer I played it, the more I wanted to play it. *Warning: Carlotta Follansbee's license-plate word game is addictive!*

"Since I am hopeless with languages," she added, almost as an afterthought, "I give myself an extra pat on the back when a combination like ABG yields a word like *abogado,* or when a group like HRU (see above list) provides *uhuru.*" *Gaekwar* isn't bad either, Carlotta. Incidentally, she points out that some children play the game very well. If yours do, it may be an indication of "giftedness"—that is, smart, as opposed to smart-alecky.

You probably already know the simplest time-tested method of increasing your vocabulary and thereby expanding your intelligence, but it's worth mentioning as a reminder: Whenever you come across an unfamiliar word first try to derive its meaning from the context in which it is used. Then write it down and when you get a chance, look it up in the dictionary. Even if the dictionary is at hand and you can look up the word immediately, write it down anyway. Writing it helps to imprint it on your memory. The exception, of course, is in the quiz that follows: If you take the time to look up unfamiliar words, it will play havoc with your timekeeping. Maybe you can put a little pencil mark next to the words you don't know and look them up later, even though they're defined, more or less, in the answers.

All right; you've stalled long enough. It's time to turn to the quiz.

# Match Wits with Mensa

## VOCABULARY TEST

Time started _____
Time elapsed _____

A favorite author of many Mensa members is Isaac Asimov. The following words were taken from some of his books.

1. Conglomeration
   a) a fire
   b) a catastrophe
   c) a clustered mass
   d) a net
   e) a matching
2. Stagnation
   a) deer
   b) a union of countries
   c) absence of activity, usually unhealthy

     d) able to be reduced to lowest possible terms

     e) inflation of monetary currencies

3. Eloquent

     a) omitting one or more words in a sentence, for effect

     b) possessing or exercising the power of fluent, appropriate, expression

     c) flowing smoothly, like a river with considerable current

     d) a building of a particular size and shape

     e) dangerous, because of certain characteristics

4. Sibilant

     a) children having one or both parents in common

     b) a Greek character who could foretell the future

     c) a substance that dries up moisture

     d) having a hissing sound

     e) living in, or being a citizen of, Sibilis

5. Apocryphal

     a) biblical

     b) spurious, mythical, of doubtful authenticity

     c) written anonymously

     d) pertaining to the Antipodes

     e) handwritten

6. Inveigle

     a) to rail against

     b) to dress in veils, as for a dance

     c) to beguile or deceive

     d) invert

     e) to turn into another object, as by magic

7. Sordid
    a) dirty, squalid, mean, despicable
    b) deaf, hard of hearing
    c) a type of acid
    d) a thing of small value, a trifle
    e) a scab

8. Antagonism
    a) a country in Asia Minor
    b) active opposition
    c) a predecessor
    d) an antidote to poison
    e) a flower cluster on a single stem

9. Mountebank
    a) an Alpine banking organization
    b) an Italian flower
    c) a charlatan, a quack
    d) a card game involving cheating
    e) enveloped in a crust

10. Legerdemain
    a) a kind of imported handgun
    b) the Italian name for the town of Leghorn
    c) sleight of hand, conjuring tricks
    d) a former prime minister of France
    e) the title of a famous poem by Keats

11. Implicit
    a) implied, although perhaps not expressed
    b) built-in guarantee
    c) not legal
    d) a medieval household tool
    e) above and beyond the usual

12. Hegemony
    a) a musical mode
    b) a form of Greek poetry
    c) the opposite of entropy
    d) the predominance of one state in a confederacy
    e) the act of analyzing the linguistic structure of words

13. Periphery
    a) outer surface, circumference; a surrounding region or area
    b) traveling widely
    c) a hemispherical shape
    d) a variety of worm-like creatures that inhabit Africa
    e) an angle of more than 90°

14. Solicitous
    a) all alone, without company
    b) anxious, troubled, or deeply concerned
    c) involved with a solicitor or lawyer (especially British)
    d) being perfectly united, or of one opinion, with a group
    e) the theory that involves the study of knowledge

15. Archaic
    a) of, or pertaining to, arches
    b) pertaining to archangels
    c) retention or imitation of what is old or obsolete
    d) a former variation of the word archery
    e) of or pertaining to rainbows

16. Kinetic
    a) relating to the movies, or moving pictures

b) related to cattle, or kine
c) producing or causing motion
d) related to touching
e) related to the science of numbers

17. Ulterior
   a) outside the walls of a building
   b) beyond the main point, beyond what is evident
   c) relating to Ireland
   d) painted exterior walls
   e) the finest of its kind

18. Plutocracy
   a) rule of the wealthy
   b) rule of Pluto in the Underworld
   c) rule by the smartest
   d) rule of the masses
   e) rule by the majority

19. Prerogative
   a) ruling powers of a state
   b) enjoyed by exclusive privilege
   c) original laws, prior to amendment
   d) newspaper freedom of information
   e) payment for special rights

20. Luminescent
   a) emitting sounds
   b) multicolored lights
   c) glittering
   d) related to a particular family of plants
   e) emitting light other than as a result of incandescence

Time finished _____

3

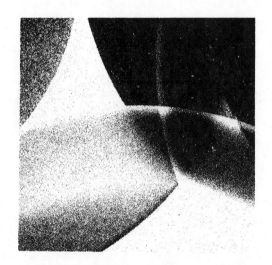

# ANALOGIES

# Warm-Ups

Instructions for this practice quiz are the same as for the others. Try each of the puzzles, see how well you can do and keep score. After you check your answers, try to find where you went wrong in the ones you missed. When you feel you are ready, try the timed test, which will match you against Mensa members who took the same test.

1. 6 is related to 36 as 4 is related to:
   a) 8   b) 16   c) 24   d) 44   e) 34
2. Stalactites are to stalagmites as ceiling is to:
   a) roof   b) floor   c) windows   d) cave
3. A square is to a cube as a circle is to a:
   a) pyramid   b) cone   c) sphere   d) octagon
4. Books are to libraries as weapons are to:
   a) tents   b) guns   c) soldiers   d) armories
5. A medal is to bravery as wages are to:
   a) money   b) work   c) hours   d) unions

6. Star is to rats as reward is to:
   a) mice   b) ransom   c) drawer   d) fame
7. A rainbow is to the East as the Aurora Borealis is to:
   a) Northern Lights   b) South   c) North
   d) color
8.

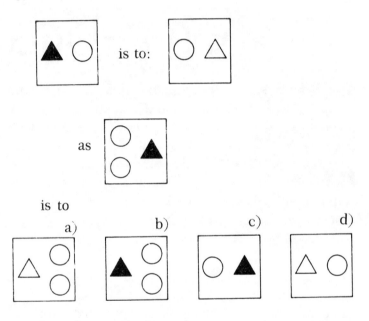

9. Clouds are to rain as springs are to:
   a) river   b) summer   c) weather   d) boats
10. £ is to England as ¥ is to:
    a) France   b) Japan   c) Yemen   d) Australia
11. Wimbledon is to tennis as Pebble Beach is to:
    a) swimming   b) golf   c) sailing   d) running

12. Gutenburg is to printing as Mercator is to:
    a) books  b) chemistry  c) maps  d) astronomy
13. Silver is to metal as oats is to:
    a) grain  b) horses  c) cake  d) food
14. A well is to a cellar as a cave is to a:
    a) hill  b) basement  c) valley  d) river
15. Skin is to people as carapace is to:
    a) lions  b) cats  c) shellfish  d) birds
16. Solar is to sun as terrestrial is to:
    a) moon  b) stars  c) earth  d) planets
17. GRAIDAM is to DIAGRAM as DOLENG is to:
    a) LENGTH  b) GOLDEN  c) GLADDEN  d) OLDING
18. The Leaning Tower is to Pisa as the Tower Bridge is to:
    a) New York  b) London  c) Edinburgh
    d) Paris
19. Zeus is to Jupiter as Hermes is to:
    a) Cupid  b) Hercules  c) Mercury  d) Venus
20. Daimler is to automobiles as Hughes is to:
    a) motorcycles  b) airplanes  c) gliders
    d) motorboats

# Analyzing Analogies

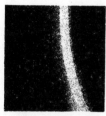 An analogy is a comparison of things that are somewhat alike. A camera is analogous to the human eye. A computer is analogous to the human brain. An education is analagous to a set of tools.

All too often, *education* is mistaken for *intelligence*. "He must be pretty smart; look at all the degrees he has." Unfortunately, nothing could be further from the truth. Education is simply the acquisition of information and an indication of the ability to make such acquisitions. It would be relatively easy for me to acquire a first-rate set of woodworking tools, but that wouldn't make me a good carpenter. Whether you are an artist does not depend on how many paints, brushes, canvases, and easels you can acquire. To be a good carpenter, I must first have carpentry skills. To be an artist, you must first have talent.

An education is precisely analagous. A skilled carpenter can construct marvelous devices with a good set of tools, just as a talented painter can create masterpieces with the right appurtenances. But give the carpentry tools to the artist and the paints to the carpenter, and, unless either or both happen to be twice blessed, the results are likely to be discouraging. In the same way, if you give a quantity of facts or information to a dimwit, you will have an educated dimwit, who is likely to ignore—or, worse, misuse—the tools. If you doubt that, take a minute or two and search your memory. If you are over twenty-one, you will more than likely recall a teacher, a physician, a lawyer, a clergyman, a boss, a psychologist, or any other member of a highly-educated calling for whom the word "dummy" is almost a kindness.

One of the elements in that nebulous, indefinable quality we call "intelligence" is the ability to relate things—objects, people, events, circumstances—to other things. The facts—the tools one uses—have an effect on the job one does, but the *way* those tools are used have a much greater effect. A really good carpenter who understands how things relate to each other can do a respectable job with the tools and materials on hand, but a klutz will botch the job, no matter how well-equipped his workshop.

What has all this to do with analogy quizzes? This type of quiz tests two factors: To some extent, it tests your general store of knowledge, your toolkit. More important, however, it tests your ability to see how things relate to each other, how ideas can connect. If you know you can do that, you can begin seeking relationships, connections, in all sorts of circumstances. For example, if, as mentioned earlier, the camera is analogous to the human eye, then the reverse must be true. Perhaps, then, the basic principles of cameras could be adapted to replace a human eye that has failed. It should come as no surprise to you that the technology for doing just that exists and that experimenters and researchers are very near the full development of artificial "eyes" that serve more than cosmetic purposes.

When we asked Mensans to tell us how they improve and develop their own intelligence, we did so in an open-ended manner, without specifying categories as such. It is interesting, therefore, that several responses, while not addressing the specific topic of analogies, nevertheless alluded to analogical thinking and attitudes. My favorite reply is from E. W. Paulson, of Rosebury, Oregon. Mr. Paulson's letter was handwritten on a yellow legal pad. Across the first page is a pencilled outline of a left hand. "I know you said typed, double-spaced, 8½ × 11, white . . . the pencil mark around my hand explains why I can't type. . . ." Indeed it does. I have never met Mr. Paulson and know nothing about him (other than the fact that he is a Mensan, and the information given in his letter), but it is reasonable to assume that he suffers from swollen hands, making typing quite impossible. Analogies, you see, are an important first step to deductive reasoning. But back to Mr. Paulson's letter:

The fourth grade was the best of my twelve years in school. After about three weeks of putting up with my deviltry because I had lots of time to think of things, the teacher got me by the ear and sat me down by one of the other kids with strict orders to spend my time helping him. Ralph wasn't dumb; he was just slow to catch on. The challenge of getting him to understand was fun. In the process of explaining or trying different approaches to the problems, I learned a great deal more about [the] subject myself. My deportment went from undesirable to exemplary, and Ralph's grades [changed] from D's and F's to B's and C's. For me, school changed from a bore to a fun challenge and Ralph changed from hating school to almost liking it. That little Swedish girl who put me to work to keep me out of her hair is now, more than fifty years later, my favorite of all the teachers I had.

I find, yet today, that if I have to explain something to someone who finds it hard to understand, I have a better view or grasp of the concept when I have tried several approaches so the other person can understand. I get more than I give. In trying to put things together to make a picture for someone else I get a clearer one for myself.

It must be a source of considerable satisfaction to E. W. Paulson to know that for half a century he has been able to use his ability to show how things relate to each other, and how those relationships in turn relate to individuals, all the while helping others *and* developing his own awareness of the world around him.

Let's get back to those tools. No matter how skilled you may be, it's almost impossible to do any job without tools—the more tools and the higher their quality, the better the result. Thus, in order to be really adept at visualizing relationships—i.e., analogies—one should attempt to acquire tools. Betty C. Dillingham, of Houston, disclaims any tricks or devices. "To keep my mind in shape," she says, "I simply exercise my curiosity. Frequently, regularly, and unstintingly." She is, by her own admission, "addicted to the printed word. . . . In addition to reading," she continues, "I observe everything my eyes behold or other senses reveal. Having made an observation . . . curiosity is aroused, and I'm off on another mind-stretching adventure, major or minor."

The concept of teaching, explaining, and even learning by analogy seems to be commonplace in the intelligent mind, so much so that it is often used without much premeditation. Jean Hopkins Jackson, a Los Angeles Mensan, wrote to describe a mind-improving technique that, while interesting, I am reluctant to recommend because I believe it requires a skill that at best is difficult to acquire, and, I suspect, is probably inherent. Despite the typical childhood admonitions about doing homework while listening to television (or, depending upon one's age, the radio), Jean can, in fact, read and listen to her radio at the same time. Not only that, but "in a classroom, I now [simultaneously] read textbooks and listen to the lecturer." (She did not explain, and I dared not ask, how she takes notes.) How does she do it? To describe the process, she uses an analogy, albeit one that she is not at home with. "I seem to be able to juggle both tracks; something, I guess, like both tracks on a tape recorder, although I am not too familiar with that technology."

Familiar or not, what could be clearer?

Now, see how well you can do with analogies. As we've pointed out more than once, these quizzes are intended mostly for fun. Still, developing the ability to see analogies, and acquiring the information with which to do so, could significantly change how you work, think, and relate to people. Practice. It's worth it.

# Match Wits with Mensa

## ANALOGIES TEST

Time started _____
Time elapsed _____

Choose the word or number in the second pair that is most closely related to the first. For example: Apple is to pear as veal is to a) pork b) fish. The answer would be a, since apple and pear are both fruit and veal and pork are both meat.

1. Potatoes are to peanuts as apples are to:
   a) bananas  b) lilies  c) peaches  d) tomatoes
   e) cucumbers
2. Spain is to Argentina as Portugal is to:
   a) Trinidad  b) Brazil  c) Mexico  d) Guyana
   e) Canada
3. Celsius is to 0° as Fahrenheit is to:
   a) 100°  b) 0°  c) 32°  d) 212°  e) 112°

4. Drachma is to Greece as peseta is to:
   a) Mexico  b) Italy  c) Canada  d) Brazil
   e) Spain

5. Loops is to spool as straw is to:
   a) pinker  b) hay  c) painting  d) warts
   e) rosy

6. Napoleon is to Melba as macadam is to:
   a) roads  b) poinsettia  c) overshoes  d) trees
   e) food

7. Rich is to money as leafy is to:
   a) vase  b) foliage  c) mountain  d) flower
   e) dog

8. The number 2 is to 8 as 5 is to:
   a) 15  b) 100  c) 125  d) 10  e) 60

9. 1789 is to France as 1649 is to:
   a) Germany  b) Switzerland  c) New Zealand
   d) United States  e) England

10. The letter A is to E as B is to:
    a) C  b) D  c) G  d) H  e) Q

11. Retort is to chemist as ramekin is to:
    a) painter  b) engineer  c) dressmaker  d) cook
    e) lawyer

12. Black Beauty is to horse as Lassie is to:
    a) cow  b) bird  c) dog  d) whale  e) camel

13. Palette is to artist as kiln is to:
    a) potter  b) painter  c) goldsmith  d) writer
    e) cook

14. Ceylon is to Sri Lanka as Constantinople is to:
    a) New Constantine  b) Leningrad  c) New
    York  d) London  e) Istanbul

15. *The Raven* is to Poe as *Gone With The Wind* is to:
    a) Mitchell  b) Keats  c) Robbins  d) Susann
    e) Blake
16. Star is to constellation as constellation is to:
    a) sun  b) earth  c) galaxy  d) planetoid
    e) moon
17. Onions are to leeks as crocuses are to:
    a) apples  b) saffron  c) tulips  d) lilacs
    e) bananas
18. Reagan is to Carter as Truman is to:
    a) Dewey  b) Jackson  c) Kennedy  d) Roosevelt  e) Johnson
19. Halley is to comet as Broca is to:
    a) printing  b) tires  c) automobiles  d) brain
    e) fruit
20.

is to:

Time finished _____

# 4
# MATHEMATICS,

# REASONING, & LOGIC

# Warm-Ups

1. Five men raced their cars on a racing strip. There were no ties. Will did not come in first. John was neither first nor last. Joe came in one place after Will. James was not second. Walt was two places below James. In what order did the men finish?

2. A soldier has been captured by the enemy. He has been so brave that they offer to let him choose how he wants to be killed. They tell him, "If you tell a lie, you will be shot, and if you tell the truth, you will be hanged." He can make only one statement. He makes the statement and goes free. What did he say?

3. You go shopping with $60. You spend 1/4 on clothes, $30 for equipment for your home computer, and 10 percent of your original money on some food. How much do you have left?

4. If Sally's daughter is my son's mother, what relationship am I to Sally if I am male?

5. In the following series of numbers, fill in the missing number: 35, 28, 21, \_\_\_\_

6. By following the same rules used for the signpost, how far is it to Moscow?

New York 10 miles
Perth 5 miles
Moscow ?

7. A cup and saucer together weigh twelve ounces. The cup weighs twice as much as the saucer. How much does the saucer weigh?

8. What figure should come next in the following series?

9. Paul usually beats Patty at croquet, but loses to Joe. Tom wins most of the time against Patty, and sometimes against Paul, but cannot beat Joe. Who is probably the worst player?

10. A rule has been followed to make each of the sample words in parentheses. The words in parentheses are related to the words in both the first and last columns. Using the same method, fill in the missing word.

|       |         |       |
|-------|---------|-------|
| tend  | (teal)  | also  |
| evert | (even)  | enter |
| late  | (_____) | stone |

11. You are working in a store where they have been very careless with the stock. Three boxes of socks are incorrectly labeled. The labels say Red Socks, Green Socks, and Red and Green Socks. How can you relabel them correctly by taking only one sock out of one box?

12. Following the same rule that has been used to place the following numbers, add the next two numbers in their proper places:

| 1 | | 4 | 7 | |
|---|---|---|---|---|
| 2 | 3 | 5 | 6 | |

13. Joe has red hair. Some people with red hair have terrible tempers. Therefore, Joe has a terrible temper. True, false, or uncertain?

14. Your friend has invented a new variety of paper-and-pencil game, like tic-tac-toe, but three in a row *loses*. Below is the diagram of a game. You are o and it is your turn. What move must you make? (Remember: Three in a row loses.)

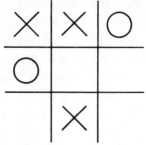

15. What two numbers come next in the following series?

1   6   2   7   3   8   ?   ?

16. A woman collects antique snuff boxes. She bought two, but found herself short of money and had to sell them quickly. She sold them for $600 each. On one she made 20 percent and on the other she lost 20 percent. Did she make or lose money on the whole deal? And how much?

17. A forty-foot length of chain, of uniform weight per unit of length, hangs between two buildings, attached at the same height at both ends. The shape of this chain is called a "catenary." If the distance from the points of suspension to the lowest point of the chain is twenty feet, how far apart are the buildings?

18. There are four seats in a row at a concert. Philip will sit next to Sally, but not next to Gerald. If Gerald will not sit next to John, who is sitting next to John?

19. A man hires a taxi to meet him at the railroad station at 3 p.m. to take him to an appointment. He catches an earlier train and arrives at 2. He decides to start walking, and is picked up en route by the taxi. He arrives twenty minutes early for his appointment. How long did he walk?

20. A woman buys two dozen apples and one dozen oranges. She makes a pie with half of the apples and squeezes six oranges for juice. Next time she goes to the store, she buys half as many apples and oranges as she has left. How many pieces of fruit does she then have altogether?

## BONUS:

The Mensa diet, which follows, was invented by Jerry Salny at an air force base during World War II, while trying to cool off and lose weight at the same time. It has been printed in numerous Mensa publications and in another quiz book, which said it could not be solved. It can.

# The Mensa Diet

Everybody knows that losing weight is a matter of burning up more calories than are taken in. Everyone also knows that a calorie is that amount of heat required to raise the temperature of one gram of water (pure water, under standard conditions) by one Celsius degree.

Let us take a glass of scotch and soda filled with ice. Assuming that this is 200 grams (200 cc), and neglecting the fact that scotch can lower the freezing point, and overlooking the bubbles in the soda, the temperature must be 0° Celsius, since the glass contains melting ice.

Drink the scotch and soda.

Somehow, the body must supply enough heat to raise the 200 grams to body temperature, or 37°C. The body must supply 200 grams × 37°C or 7,400 calories. Since all the calorie books show scotch as having 100 Calories per ounce, and none at all for the soda, we should be able to drink scotch and soda all day and lose weight like mad.

This has been tried, and although the experimenter hasn't lost any weight in the process, he doesn't worry about it much anymore. Why doesn't it work?

# Adding It Up

Why lump mathematics, reasoning, and logic questions together in a single group?

When that question was put to our test maven, Dr. Abbie Salny, she replied, "Many people don't like to be confronted with a lot of math questions at one time. They get bored. Some even become intimidated." Of course, there are many people who love math problems, but they seem to be a minority. Also a minority, but nevertheless present, are those who simply hate math, primarily because they can't seem to get it right. If math were the only criterion for the IQ score that qualifies for Mensa membership, I wouldn't even have tried to make it; I consider it an exceptional day when I can get my checkbook to balance on the second try. (I am, perhaps, one of the few people who actually was entitled to a tax refund after an Internal Revenue Service income tax audit;

I had made a serious error in adding up my gross income. Gross.)

There is another good reason for grouping mathematics, reasoning, and logic together: If you consider it for a moment, you'll see that it's reasonable and logical—it all adds up.

There's no arguing with mathematics. There can be only one right answer. To be sure, there is often considerable argument as to how to arrive at that answer, which is why people highly skilled in math often come up with different answers to the same problem. The more complex the problem, the likelier it is that there will be more than one right answer. Wait a minute—didn't I just say that in mathematics, there can be only one right answer? That's where reasoning and logic come in. If you know your stuff, you'll follow the mathematical steps, in logical order, to arrive at a solution.

Frequently, such logical processes are somewhat abstract, perfectly applicable in "pure" math, but something less than practical in real life. If you're confronted with a problem that begins "Assume you are travelling at the speed of light," you don't have to be a mathematician to realize that you're dealing with an exercise in mental gymnastics and not something you're likely to come across in your daily routine. So it is sometimes necessary to attack a problem from the standpoint of what is logical, and then examine it in terms of what is reasonable. Life, alas, is not always logical. (It is in these quizzes, however, so there's no need to worry about that, at least for now.)

It can be fun and profitable to massage the mind with self-imposed math problems. Brenda Evans Hart discovered, some years back, "that amid the hustle and insanity of Houston traffic, if I didn't figure out a way to calm myself and develop patience, I would either die of a heart attack or ram the nearest car." She began by tuning in the local classical-music station and found that "the metronome-like beat [of the music] had a calming effect on my nerves." An interesting observation: Have you ever noticed the close relationship between music and mathematics—half- and quarter-notes, the numerical designations of tempo (a waltz is played in 3/4 time), the numerical divisions of sections of music (eight bars to the measure), etc.? Brenda soon found that while the music calmed her, she needed something to occupy her more-tranquil mind, so she began devising math problems relevant to her surroundings. "If I live twenty miles from work," she writes, "and take two hours to get home, having stopped on the freeway forty-five times, what is my average speed . . . and can I walk it faster?" This, she claims, had an additional soothing effect. "Before I knew it, I was home, out of traffic, and feeling fine.

"I took this addictive serenity from my car into my home," she wrote, "and found myself working old college-text calculus problems to the sounds of Bach whenever I found life getting to be too much." (To each his own: I'll keep the Bach and swap the calculus problems for a book of British crossword puzzles, thank you.) Brenda moved her mental gymnastics into the office ("My boss thought I was very busy and was, therefore, pleased"), and then added to them by playing a variation of the "Dictionary" game (described in the Vocabulary section). That, in turn, led to a love affair with the English language and a desire to improve her use of it.

While she heartily recommends these methods of improving one's own intelligence, she includes two cautionary notes: First, she insists that it must be a continuous effort, on the premise that, as with some other activities (such as sex), if you don't use it you'll lose it. Second, she is a staunch advocate of physical fitness. Nevertheless, she insists that her techniques work, at least for her. "If the ability to make a high score on a test is an indication of being smart," Brenda Evans Hart writes, "then, yes, I am smarter today than I was a few years ago because a few years ago, my test scores would not have gotten me into Mensa. I attribute this to a sharpening of my analytical skills in an attempt to cope with insanity and boredom with mental order and physical good health." She signed her letter, "Sincerely," and I believe her.

In any argument or debate, the winner usually has reasoning and logic on his or her side (although they are all too frequently overshadowed by emotion and prejudice). Nancy Reller, of Kent, Ohio, has developed a technique that sharpens her own thinking and arms her with reasoning and logic when the situation calls for it. Her inspiration also struck in the midst of traffic. "On the way to work one morning," she relates, "I was listening to a discussion [on the radio] on whether eighteen-year-olds should have the vote. The announcer asked listeners to call in with their opinions and I decided to call as soon as I got to work, since it was a subject on which I had strong feelings. That was when it hit me that I didn't really know exactly what my opinion was, much less being able to put it clearly and in a few words."

The realization shocked her, because she felt that the subject was one in which she was well versed. It is also a sign of her intelligence—at least in my opinion—that she was able to face the fact that she didn't know. "Forgetting the phone call," she continues, "I started putting down on paper everything I could think of on the subject, important or not." In a one-woman brainstorming session, she discovered that what at first had seemed unimportant took on new prominence. She studied her list, selected what she considered "the best of the facts," arranged them in a logical and reasonable sequence, "and from that composed a paragraph. This was studied in turn, and the whole thing rewritten, several times. Finally, I could say, 'This—briefly—is my opinion.'" And I guess that it would be difficult to argue against it.

Using mathematical precision, logic, and reasoning, however, seems to be the province of those with orderly minds. What resources are available to those of us whose thoughts—and even deeds—seem to be scattered all over the place? Since logic and reasoning appear to have been missing from the package handed me at birth, I have had to find adequate substitutes. My own method should win me a certificate of appreciation from the people who manufacture index cards. When I have to put together an article or a book, I do all my research, including taped interviews, and then carefully review everything, extracting facts or other useful bits of data—impressions, quotes, "color," etc. Each bit of data is transferred to a separate index card (not necessarily physically; I often use a simple cross-referencing system). I then begin jotting down, on more cards, those general elements that have to be included in the work. These are done helter-skelter, as they occur, with no attention to detail or order, and each idea earns its own card. I then arrange the idea cards in what strikes me as a logical sequence. I now have a working outline and I simply drop the "fact" cards behind the appropriate idea cards. The next step is to arrange the cards in each section in some sort of sensible sequence, at which point, there's nothing left to do but the writing. It seems to work. How well it works you can judge for yourself: you are holding the product of such an effort in your hands right now.

Richard Hazelett, of Provo, Utah, has found an elaborate variation of this technique to be helpful in increasing his knowledge and intellectual prowess. In an essay (previously unpublished) entitled "How Not to be Scatterbrained—Sometimes," he writes: "In order to improve my mind and also to get things done, I write on a *separate* pocket-sized slip of paper each idea, problem, chore, or citation to search in a library. I keep the problem-slips in my wallet, as Lincoln used to keep them in his stovepipe hat, and then I go over them at odd moments." The idea slips are sorted by projects. "If the object is an article or book," he claims, "it almost writes itself that way," a claim that I can wholeheartedly support. "Chores are sorted according to priority or convenience." Lest one get the impression that Richard's wallet is enormous, he adds that something on the order of a hanging-folder file is extremely useful.

Thus, even if you are not mathematically inclined, and fail to arrange your ideas—or even your life—in a logical way, and tend to let emotions overcome reason, there are ways to compensate.

All you have to do is think logically and reasonably about how to be logical and reasonable.

# Match Wits with Mensa

## MATHEMATICS, REASONING, AND LOGIC TEST

Time started _____
Time elapsed _____

1. A man goes to visit his friend thirty miles away. He doesn't mind speeding, so he travels at 60 miles per hour and arrives in half an hour. On the way back, however, he has a little trouble with his car, and it takes him an hour to reach home. What was his average speed for the round trip?

2. You are in a country where there are only liars and truthtellers, and they cannot be told apart by sight. You set out on a dangerous trip, because there is a fork in the road that can lead either to a crocodile swamp or to safety. When you reach the fork, the signpost is gone, but there are two

men standing there. You know that they will answer only one question between them. What question can you ask either of them that will tell you which road is safe?

3. A horse salesman went to a horse auction with a certain number of horses. To his first customer, he sold half his horses, plus half a horse. To his second, he sold half of what he had left, plus half a horse. To the last, he sold half of what he had left, plus half a horse. Each of his customers received whole horses, however, not half horses, and he had no horses left. How many horses did he start out with?

4. 0  1  2  3  4  5  6  7  8  9 = 1

   Put the appropriate plus or minus signs between the numbers, in the correct places, so that the sum total will equal 1.

5. A man went into a jewelry store and bought a $75 chain, giving the clerk a $100 bill. He returned a few moments later and bought a new catch, giving the clerk a $20 bill and receiving $5 in change. Later, the bank told the store that both the $100 bill and the $20 bill were counterfeit. Ignoring markup, overhead, cost of merchandise, etc., how much money did the store lose?

6. You are playing a new game of tossing cubes with numbers on them. The numbers are given below. The winner is the one who first reaches 100, using the fewest numbers possible, and no

repeats. Which numbers do you need?

5   17   19   37   41   46   50   66

7. Robert and Rose went shopping for presents together. They had a total of $264 between them. Rose had $24 more to begin with but she spent twice as much as Robert and ended up with two-thirds as much money as Robert. How much did Robert spend?

8. Next week I am going to have lunch with my friend, visit the new art gallery, go to the Social Security office, and have my teeth checked at the dentist's. My friend cannot meet me on Wednesday, the Social Security office is closed weekends; the art gallery is closed Tuesday, Thursday, and weekends; and the dentist has office hours only on Tuesday, Friday, and Saturday. What day can I do everything I have planned?

9. If a jet has a value of 1, and a plane has a value of 2, what is the value of a Concorde?

10. Complete the series by adding the next number:

0   0   1   2   2   4   3   6   4

11. Multiply by 6 the number of 9's followed by 2, but not followed by 7, in the number below:

9256312397986413492892 9596

12. X is less than Y; Y is not equal to Z. Therefore the statement that: X is not equal to Z, is:

a) correct   b) incorrect   c) undetermined.

13. A man bets $24 and gets back his original bet and $48 additional. He spends 25 percent of his winnings at a restaurant to celebrate, and 50 per-

cent of his winnings to buy a present for his wife because he was so late, and his salary was $240, from which he made his original bet. How much money does he lave left when he finally arrives home?

14. What is the next number in the following series:
    − 2  4  − 12  48  − 240  ____

15. You are at a meeting at which there are only liars and truthtellers. A woman comes up to you and says that the chairman of the meeting told her he was a liar. Is she a liar or a truthteller, and how do you know?

16. Three youngsters on our street went shopping for clothes in a very unusual clothing store. The owner charges $3 for a tie, $3 for a hat, and $5 for a shirt. How much would a jacket cost?

17. How many minutes is it before six o'clock if fifty minutes ago it was four times as many minutes past three o'clock?

18. A man just finished painting his house and needs something more. At the hardware store the clerk shows him what he wants and says, "one is $1.". "Fine,"says the man,"I took 600, so here's $3." What had he bought?

19. How many odd pages are there in a book 479 pages long?

20. What is the missing number in the following sequence?
    3  7  15  ____  63  127

Time finished _____

5

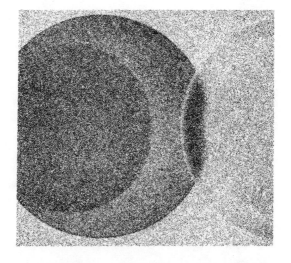

# CLASSICS

# Warm-Ups

1. If a teenager and a half can eat a pizza and a half in a day and a half, how many pizzas can a dozen teenagers eat in three days?
2. How far can a dog run into the woods?
3. Which is heavier, a pound of gold or a pound of feathers?
4. In a strange town, there are only two barbers. Looking into the barber shops, you see that one barber is messy and disorganized, and has a terrible haircut. The other barber is neat and tidy, and has a beautiful haircut. Which one do you pick to cut your hair, and why?
5. Sally comes to school one day, and for Show and Tell announces to her kindergarten class that today is the birthday of both her father and her grandfather, and what is more, both are exactly

the same age. Her teacher tells her that is impossible, but Sally insists that she is right. Can she be?

6. If you have black socks and brown socks in your drawer, mixed in the ratio of 4 to 5, how many socks will you have to take out to make sure of having a pair the same color?

7. Six thousand, six hundred six dollars is written $6,606. Now write eleven thousand, eleven hundred eleven as fast as you can.

8. There is a low railroad trestle in your town. One day you see a large truck stopped just before the underpass. When you ask what's happened, the driver tells you that his truck is one inch higher than the indicated height of the opening. This is the only road to his destination. What can he do to get through the underpass the easiest way?

9. Even if you never had a word of Latin, you should be able to read and understand the following poem:

> O sibili si emgo.
> Fortibuses i naro.
> O nobili demis trux.
> Vatis inem? Caus an dux.

10. I have two coins that add up to 55¢. One of them is not a nickel. What are the two coins?

11. Punctuate the following sentence so that it makes sense:
Jim where Bill had had had had had had had had had was right.

12. On your bookshelf you have three books in a set,

Volumes I, II, and III. Unfortunately, you also have a book worm who is eating up your books. The books are each two inches thick, and the covers are each a half inch thick. If the hungry bookworm starts at the outside front cover of Volume I and eats through to the last page of Volume III before you find him, how many inches of book material has he eaten?

13. Divide 100 by 1/2 and add 10. What do you have?

14. You have just tossed a coin that has come up heads for the tenth time in a row. What is the probability that it will come up heads the next time?

15. A man is stalking a bear that has attacked his camp. He reports later that naturally he went south. What color was the bear?

16. A young explorer called his expedition chief in great excitement to report that he had just found a golden coin marked 6 B.C. The expedition chief fired him. Why?

17. Sam Jones lives on the eighteenth floor of an apartment building. Every morning when he goes to work, he gets on the elevator, presses the ground floor button, and rides down. Every night when he comes home, if he is the only one in the car, he gets off at the sixth floor and walks up the rest of the way. He would prefer to ride. Why does he walk?

18. John wants to win a club election very badly, but there are two other candidates and all have re-

ceived an equal number of votes. They decide to settle the election by pulling the winning name out of a hat. John writes one opponent's name on the top part of a sheet of paper, his own in the middle, and the other opponent's name on the bottom. Then he tears them apart, places the strips in the hat, and offers to draw out a name. How does he make sure he wins, even though he is adequately blindfolded?

19. A poor but honest knight wants to marry a beautiful princess, and she wants to marry him. The king offers the knight a choice. He can draw one of two slips of paper from a golden box. One will say "Marriage," the other "Death." The princess manages to whisper to her suitor that both slips say "Death." But the knight and the beautiful princess are wed. How did he accomplish this?

20. One store in town is selling a small radio for $20. Its rival is advertising the same radio on sale for only one thousand, nine hundred ninety-nine pennies. How much will you save by buying it on sale?

# Classic Conundrums

 If some of the practice questions you've just gone through seem familiar, it's because they've been around for ages. Many of them are tests of knowledge, logic, and reasoning ability. And many of them are so-called "trick" questions. The relationship of trick questions to intelligence is worth looking at a little more closely.

In the not-too-distant past, the expression "native American intelligence" was commonplace. These days, however, it seems to have lapsed into disuse. Why? Has native American intelligence ceased to exist? Have we, as a nation, lost our ability to think? Probably not. I admit that mine is a personal and untested theory, but I believe that over the years, we have been culturally conditioned to abandon thinking as unnecessary. Everything—news, information, entertainment, medical care, food, merchandise—is provided in neat packages, predigested, preconditioned: Just add water, batteries not included. We've lost the habit of thinking for ourselves.

Intelligence implies the ability to think, and an IQ score implies the existence, to a greater or lesser degree, of intelligence. But that IQ score is an index of a potential. Whether the size of that potential is variable or expandable within a given individual is the subject of considerable debate. The extent to which that potential is used, however, is not debatable: Either you use it or you don't. With the best of intentions, it is difficult to use if it is confined by boundaries.

If you've come this far in the book, then you probably have a fair idea of your own potential by now. If you think you have a high IQ, you are making a mistake if you believe that alone is enough to qualify you as "intelligent." If, on the other hand, your scores are lower than you would have liked, you are making a mistake if you believe there is nothing you can do about your intelligence. It has been said before, but it bears repeating: Use it or lose it.

You don't need any teachers, counselors, psychologists, or gurus to help you expand your intelligence. All you need is the desire to do so and the initiative to practice. Ask questions. Understand everything, even if it has to be explained several times or in a new way. Give free rein to your curiosity. Most important of all, free yourself of those mental boundaries I mentioned earlier.

That brings us back to those trick questions. What makes them tricky is that they rely on the likelihood that your thinking is conditioned to move in only one direction with respect to the information given. When you are given the answer, you feel a little foolish, perhaps even irritated, because you've been taken advantage of. That's because you instantly realize that you should have known the answer all the time, if only you'd thought about it. But you couldn't have thought about it because your thinking process was preconditioned.

Farfetched? Melodramatic? Try it yourself on relatives or friends, with these old chestnuts. First, set them up—precondition their thought processes; then zap them with the right answers and see what happens. Begin with the "Scottish Names" gambit. (This should be done orally; it's too easy to solve when seen in print.) Ask your victim to pronounce M-A-C-T-A-V-I-S-H. After he or she has done so, try M-A-C-C-A-R-T-H-Y; then M-A-C-D-O-U-G-A-L. You can use any other "Mac" names, as long as they are legitimate. After each name has been pronounced in turn, ask the sucker to pronounce M-A-C-H-I-N-E-S. As you can see, that spells *machines*, but if your victim doesn't answer with "MacHines," it's safe to assume that he or she has fallen into the trap before. By spelling out the "Mac" names first, you will have effectively preconditioned the listener's thinking, leading it straight down a predetermined—and totally incorrect—path. Talk about tricky.

Here's another one that is better spoken than written. How do you pronounce:

C  H  O
P  H  O
U  S  E  ?

Again, you're setting your victim up by placing the letters in groups of three (as I have attempted to do by arranging them in a square), again preconditioning thinking. As a result, you're likely to get an answer approximating something like "Show - foe - use." What kind of a word is that? No kind, of course. Did you fall into the trap? Did you allow me to dictate your thought processes, or were you able to break through the boundaries and simply string the letters out in a row to arrive at *chophouse*? (Not many young people may be familiar with that word to begin with. Never mind; this gambit works almost as well with *flophouse*.)

One more supposedly trick question, this one to demonstrate how it isn't even necessary for you to set the person up; you can simply take advantage of the preconditioning that already exists. Punctuate the following: TIME FLIES I CANT THEYRE TOO FAST. Most people will stick in the missing apostrophes immediately, but then they're stymied. Look how simple it is, once you free up your thinking (the quotation marks are a little added refinement to aid comprehension): "Time flies." "I can't. They're too fast." Still doesn't make sense? Look again. The problem is that you're already familiar with the cliche, "Time flies." In that expression, *time* is a noun and *flies* is a verb, and your conditioning leads you to assume that it has to be that way. It doesn't. Read the punctuated sentence again, but this time consider *time* as the verb and *flies* as the noun. Tricky? Only if you insist on retaining the strictures placed on your mind, on your native intelligence.

If you think these mental somersaults are of little value in the real world, try paying closer attention, say, to television commercials. When the announcer tells you that a particular brand of toilet paper has more sheets per roll than the leading competitor, he is telling the truth. The assumption is that *you* will assume—because it's implied, although not actually stated—that all toilet paper sheets are the same size. But if you compare brands in the supermarket, you may find that in fact, the total quantity is exactly the same, because although one brand has more sheets, the individual sheets are smaller.

There are other benefits to opening your mind, to attempting to see familiar things in new ways. There are several names for what results—imagination, creativity, insight, even intelligence.

The sermon being preached here is a simple one: Whatever role heredity may play in intelligence, environment plays at least as important a role. The only way to improve, enhance, and develop your intelligence is first, to decide to do it, and then, to do it.

Most Mensa members apparently agree. Vicky Edwards Gehrt is a freelance journalist who lives in Villa Park, Illinois. She conducted an informal survey among her fellow Mensans to use as the basis for an article she's working on and prepared a short summary for this book. Here is her report:

*In a survey I conducted with 327 members of Mensa, I asked participants to describe the major environmental factors they considered responsible for their intelligence. The responses provide a guideline for those who wish to assure themselves that they are not letting their potential go to waste.*

*The foremost consideration was reading. Many respondents noted that their parents read to them when they were children. Parents were also influential by providing reading materials in the home, by encouraging the use of the public library, and by setting an example by their own reading habits.*

*Intelligent people tend to be heavy readers throughout life. They read for information and entertainment. Although the reading habit should ideally be established during childhood, it is possible to develop a love for reading at any age. . . . Intelligence needs to be nourished with a steady supply of newspapers, magazines, and books.*

*Several participants also mention personal drive as a factor in intelligence. They believe that the desire to learn is vital, and take every opportunity to fulfill that desire. When they encounter a new concept, they find out more about it; when they discover a new area of interest, they delve into it wholeheartedly; and when they have questions, they find answers.*

*Other considerations in the development of intelligence noted by participants include the following:*

*Playing word games and doing word puzzles; playing strategy games; limited television viewing; enrichment activities (lessons, education courses); cultural activities (concerts, theater, museums); travel; hobbies, collecting, pursuit of personal interests; contact and conversation with intelligent people.*

That seems to sum things up nicely, especially the part about contact and conversation with intelligent people. If that appeals to you, consider joining Mensa. You'll find the address in the back of this book. But first things first.

# Match Wits with Mensa

## CLASSICS TEST

Time started _____
Time elapsed _____

This is a collection of many of the old time puzzles and "foolers" that you have read and heard for many years, in one form or another. How many do you remember? If you don't remember them, can you figure them out?

1. A man wants to grow a tree very quickly. He buys some special tree seeds that double in height every day. On the tenth day, the tree is twenty feet high. On what day was it five feet high?

2. A snail is climbing out of a well. The well is twenty feet deep. Every day the snail climbs up three feet and every night he slips back two feet.

How many days will it take him to get out of the well?

3. A man moors his boat in a harbor at high tide. A ladder is fastened to the boat, with three rungs showing. The rungs are twelve inches apart. At low tide the water level sinks twenty feet. How many rungs of the ladder are now showing?

4. If there are twelve one-cent stamps in a dozen, how many two-cent stamps are there in a dozen?

5. A child is injured in an accident and rushed to the hospital. The doctor takes one look at the child and says: "I can't treat him, that's my son." The doctor is not the child's father. How do you explain this?

6. There is a family party consisting of two fathers, two mothers, one grandfather, one grandmother, two sons, and one grandson. Only five people are there. How is this possible?

7. You are very tired and go to bed at 8 P.M. However, you have a very important appointment at 10 A.M. the next day and don't want to oversleep, so you wind up your alarm clock and set it for 9. How many hours do you sleep?

8. Your doctor gives you six pills and tells you to take one every half hour. How long does it take you to use up all of the pills?

9. How many months have twenty-eight days?

10. How many pairs of animals did Moses take on the Ark?

11. What is the next letter in this series? O T T F F S S E N ?

12. You have two pencils, a good one and a cheap one. The good one cost $1.00 more than the cheap one. You spent $1.10 for both. How much did the cheap one cost?
13. You are cutting a board twelve feet long into one-foot pieces. How many cuts must you make? (Stacking the pieces is not allowed.)
14. A fly is flying between two boys on bicycles who are pedalling toward each other at 10 miles per hour. The fly reaches one boy, reverses immediately, and flies back to the other boy instantly, repeating the process each time. The fly is flying at 60 miles per hour. The boys meet in thirty minutes. How far has the fly flown in that time?
15. You are driving alone on a dark night, and pass through Dogpatch (you can see its name on the City Hall). About half an hour later, you reach a five-way crossroads, but the sign has been uprooted and is lying in such a position you cannot tell exactly how it stood. How do you find out which of the roads leads to Crosspatch, your destination? (You are not allowed to invent a convenient passerby).
16. In thirty seconds or less, give the number that is double one half of 99,637,543,667,345.
17. A very fast train runs from A to B in an hour and a quarter, but on the return trip it takes 75 minutes under identical conditions. Why?
18. What word, when you add additional letters, becomes smaller?
19. Does Canada have a 4th of July?

20. Under international law, if a plane crashes in the
middle of the Atlantic, where would the survivors
be buried?

Time Finished ⸺⸺⸺⸺⸺

# ANSWERS

# TRIVIA WARM-UP ANSWERS

1. El Greco, the painter.
2. Hungary.
3. Phileas Fogg (and his valet, of course).
4. Wine.
5. Australia.
6. George Orwell; all three are pen names, but the other two are female.
7. They are both tidal islands, cut off from the mainland at certain tides, and a chapel sits on each.
8. Off the coast of Newfoundland, Canada; they belong to France.
9. Butcher, baker, and candlestick maker.
10. The Richter Scale.
11. Trees; there are living sequoias that are believed to be several thousand years old.
12. **Alaska—also the westernmost; the 180th parallel runs through it, so it is both.**
13. Brasilia.
14. From Captain Boycott, a land agent in Ireland who was ostracized for refusing to reduce rents.
15. At Lake Success, in New York.
16. Your wife.
17. Probably not; a lycanthrope is a werewolf.
18. Feast of St. Stephen.
19. **Tanganyika**
20. Ursa Major.
21. Aphrodite.

22. For engineering canals: Suez and Panama.
23. Canada and the United States, on the west coast.
24. 7 A.M.
25. In southern New Jersey.

# TRIVIA TEST ANSWERS

Listed after each of the following answers is a percentage figure that represents the percentage of Mensa members taking this quiz who answered correctly. Give yourself one point for each correct answer. If you answer a question that fewer than 15 percent of Mensa members answered, give yourself double credit for that answer.

The average number of right answers obtained by Mensa members was twelve. The average time taken was seven minutes.

1. Voltaire. (33%)
2. Francisco Pizarro. (55%)
3. Sweet white wine. (33%)
4. In London, England. (41%) (One member answered: "In a communist plot.")
5. Finland. (10%)
6. They are basically wingless; they can't fly. (48%) (Incidentally, the kiwi is *not* extinct.)
7. A three-panel painting. (55%)
8. Cellini, who was a sculptor, not a painter. (37%)
9. Pain, which is measured in dols. (17%)

10. The number 13. (72%)
11. Henry VIII; she was Catherine of Aragon, his first wife. (52%)
12. Mark Twain. (93%)
13. Styx. (85%)
14. Portugal; however, Lusitania also included some of Spain. (10%)
15. Alben W. Barkley, Harry S Truman's vice president (v.p. = "veep"). (31%)
16. Dynamite, or explosives. (83%)
17. Guernsey, Jersey, Alderney, Sark, and Herm—any two. (31%)
18. Ceylon. (12%)
19. Archery. (72%)
20. Heraldry. (86%)
21. Spinach. (50%)
22. Pt. (33%)
23. Generally southeast. (59%)
24. Denmark, although it was recently granted home rule in many areas of legislation. (55%)
25. On Staten Island, New York, having crossed from Bayonne, New Jersey. (14%)

# VOCABULARY WARM-UP ANSWERS

1. c) His intelligence, as measured, was *paramount*.
2. d) The explorer photographed the *pagans'* religious rituals.

3. c) The doctor's explanation *allayed* the woman's fears.

4. d) The girl assumed the pose of a *suppliant* before her tormentor.

5. c) Many emperors hope to found a *dynastic* line.

6. b) *Feudal* laws were very exact on the duties and obligations of lords and vassals.

7. b) The actor *improvised* his speech when his co-star forgot her lines.

8. b) The movie studio put the mousy aspiring actress through a veritable *metamorphosis*; now she looks like Jean Harlow.

9. a) The spoiled child went into a *paroxysm* of anger when he was refused a new toy.

10. d) You could never be sure of her actions, since she usually behaved in a *capricious* manner.

11. d) The king said the entertainment presented to him was unsatisfactory because it was too *plebian*.

12. c) The crusading newspaper referred to the gambling casino as a "den of *iniquity*."

13. b) The man who suddenly acquired a great deal of money built a *pretentious* home in the Country Club section.

14. b) Mensa is now *extant* in dozens of countries in the world.

15. d) The woman was greatly *perturbed* when she lost her purse.

16. c) The traitorous Duke was arrested for trying to *usurp* the throne.

17. c) Hamlet saw an *apparition*, the ghost of his father.
18. d) My former teacher, who was an expert in *circumlocution*, could take a paragraph just to say, "Hello."
19. a) The new congressman found a *staunch* ally in the senior representative from his own state.
20. b) People do not wish to live in areas where there are *noisome* vapors.

# VOCABULARY TEST ANSWERS

Again, the numbers in brackets after each answer show the percentage of Mensa members who gave the correct answers.

The average Mensa member who took this test got eighteen right. The average time taken was five minutes. Twenty-two percent of the Mensa members who took this test received perfect scores.

1. c) There was a *conglomeration* of objects on the cluttered table. (96%)
2. c) Economic *stagnation* is usually undesirable for a country. (100%)
3. b) *Eloquent* speech is not always accompanied by wisdom. (96%)
4. d) A snake makes a *sibilant* sound. (75%)

5. b) Many anecdotes told about famous people are probably *apocryphal.* (56%)
6. c) He was *inveigled* into an illegal card game by the clever gambler. (85%)
7. a) The reasons for the murder were the usual *sordid* ones. (100%)
8. b) *Antagonism* between nations is often deep-rooted. (100%)
9. c) Many alleged cures for disease are promoted by *mountebanks.* (88%)
10. c) A good stage magician is usually skilled in *legerdemain.* (96%)
11. a) The competency of many people is *implicit,* until they demonstrate otherwise. (96%)
12. d) Having one state far more powerful than the others in an alliance usually results in *hegemony.* (70%)
13. a) The surveyors walked the *periphery* of the area they were working on. (96%)
14. b) The mother was very *solicitous* of her sick child. (88%)
15. c) The word *thou* is often considered an *archaic* usage. (100%)
16. c) Ballet is considered a *kinetic* art. (100%)
17. b) There is sometimes an *ulterior* motive behind seemingly simple actions. (93%)
18. a) *Plutocracy* is derived from the Greek words for *wealth* and *rule.* (78%)
19. b) Each branch of the American government has certain *prerogative* powers not enjoyed by the other branches. (93%)

20. e)  Fireflies are *luminescent*. (96%)

# ANALOGIES WARM-UP ANSWERS

1. b)  16, the number 4 squared.
2. b)  Floor—top and bottom.
3. c)  Sphere; three- and two-dimensional.
4. d)  Armories, where weapons are stored.
5. b)  Work; a reward for effort in each case.
6. c)  Drawer—the word reversed.
7. c)  North; locations are given.
8. a)  Reversed and missing color.
9. a)  River; in each analogy, the second word represents the source of the first.
10. b)  Japan—the sign is for the Japanese yen.
11. b)  Golf.
12. c)  Maps.
13. a)  Grain.
14. c)  Valley—the second analogy pairs natural hollows or holes; the first pairs man-made ones.
15. c)  Shellfish.
16. c)  Earth.
17. b)  GOLDEN—an anagram.
18. b)  London.
19. c)  Mercury; Zeus and Hermes are Greek names of gods; Jupiter and Mercury are the Roman forms.
20. b)  Airplanes.

# ANALOGIES TEST ANSWERS

The percentage after each question shows the percentage of Mensa members who got that question correct. No one received a perfect score. The average score was fifteen correct. The average time was just over ten minutes. (The highest score, nineteen correct, was accomplished in three minutes!)

1. c) Both grow on trees as potatoes and peanuts both grow underground. (71%)
2. b) Both of the second pair speak Portuguese, as both of the first pair speak Spanish. (86%)
3. c) 32° is freezing on the Fahrenheit scale, as 0° is freezing on the Celsius scale. (86%)
4. e) Pesetas are the monetary unit in Spain, as drachmas are in Greece. (34%)
5. d) Each is the reverse of the word. (67%)
6. b) The first pair are names of people applied to food; macadam and poinsettia are the names of people applied to objects. (10%)
7. b) Foliage refers to leaves. (87%)
8. c) The number cubed: 2 × 2 × 2 equals 8; 5 × 5 × 5 equals 125. (81%)
9. e) The year when a revolution took place. (33%)
10. a) The first pair is the first two vowels, the second is the first two consonants. (20%)
11. d) A ramekin is a small baking dish. (57%)
12. c) Both are famous animals of their kind. (81%)
13. a) Potter. (95%)

14. e)  Istanbul is the new name of Constantinople, as Sri Lanka is the new name of Ceylon. (80%)

15. a)  Margaret Mitchell wrote *Gone With The Wind*. (80%)

16. c)  Each is part of a larger grouping. (89%)

17. b)  They are members of the same family. (14%)

18. d)  Carter preceded Reagan and Roosevelt preceded Truman, as U.S. president. (71%)

19. d)  Both were scientists who studied astronomy and the human brain, respectively. (67%)

20. b)  Top and bottom lines reversed, right to left reversed. (89%)

# MATH, REASONING, AND LOGIC WARM-UP ANSWERS

1.  James was first, followed by John, Walt, Will, and Joe.

2.  He said, "I will be shot." If he were shot, it would be the truth, and if they hanged him it would be a lie. So they set him free.

3.  $9.00; do one step at a time.

4.  Sally's son-in-law.

5.  14; it is the 7 × multiplication table backwards.

6.  10 miles—5 miles per vowel in the word.

7.  4 ounces, or 1/3 of the total weight.

8. The second white figure, reversed; the pattern starts with three black stars interspersed with white figures, and then it begins again with the same figures reversed.

9. Patty, because all of the others usually either beat her or beat somebody else who beats her.

10. Last; the first two letters of the first word and first two letters of the last word are used.

11. Take a sock out of the box labeled Red and Green. You know all the boxes are mislabeled, so the box labeled Red and Green *cannot* contain two colors. If the sock is green, put the green label on that box, and switch the other two labels; if the sock is red, attach the red label and then switch.

12. 8 and 9, both of them below the line. Numbers with curved lines go below the line; straight lines go above.

13. Uncertain; it says "some," which means others don't.

14. Put your 0 in the lower left-hand corner, then he cannot avoid losing.

15. 4 and 9. There are actually two series. The first starts with 1 and continues in sequence in every other place. The second starts with 6 and follows the same procedure.

16. She lost money. From the facts given, one cost her $500 and the other $750. So she paid $1250 for them and then sold them for $1200, losing $50 in the process.

17. The buildings are together. Draw a diagram. If

you missed this one, don't feel bad. A young physicist who later won the Nobel Prize worked it out at 60 feet, using a mathematical formula for a catenary.

18. Philip. They would sit in this order: John, Philip, Sally, Gerald.
19. He walked 50 minutes; the taxi saved 10 minutes going and 10 minutes coming back.
20. Twenty-seven apples and oranges.

BONUS: There are *gram* calories and *kilo* Calories, the first spelled with a small c and the second with a capital C, and a kilo Calorie is 1,000 times greater than the other. One ounce of scotch contains 100 kilo Calories, so you take in 100,000 calories and use up only 7,400, and continue to gain weight.

# MATHEMATICS, REASONING, AND LOGIC TEST ANSWERS

The number in parentheses after each answer is the percentage of Mensa members who answered that question correctly. The average number of correct answers was twelve. The average time was twenty-seven minutes.

1. 40 miles per hour. (This is deceptive. You do not add up the time and divide by two. You figure that he traveled sixty miles—there and back—in

ninety minutes, or an hour and a half. That gives you the right answer.) (65%)

2. You ask either man: "Which road would the other man tell me was safe?" and take the opposite. If you ask the liar, he will tell you the unsafe road, because the truthteller would have pointed out the right road. If you ask the truthteller, he will tell you the truth, that the liar would have named the unsafe road. In either instance, whomever you ask will point out the unsafe road. So you take the other one. (25%)

3. Seven. The first man gets three-and-a-half, plus one-half, or four horses. The second man gets half of the three that are left, one-and-one-half, plus one-half, making two. That leaves one, so the last man gets one-half and one-half. If you start from the end and work backwards, it's easier. (45%)

4. $0 + 1 + 2 - 3 - 4 + 5 + 6 - 7 - 8 + 9 = 1$
There are probably other solutions. If you check your answer and it is correct, give yourself full credit. (55%)

5. $120—the two counterfeit bills. (55%)

6. 17, 37, 46. (80%)

7. $48. (35%)

8. Friday; just cross out days that can't be used. (80%)

9. 3—one for each vowel. (25%)

10. 8. There are two series of numbers, both starting with zero. The first is 0, 1, 2, 3, 4, in every other place. The second is 0, 2, 4, 6, 8. (20%)

11. Three 9's meet the requirements; multiplied by 6, the answer is 18. (50%)
12. c. (90%)
13. $252. (60%)
14. 1440. The first number in the series is multiplied by negative 2, the second by negative 3, the third by negative 4, and so on. (70%)
15. She is a liar. No liar would claim to be a liar, therefore she is not telling the truth. (55%)
16. $6. The storekeeper charges $1 per letter in the name of the item. (35%)
17. Twenty-six minutes. (35%)
18. His house number. (30%)
19. 240. (85%)
20. 31. Double each number and add 1 to get the next number. (85%)

# CLASSICS WARM-UP ANSWERS

1. Twenty-four. One teenager can eat one pizza in a day and a half, or two pizzas in three days.
2. Only half-way; after that, the dog is running *out* of the woods.
3. A pound of feathers is heavier, because it weighs 16 ounces. Metal is weighed in troy ounces, of which there are 12 to the pound.
4. Get your hair cut by the sloppy barber. He's the one who gave the neat barber his beautiful haircut.

5. Of course. For example, her father could be 50, and her mother's father (her grandfather) is also 50. (Her mother is much younger than her father, obviously.)

6. Only three. If you take out three socks, you are guaranteed a pair.

7. 12,111.

8. Let enough air out of the tires to lower the truck.

9. Oh, see Billy, see them go.
   Forty buses in a row.
   Oh, no, Billy, them is trucks.
   What is in them? Cows and ducks.

10. One of them *is* a nickel: a 50¢ piece and a 5¢ piece.

11. Jim, where Bill had had, "had," had had; "had had." "Had had" was right.

12. Three and a half inches. Put a set of books on the shelf and look at them. If the worm started at the *front* cover of Volume I and ate through Volume II, he would not have touched the pages of Volume I at all. Volume II, with cover, would be three inches, and the worm would eat only the cover of Volume III, another half-inch.

13. 210. If you divide a number by 1/2, you double it.

14. The chance it will come up heads is 1 in 2. A coin has no memory.

15. White. He was at the North Pole if he could only go south and the bear was a polar bear.

16. There is no way in which a genuine coin could be marked B.C. B.C. means Before Christ, and

certainly no coins were minted indicating an era marked by someone who had not yet been born.

17. He's a midget and can't reach the button for the eighteenth floor.
18. He feels for the two torn edges of the paper with his name on it.
19. The poor but honest and clever knight tears up the paper he picks, and offers the other one to the king. Since the untorn one says "Death," obviously, says the knight, the one he tore up said "Marriage."
20. You save 1¢: That is $19.99.

# CLASSICS TEST ANSWERS

Each of the answers is followed by an indication of percentage. That is the percent of Mensa members who got that particular question right. The average number of correct answers was seventeen. The average elapsed time was fourteen minutes. Of all the Mensa members who took this quiz, only 6 percent got perfect scores.

1. The eighth day. If it doubles each day, on the ninth day it was ten feet high, on the eighth day it was five feet high. (84%)
2. Eighteen days. On the eighteenth day he reaches the twenty-foot level and climbs out; he doesn't have to fall back. (56%)

3. The number of rungs showing will be the same, as long as the boat is afloat. (94%)

4. Twelve, just as there are in any dozen. (98%)

5. The doctor is a woman, and the child's mother. (94%)

6. Grandfather, grandmother, son, daughter-in-law, and grandson. The grandfather and son are both fathers, the grandmother and daughter-in-law are both mothers, and the son and grandson are both sons. (91%)

7. One hour. On a wind-up alarm, it will ring at 9, which is one hour after you set it. (97%)

8. Two and one half hours. (97%)

9. Every month has twenty-eight days; most of them also have more. (94%)

10. Noah, not Moses. (95%)

11. T, for Ten. The sequence is One, Two, Three, etc. (84%)

12. Five cents. The expensive one was $1.05. If you thought the answer was $1.00 and 10¢, that does not meet the requirements. $1.00 is not $1.00 more than 10¢, it is 90¢ more. (84%)

13. Eleven cuts. (91%)

14. The fly flies thirty miles. None of the information is important except that the fly flies at 60 miles per hour and he flies for half an hour. The fly therefore flies thirty miles. (71%)

15. Pick up the signpost, point the sign to Dogpatch back the way you came, and all of the other signs will also point the right way. (53%)

16. 99,637,543,667,345. If you take one half of any number and double it, you have the number you started with. (91%)
17. One hour and a quarter is 75 minutes; there is no difference. (84%)
18. Small. (87%). (There were some clever answers here, like *meter* and *millimeter*. If you thought up one like that, give yourself credit.)
19. Yes, it comes between the third of July and the fifth of July, but it isn't a holiday for Canadians. (91%)
20. Nowhere. You don't bury survivors. (69%)

# THE MENSA GENIUS
# QUIZ BOOK 2

*Marvin Grosswirth, Dr. Abbie Salny, and
the Members of Mensa*

Dedicated to
Jerry Salny
and
Marilyn Grosswirth
for all the obvious reasons

# Acknowledgments

To enable the reader to compare his or her results with those of a group of Mensa members, those quizzes which are to be scored were given to approximately a hundred Mensa volunteers at various meetings and gatherings in the United States; London, England; and Toronto, Canada.

Among the test takers were Sharon Bailly, Judy Bank, Steve Bank, Judy Benevy, Carol Bohlen, Mickey Bregman, Vivian Bregman, Felix Bremy, Betty Claire, Seth Cohen, Mitchell Darer, Walter D'Ull, Paul Emmons, Bob Finnegan, Harold Fleming, Tracy Franz, Mary Haigh, Peter Heinlein, Sue Kent, Keith Kizer, Anne Koval, William Krause, Landon McDonald, Paul McGuffin, Melinda Maidens, Leo Marazzo, Elizabeth Marine, Isaac Marine, Allen Neuner, Jim Parsons, George Reisman, Wendy Sailer, Dan Schechter, Is Weiner, Martha Young, Carl Zipperle, all of American Mensa, and . . .

131

Helge Totland, Norway; Rhys Baron, John Darlow, Ian McLaren, Marion Maté, Susan Watkin, Brian Yare, British Isles; Elizabeth Hickman and Chris Spiegel, Australia; Barbara Thomson, New Zealand; J. A. Barker, Graham T. Coy, Douglas Skrelky, Sue Sparrow, Canada.

Even a quick glance will reveal that there are fewer than a hundred names here. As good as we claim to be at puzzles, we were unable to decipher some of the signatures (which may account for some misspellings in the list above, for which we apologize), especially those that were missing.

Identified or not, we are grateful to all who participated.

A number of Mensans offered questions for inclusion in the book. Our special thanks to all of them, including Mike Tuchman, Warren Spears, and R. B. Lehr, and to Rush Washburne, puzzle editor of the *Mensa Bulletin,* for his special help.

Once the questions were all in, Jerome E. Salny (who claims he enjoys quizzes and was in no way coerced by the quizmaker who lives with him) proofread all of them the hard way—he worked through them.

Throughout the book, in the sections between the warm-ups and the actual tests, you'll find examples of how Mensans use their brains in practical ways. These are all actual situations, contributed by members (all of whom are identified). These are only a small portion of the wealth of stories we received. Unfortunately, space considerations do not allow us to publish them all, but we are grateful to everyone who contributed (and we are saving their submissions, should there ever be a *Mensa Genius Quiz Book 3*).

We received those stories because most of the more than a hundred local-group newsletter editors published our appeal for anecdotes. Without that sort of cooperation, this book would not have been possible. The distribution of that appeal was accomplished through the small but efficient staff at Mensa's National Office, headed by Executive Director Margot Seitelman. The American Mensa Committee (our Board of Directors), and its chairman, Gabriel Werba, gave the support, encouragement, and cooperation we needed to proceed with and complete this project.

We would be remiss in not thanking the readers of the first *Mensa Genius Quiz Book*. We're beginning to realize that gremlins are no myth. Despite our, and our editors', efforts to achieve perfection, those rotten little creatures sneak into the press room just before printing begins and move things around (which is why—if you believe the answer to one of the questions in that book—you now believe that Lassie is a whale). Of course, we received letters from our readers. Every one of them was a joy, because they were all written in the good-natured spirit of fun that we hoped would prevail in that book—and in this one.

*The Mensa Genius Quiz Book 2* really is the work of the members of Mensa. All we've done is pull it together. Nevertheless, in that pulling together, we recognize that any errors and omissions that may have crept in are our full responsibility. (For the record, Salny is the question maven; Grosswirth worked on the text sections.) We cheerfully accept that responsibility, gremlins notwithstanding.

All we ask is that you be gentle with us.

As with the first volume, a portion of the proceeds of this book go to the Mensa Scholarship Fund.

MARVIN GROSSWIRTH
ABBIE F. SALNY

*February 1983*

# Are You a Genius?

Have we met somewhere before—perhaps in the pages of the first *Mensa Genius Quiz Book*? If so, welcome back. And feel free to skip most of this introduction.

If, however, this is our first encounter, stay with us for the next few pages. The primary purpose of this little book is to provide pleasure and diversion for people who enjoy puzzles and quizzes, but it can also offer some hidden surprises and rewards. You may discover that you're a potential genius.

A GENIUS—YOU?

It's entirely possible. First, let's clear up some of the doubts many people have about the word, beginning with the canard that "genius borders on insanity." High intelligence is no more of an option on a ticket to the booby hatch than is profound stupidity, or any other mental extreme. Genius isn't so much a question of how smart a person may be as measured by a score on some test, as it is a question of how that smartness manifests itself. Some of the dearest, kindest, sweetest people we know can't read a postage stamp without moving their lips, and some of the most despicable villains in the world have soaring IQs.

Professions, occupations, and hobbies are not necessarily indicators of intelligence either. The only requirement for Mensa membership is a score on a recognized IQ test at or above the 98th percentile—in other words, in the top 2 percent of the population. (That works out to a minimum score of 130 on the most current Wechsler scales and to 132 on the Stanford-Binet, the two major sets of IQ tests.) But that membership is a varied and eclectic one. Authors Isaac Asimov and Leslie Charteris (author of "The Saint" mysteries) are members. Carolina Varga Dinicu, who, as "Morocco," performs Middle Eastern dances, is a member. So are Adam Osborne (who designed the Osborne portable computer) and Clive Sinclair (developer of the Timex/Sinclair computer). The president of the Ford Motor Company is a member, as is the president of a six-person janitorial service in New England. Members include homemakers, computer programmers, shop owners, shop clerks, postal employees, telephone linespeople, singers, physicists, journalists, doctors, lawyers, beggars, thieves, and, for all we know, an Indian chief (although, admittedly, at this writing, none has come forth). We have soldiers and sailors, teachers and students, artists and carpenters, Republicans, Democrats, libertarians, born-again Christians, atheists, agnostics, apostates, people with ten or twelve degrees, and high school dropouts.

So how does one identify a "genius"? Well, for openers, you might try checking the several dictionary definitions of the word and see if any of them applies to you. If you have a particular talent at which you truly excel, you may be a genius at the piano, or in labor negotiations, or in concocting exotic recipes. And if your IQ is in the top 2 percent of the population, then you're certainly what psychometrists would call a "genius."

## WHO CARES?

Good question. If you don't, no one else does either. Anyone who's been around Mensa long enough will eventually hear some old-timer mutter, "IQ isn't everything, but it isn't nothing either." By itself, intelligence is as useless as a fine singing voice that is exercised only in the shower. As we said earlier, it isn't how smart you are, it's what you do with your brains that matters. But first you have to know what your potential is. That's where IQ testing comes in.

Everybody knows that IQ tests have flaws and faults. Nevertheless, it's the belief in Mensa that such tests are the only tool available for measuring one's intelligence potential, and it's as worthwhile knowing what that potential is as it is knowing your height, weight, and blood type. And that's where this book can be of help.

## IS THIS BOOK AN IQ TEST?

Absolutely not! IQ tests are written, normed (that is, given to groups of people to determine how to judge scoring levels), and eventually administered under carefully controlled conditions. Many of the questions in this book, however, are similar to the types of questions found on IQ tests, so if you score well on these quizzes, chances are you'll come out well on a standardized IQ test, too. Furthermore—and perhaps more important—you can compare your results with those of the hundred or so Mensans who also worked these quizzes. That could indicate whether you're a likely candidate for Mensa.

## SUPPOSE YOU FAIL?

Forget it; you can't "fail." No one "fails" or "passes" an IQ test any more than anyone fails or passes a height, weight, or vision test, or any other test that measures a physical or mental attribute. Besides, this isn't a test. The only way you can "fail" is by failing to have fun with this book, in which case the failure is ours, not yours.

Furthermore—and this is probably the most serious criticism of IQ tests—many people, including some of the most brilliant geniuses of our time, are simply no good at taking tests. (There are, however, tips to test taking; see "How to Take a Test—Any Test," page 9.)

## WHERE DO YOU GO FROM HERE?

If you have no trouble with tests, proceed to the quizzes themselves. They've been organized into categories that are likely to appear, with variations, on many IQ tests.

At the beginning of each section is a set of "Warm-Up" questions, designed to get you in the mood. As with any warm-up exercise, it's a good idea to take it easy and proceed in a leisurely manner at first.

In the first *Mensa Genius Quiz Book*, we separated the warm-ups from the scored quizzes with little essays about how Mensa members exercise, polish, and have fun with their intelligence. In this book, we've devoted that space to showing how Mensans apply their thinking abilities to real-life situations. We've tried to use anecdotes that relate to the particular section of questions, but in all honesty, we must admit that we're stretching a little in some cases because most of the stories are really examples of logical thinking. (And just so you can prove what you've always suspected—that there's such a thing as being too smart—don't miss the epilogue.)

When you plunge into the scored quizzes, you should time yourself carefully because here is where you'll be pitting your wits against the Mensans who took the same quizzes. There are two good reasons for keeping track of the time. If you do as well as the

Mensans—that is, if you get as many right answers within about the same time—then you'll have a good indication of how you stack up against people whose IQs have been certified by valid tests. If, however, you don't do as well—that is, if you get as many right answers, but it took you longer to get them—that could indicate that you don't work well under pressure, and that's worth knowing, too.

In any case, if you really don't care about any of this, then just work the questions, at your own pace and as the time and mood suit you, just for the sheer pleasure of it.

If you discover that you have a "genius" for coming up with alternative right answers that we may have missed, double-check your results, and if you're certain you're correct, give yourself a double score for that question. And please tell us about it.

Above all, have fun. After all, that's what this book is really all about.

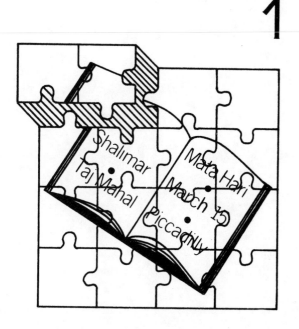

# TRIVIA

# Warm-Ups

1. Everyone has heard of Piccadilly in London. What does the name come from?
2. Who was the husband of the writer who wrote *Frankenstein*?
3. What is the British equivalent of West Point for training officers?
4. Sylvaner, Niagara, Sirah. What are they?
5. What is the wife of a baronet called?
6. Why can Princess Diana of England become queen some day, whereas Prince Philip can't become Queen Elizabeth's king?
7. What is a marriage between a commoner and royalty called, wherein the right of succession is abandoned?
8. The plate or badge on the bumper reads: CH. Where did the car come from? (Or at least, where did the owner buy the plate?)
9. If your baggage was labeled ORD, what airport in the United States would you expect to land at?

10. The family of a famous founder of a famous American university came from Stratford-upon-Avon. Who was the founder and what is the name of the university?

11. When the Pilgrims landed in what is now Massachusetts, they were greeted by an Indian, Squanto. What language did he speak?

12. The Plantagenets ruled England for many years. What does the name Plantagenet come from?

13. A brilliant hair color was named after an Italian painter. What is the hair color and who was the painter?

14. Where did Romeo and Juliet live?

15. She was Mrs. John Rolfe socially. Every schoolchild knows her by her first name. What is it?

16. T. E. Lawrence was strongly identified with what country?

17. According to the rhyme, what is the fate of Saturday's child?

18. Where did Peter Rabbit's father meet his doom?

19. In which of Beethoven's symphonies is Schiller's *Ode to Joy*?

20. Who was Mary Tudor's more famous sister?

21. What's the name of the drinking song whose music was used for "The Star-Spangled Banner"?

22. Where did Molly Malone of "cockles and mussels" fame live?

23. Of what country is Bernardo O'Higgins a famous national historical figure?

24. In what war did Winston Churchill serve as a war correspondent?

25. Where is the Taj Mahal?

# No Small Matter

Among the various quizzes, puzzles, and contests one is likely to come across in Mensa publications and at parties, meetings, and even conventions, *trivia* questions rank high. It sometimes seems that the older a person is, the more he or she enjoys trivia quizzes, probably because trivia and nostalgia are inexorably intertwined.

It may be argued that there's not terribly much value per se in remembering the name of Gene Autry's horse (and I don't). But the simple act of attempting to conjure up that long-forgotten detail brings a flood of memories about a boyhood in which Saturday mornings were spent trudging through the neighborhood with empty milk and soda bottles in the hopes of recovering enough of the "deposit" (a kind of ransom paid to the storekeepers to ensure that the bottles would be returned) to pay the afternoon admission price to the Supreme Theatre in Brooklyn, with, perhaps, enough left over for a box of Mason's

Dots or Jujubes, thereby sustaining a thriving neighborhood dental practice.

However, apart from providing fun and a challenge to one's memory, and evoking frankly sentimental nostalgia, trivia has its practical aspects, too. The ability to store and recall seemingly obscure and unimportant—that is, "trivial"—facts is an integral component of a sharp intuition. If you're a veteran of the first *Mensa Genius Quiz Book,* then you are already aware of my conviction that intuition is not only a real attribute but a valuable one. (Intuition can be defined—perhaps a trifle simplistically—as the ability to rapidly "program" a set of facts randomly drawn from a vast storehouse of "trivial" data stored somewhere in the brain.)

I regard intuition as a form of intelligence. As with all forms of intelligence, people may vary in their overall intuitive capacities and skills. But, also like all forms of intelligence, intuitive abilities are not enough. To work well, even to work at all, intuition needs input, a mental storehouse full of tiny scraps of information for the mind to draw on as the need arises and circumstances dictate.

Basically, what we're talking about is a matter of magnitude. "Intelligence" requires inputs of significant data. Intuition requires inputs of seemingly insignificant data, details that you're not likely to remember consciously but that your subconscious retains and brings to the fore when a decision—major or minor—has to be made quickly.

To be sure, one person's "education" may be an-

146

other person's trivia, and it isn't always easy to distinguish between the two. As an evening session student at the Baruch College of Business and Public Administration (City University of New York), I took a required course in advertising. One of the questions on the midterm examination dealt with postal regulations: "How would you mail 5,000 advertisements . . . ?" In answering, the student was expected to have cited chapter and verse of some boring postal ordinance which I could never remember. I responded with something about turning it over to the head of the mail room with instructions to let me know the fastest and most economical means of getting the mail out, pointing out that it was his job to know postal regulations, not mine. I got full credit for the answer, along with a note from the instructor requesting that I not discuss it with any of the other students.

Hans G. Frommer, American Mensa's second vice-chairman, is another person who, as a student, preferred coping with trivia to memorizing it. During his early years in engineering school, he had a chemistry professor who avoided written exams by orally testing two or three students during each period before proceeding to new material. "He would test alphabetically," Hans wrote, "so we knew about when our turn would come.

"I was an extremely lazy student," he claims, "trying to get by with a minimum of study. Consequently, I postponed studying some twenty different elements in inorganic chemistry until the last minute. Finally, I started with the two easiest ones—gold and silver—and got them down pat." That, he felt, would hold him for a while. But when he showed up in class, he made the unhappy discovery that because of several absences, the student who was ahead of him alphabetically was being called, and Frommer would certainly be called upon next. "I panicked," Hans admitted, "but then I had an idea. The prof always looked at each student's notebook and picked one of the subjects from it. I quickly creased my notebook so it would fall open at 'Gold' and underlined the heading with red pencil. For good measure, I did the same with 'Silver.' I had barely finished when my name was called.

When his turn came, as he knew it must, Hans handed his professor the notebook, "and it practically fell open to 'Gold.' 'Well, Frommer, tell me something about gold.' I rattled off all the data, uses, compounds, etc., and was ready to sit down. 'Not so fast,' he said. 'That was very good, but not enough.' Again he leafed through my notebook. It did its job and stopped at 'Silver' . . . [and] shortly thereafter I sat down with an A and spared myself studying up on eighteen other elements. Was it smart? I doubt it," he concluded with appropriate self-effacement.

Perhaps the smartest thing he did was not to have used a ring-binder type of notebook.

Some people can't seem to ignore a challenge, no matter how trivial it may be. Consider Sandra Stright, of Walnut Creek, California, who could have waited a few moments to solve a minor problem but who couldn't resist the opportunity of finding a clever way to work it out herself.

"One day at the office," she said, "I was trying to put a memo I'd written up on a metal bulletin board with a magnet. The bulletin board is too high for me to reach, so I usually get one of the taller people in the office to put things up for me, but this time no one was around who could reach it any better than I could. I could hold the paper up high enough by grasping it at its bottom edge, but I couldn't reach high enough to place the magnet."

There were three possible ways to deal with this problem: (1) Stand on something. (2) Wait for a tall person to appear. (3) Find a way that nobody else might have thought of. Clearly, the first two choices were unacceptable. After a couple of minutes' thought, inspiration struck. Instead of holding the paper to the bulletin board and then placing the magnet against the paper, Sandra attached the magnet to the staple holding the two sheets of paper together at the top, grasped the pages at the bottom, and, carefully stretching and balancing, got the magnet to touch the bulletin board. A co-worker who had observed the whole exercise characterized it as "Outrageous!" "It worked, didn't it?" was Sandra's unassailable response.

Cutting costs in a business enterprise is hardly trivial, but it sometimes takes imagination and intelligence to recognize that solutions may lie in seemingly unimportant, routine operations. As a new partner in a small typesetting company, Roberta L. Sniegocki, of

Chicago, was seeking ways of reducing expenses. One day, while reviewing recording procedures with the bookkeeper, Roberta discovered that hours were being wasted posting figures. Each employee would fill out a time sheet, from which the bookkeeper would transfer the numbers for per-job costing and billing.

Roberta devised a simple method of record keeping by designing a form that "traveled" with a job through each of the shop's departments; employees made appropriate entries as the job entered and left their section. This method eliminated considerable copying, transferring, calculating, and, not incidentally, margin of error. "After some argument about what 'everyone else' in this business does, . . . I put the new system to work. And," she admits freely, "it's been great. Now the bookkeeper has time to do all the Xeroxing, make trips to the post office—even water the plants."

What does a manufacturer do with unusable scraps? A simple—even trivial—question. "Unusable" means there is no market for them. There is, therefore, only one answer: throw them away. But people like Kathy Jones tend to be dissatisfied with simple answers, especially if such solutions are aesthetically offensive.

Kathy is a principal in Kadon Enterprises, Inc., a company that manufactures Quintillions, which Kadon promotes as "the aristocrat of strategy games." The company's advertising describes the game best:

Based on a geometric phenomenon recognized for

thousands of years—the 12 possible ways to join 5 squares—QUINTILLIONS moves these famous shapes into the third dimension and adds five fascinating games . . . plus hundreds of super puzzle challenges in 2-D and 3-D.

The sets are laser-cut from high-quality, matched-grain hardwood. There are, of course, scraps. But what aesthete could bear to part with "scraps" that also happen to be beautifully cut pieces of fine wood? Certainly not Kathy Jones and company. The solution? On the same sheet describing the game is an advertisement for "Quint-Art Sculptures—certified one-of-a-kind originals, signed and numbered editions to titillate the eye and the mind . . . in solid hardwood, permanently bonded into intriguing abstracts, witty animal and people forms. Special themes or subjects available by commission."

"I have a lot of . . . trivial items of no particular interest," Kathy said, "just routine craziness, like hanging wastebaskets on the wall so the dog won't raid them. . . ."

To fully appreciate the mental and artistic dexterity with which Kathy treats "trivialities," send a stamped self-addressed envelope to Kadon at 1227 Lorene Drive, Pasadena, MD 21122, for a copy of the company's flyer.

And if you now fully appreciate the uses of trivia, proceed to the quiz on the next page.

# Match Wits with Mensa

## TRIVIA TEST

Time started _____
Time elapsed _____

1. Where are the Islets of Langerhans?
2. Margaretha Geertruida Zelle (or alternate spellings, depending upon your reference) is better known by another name. What is it?
3. What was the previous name of the country now called Zimbabwe?
4. What is a *roman à clef*?
5. Give an example of a *roman à clef*.
6. What is a patten?
   a) a shoe   b) a song   c) a book   d) a typeface
7. "Pale hands I loved, beside the Shalimar" is a line from an old song. What is the Shalimar?
8. For whom was January named?

9. Isaac Walton is famous as an author in what field?

10. Ems, Roman, Bodoni, serif: What field are we talking about?

11. Some countries call it a ground nut. What is it usually called in the United States?

12. In what direction does the St. Lawrence River flow?

13. What do Bath, Aix-les-Bains, and Baden-Baden have in common?

14. Clarence Day wrote a book that became a very famous play. What was its name?

15. Another word for *jail* is *clink*. What is its derivation?

16. *Hyperbole* is used in what field?
    a) mathematics   b) language   c) music
    d) history

17. If you want a plant to come up again next year in your garden, should you buy an annual or a perennial?

18. Blue denim is typically American. Where did the word *denim* originate?

19. Name the Three Musketeers and the fourth member of their group.

20. "Under a spreading chestnut tree/The _____ stands." Who or what is standing there in the shade?

21. Where is the Southern Cross?

22. Where did the dodo bird live before it became extinct?

23. Who was Joseph N. Niepce's world-famous part-
    ner and colleague, whose name has passed into
    the language?
24. What date is the Ides of March?
25. What was the symbol of the 1939–40 New York
    World's Fair?

*aperient*

# VOCABULARY

# Warm-Ups

The warm-up words are taken from the works of Isaac Asimov, Mensa's favorite international vice-president and one of its favorite writers.

1. Medley
   a) interfering or nosy
   b) a type of fruit
   c) motley, varied; music consisting of parts of other pieces
   d) uninteresting, flat, dull
   e) pertaining to the Medes (of the Medes and Persians)
2. Injudicious
   a) against the law
   b) subject to legal penalties
   c) within the walls
   d) lacking sound judgment or discretion
   e) willfully injurious in deed or language

3. Deputation
   a) argumentativeness
   b) forcible removal to another place as punishment
   c) showing signs of insanity
   d) dispossession or loss
   e) a group or individual appointed to go on a mission on behalf of another or others
4. Antidote
   a) a brief tale relating something of momentary interest
   b) running in opposite directions around an axis
   c) the curved elevation within the outer rim of the ear
   d) a remedy against poison or an attack of disease
   e) the opposite side of the world
5. Volition
   a) the act of flying
   b) electricity as measured by volts
   c) to volunteer as a worker in an organization
   d) the act, power, or faculty of willing or resolving
   e) speaking with extreme fluency
6. Hazardous
   a) a wordy or roundabout way of speaking
   b) full of risk, dangerous
   c) a line that forms a boundary, or, loosely, any surrounding area
   d) a form of Greek column
   e) a hermit

7. Rigmarole
   a) a form of horse harness
   b) difficult, impossible; a severely tedious task
   c) a succession of incoherent statements, a rambling discourse
   d) a fancy suit of clothing, a costume
   e) a small channel, gutter, or groove
8. Circumscribe
   a) to mark out the limits of, to restrain, to abridge, to draw a line around
   b) carefully, with due regard for common sense
   c) an accent mark over a letter (of Greek origin)
   d) the adjuncts of an action or fact
   e) to write in a circular form, using flowery language
9. Empirical
   a) relating to an empire
   b) based chiefly on experience
   c) pertaining to an adventurous or chivalrous undertaking
   d) related to the study of science
   e) related to New York State
10. Affront
   a) the decorated facade of a building
   b) the false front used sometimes for theatrical performances
   c) an architectural style
   d) an insult, a word or act of intentional disrespect
   e) to disturb, startle, or frighten

11. Petulant
    a) displaying peevish impatience, or (rare) pert, insolent, or rude
    b) full of petals, flowery (obsolete)
    c) pertaining to the keeping of household pets
    d) a species of the genus *Petunia*
    e) an oily hydrocarbon obtained from turpentine

12. Assiduous
    a) a contract of convention between a ruler and his people
    b) a sitting of a legislative body
    c) constant in application, persevering, unremitting
    d) related to the Weights and Measures Bureau
    e) a slender spear or sword (obsolete)

13. Sardonic
    a) bitter, scornful, mocking (usually, of a smile or laugh)
    b) pertaining to a native of Sardinia
    c) pertaining to sardines
    d) pertaining to a sarcophagus
    e) a type of Greek actor in Attica

14. Incongruous
    a) badly fitting, as clothing
    b) disagreeing in type or character, inconsistent
    c) unpleasant, disagreeable, argumentative
    d) unable to be consoled, extremely sad
    e) without money, bankrupt

15. Chronal
    a) on a record or register
    b) of or relating to time (rare)

    c) pertaining to many colors
    d) staining by immersion in coloring matter
    e) pertaining to the larvae of insects

16. Invocation
    a) a dedication to a career
    b) a test designed to measure aptitudes
    c) a calling-upon (usually a deity) for help, a prayer
    d) a liniment
    e) loud shouting

17. Iridescent
    a) recurring at frequent intervals
    b) displaying colors like those of the rainbow
    c) not able to be fixed or repaired
    d) nonnegotiable, as a check that is unsigned
    e) shining blue-white

*"Prolix Prose" consists of well-known proverbs or sentences cast in extremely verbose language. Give the original of each sentence disguised in this form:*

18. It is considered to be extremely injudicious to investigate with extreme care the oral cavity of an *Equus* which has been provided to one gratis.
19. It is possible to avoid thrice three in repairs if the initial step of repairing a rent or damage is initially made with a filament attached to a sharp, pointed piece of steel with a hole in one end.
20. A superfluity of persons able to prepare edible comestibles sometimes can damage the preparation of a liquid intended for consumption.

# A Way with Words

One of the more common complaints that arise in any discussion about intelligence, particularly among critics of IQ tests, is that intelligence is difficult to define. Somehow, the compilers of the *Oxford American Dictionary* (Avon Books, 1980) had no such difficulty:

> **intelligence** *n.* 1. mental ability, the power of learning and understanding . . .

What could be plainer?

Yet, somehow, that definition is perhaps not as simple as it appears. It raises some additional questions: How does one define *power, learning,* and *understanding*? Suppose, for example, Joyce and Harry are given the same set of facts and arrive at the same conclusion. It could be argued that they are of equal intelligence. But what if Joyce arrives at her conclusion in thirty seconds and Harry takes forty-five seconds; does that mean Joyce is a little more intelligent than Harry? (Probably; that's why most IQ tests are timed.)

And how much "learning" are we talking about? Who is the more intelligent, the person who loves mathematics and delves into its seemingly infinite elegances, or the one who "understands" the need for speed and accuracy and therefore learns to operate an electronic calculator with skill and efficiency?

Furthermore, how much of the "power" to learn and understand is dependent upon what one is given—taught, if you will? Several years ago, a television program about IQ tests attempted to demonstrate the effects of environment on IQ scores by describing a test that was administered to a group of inner-city black children. The vocabulary section included the word *lark*. Almost every kid failed to answer because the answers from which they had to choose did not include *car* or *cigarette*, two products with the brand name "Lark" that were being heavily advertised at the time. It hardly seems fair to denigrate the kids' intelligence because circumstances limited their knowledge of birds to pigeons and sparrows.

For decades, IQ test designers have been struggling with the problem of a "culture-free" or "culture-fair" test, one that does not depend on education—a package of learned facts—for successful completion. (They seem to be succeeding; Mensa now has such a test available, and present indications are that it really works, although some psychologists still do not agree that a culture-fair test really exists.) Such tests are really intended as a kind of convenience; you can't take an English or Italian test and translate it into Swahili or Urdu and expect it to be effective; adjustments have to be made. Rather than attempt to fine-tune every test for the linguistic and cultural differences each language requires, it would be better—and easier—to have a culture-free test, a goal that has not yet been completely met.

None of this negates, however, the importance of language in both the determination and the use of intelligence. The "power to learn and understand" is really the ability to communicate, which is the ability to send and receive information and ideas.

Clearly, then, the ability to learn and understand rests solidly on a foundation of words. As the writer and language critic Donna Woolfolk Cross wrote, "In order to understand a thing, you must first be able to describe it." If words are essential to learning and understanding, and if the ability to learn and understand is a mark of intelligence, then it follows that any attempt to measure intelligence must include a measure of one's ability with language, which is why vocabulary and reading comprehension are such important elements of IQ tests.

People who do well on IQ tests are likely to have an affinity for words. That probably explains why Mensans enjoy word games and puzzles so much. Many Mensans are fond of inventing their own word games. Puns, anagrams, double-entendres, spoonerisms, limericks, and other forms of word play abound in the organization's publications and at get-togethers. While some of us rail vigorously against abuses of the

English language, we have no qualms about inventing, as the occasion dictates, our own words. (My own latest creation, arising from the need to describe that which a friend of mine does best, is *hypochondriate*. It's a verb, and whenever I use it, the listener always understands, instantly, what I mean. Also, I will seize this opportunity to record, for posterity, that I was the first person to create a new word of departure, one that will eventually replace *good-bye* or *so long*. In 1980, at the Mensa Annual Gathering in Louisville, Kentucky, I predicted that our progeny will take leave of each other by waving and calling out: "Hand!"—an acronym for the execrable "Have a nice day!" In the South, of course, the word will be HANDY—"Have a nice day, y'all.")

Perhaps it's a reflection of the importance of words that while Mensans have a marked propensity for using them, they don't like to waste them. Most intelligent people have little patience with jargon, corporate or professional gobbledygook, or unnecessary verbiage. Case in point: Hans Frommer, the clever but lazy student with the trick notebook whom we met in the Trivia chapter. Apparently, Hans managed to graduate despite his scholastic lassitude and eventually landed a job with Caterpillar Tractor in Milwaukee. "I was making a monthly report at work," he recalls, an inventory of damaged and broken tools. "It took five hours every month, and I had no idea what use was being made of it. The report was Greek to me, [and] I resented the time it took.

"So, one day," he continues, "I told the boss that I

not only hated to do it, but that it was worthless and he should quit making me do it."

"How do you know it's worthless?" the boss asked somewhat patronizingly.

"Because," Hans replied, "I am six months behind, and nobody has asked for it." The reports were discontinued shortly thereafter.

Understandably, Frommer has become something of an expert in cutting corners to save time. Unable to resist the lure of words, he has compiled an eminently useful pamphlet called *Time Savers* that covers the home, office, kitchen, tax time, and travel. You can have a copy by sending $2 to Lakeshore Publishing, 12360 N. Lakeshore Drive, Mequon, WI 53092.

Rod Vickers, writer, artist, and recently retired entrepreneur of Shawnee, Kansas, used to be regional vice-chairman of American Mensa. Each of Mensa's nine national regions has a number; they also have names. Vickers's domain, encompassing a somewhat amorphous area in the middle of the country, was saddled with the Central Northwest Region, a name that somehow displeased its official representative. Consequently, Vickers was appointed, by the chairman, as a committee of one to come up with a suitable designation for the area. He would regale the American Mensa Committee with his newest offer at each meeting, supporting the proposed name with outrageous, and outrageously verbose, "reports." He finally stopped when one of his names missed becoming official by a single vote, but it is a lasting tribute to his linguistic skills that to this day, Region 7, while still officially known as the Central Northwest Region, is informally and affectionately referred to as "The Great Buffalo Chip Region."

Rod's skill with words is best manifested by his ability to give something resembling credence to what turns out to be, on reflection, exquisitely idiotic. When asked to contribute anecdotes on quick-thinking problem solving for this book, he included the following in a group of several offerings:

> My daddy sent me out when I was just a little tyke and gave me just two bullets, because we needed two squirrels for stew. I wasted one of the bullets shooting a tin can, and knew I was in trouble. My daddy was a believer in corporal punishment, and he acted often on his belief. So I waited until I saw two squirrels sitting side by side, and shot and swung my gun at the same time. Got them both.

He almost got me with that one.

Like Frommer, Vickers enjoys playing and working with words, but has never much liked wasting them. As a child, he quickly hit upon a method for dealing with what was once a common version of that problem, and it is passed along here in the event that there are still teachers who insist that obstreperous students be made penitent the old-fashioned way: "I learned to get through five hundred repetitions of a phrase very quickly," he claims, "if it would fit on one line. By grasping in a line four or five pencils held together by rubber bands, it is possible to write four or five lines of material at a single pass." At this point, it's a little difficult to trust Rod Vickers's credibility, but at least this sounds more plausible than killing two squirrels with a single bullet.

Sometimes words fail, even for those who use them professionally. H. R. "Dick" Horning is now public relations director for the Miami Dolphins, but in 1949 he was fresh out of college and had an urge to see the world. He wound up in Australia, where he landed a job as a reporter. The following year, Dick decided to move to Hong Kong in search of further adventures. Among the passengers on the ship was one Tony Ang, a Chinese seaman who had jumped ship six years earlier, had married an Australian woman, begun raising a family, and become a solid, hard-working citizen. Unfortunately, Tony was on Dick's ship because he was being deported as an illegal—and "undesirable"—alien, in keeping with what was then Australia's "white only" immigration policy. Dick had met Tony earlier, but it was aboard the ship to Hong Kong that he got to know and befriend the luckless ex-sailor, his pregnant wife (who had insisted on accompanying him), and their three sons.

In Hong Kong, Dick joined the *China Mail*, one of the major English-language papers in the Far East. "I did not think of Tony and his family for several months," Dick wrote. Then, almost on impulse, he decided to look up his shipboard companion.

Dick found the Angs in Kowloon, the "mainland" half of Hong Kong, living in a slum and down to the last of their savings. There was no work, and no prospects of any kind for survival in the immediate or long-range future. Tony Ang was seriously and dispassionately considering doing away with himself and his family, rather than have them endure the pain and humiliation of starving to death.

The reporter decided to use his major asset—his words—to help the Angs.

"I . . . worked out an 'open letter' to [the Australian] Immigration Minister . . . from Mrs. Ang," Dick later reported. "She knew little of writing, so I wrote it, freely expressing my outrage." He then got the Hong Kong Bureau Chief of United Press to run the open letter over the international news wires. Australia was in the midst of a heated election campaign, and the local press was eager to publish Mrs. Ang's ghost-written appeal. Within days, Australia had a new government, and the Angs were invited to return.

The family went back home, and Dick Horning lost contact with them. Twenty-five years later, in anticipation of a visit to Australia, he decided to attempt to find Tony Ang once again. This time, however, his method was brilliantly simple. He wrote to the Australian Embassy in Washington and asked for a listing of all the Angs in the Sydney telephone directory. There were four. He wrote to "Anthony Ang," and eventually received a reply from Tony's son, Dennis, who informed him that although his father had since died, all the other Angs were prospering. Dick's words had helped save a family from virtually certain extinction.

But what about that failure of words? Although Dick Horning had found the Angs in the Kowloon slum, he cannot, even now, explain how he did it. "There were no directories of any kind available," he reported, and he knew that the local immigration authorities would have nothing more than a record of the Angs' entry. "Yet," he recalled, "I remember taking a Walla Walla boat to . . . Kowloon, getting on a . . . bus . . . and riding for some three miles and impulsively getting off." He asked a Chinese clerk in a corner tobacconist's shop if he knew where the Chinese man with the Caucasian wife lived. "Oh, yes. I will show you," came the reply, and the clerk walked a block with Dick and pointed out the Angs' shack. "I still do not have the faintest idea how I 'knew' where to find the family in the teeming squatters' huts on the Kowloon side," he claims. "I have resolved the mystery as either a memory failure on my part in recalling how I knew, or by accepting the idea that I really wasn't the one who searched them out, after all."

There are, he suggests, powers beyond those of learning and understanding.

Now try your own power of learning and understanding with the vocabulary quiz, and match wits with Mensa.

# Match Wits with Mensa

## VOCABULARY TEST

Time started _____
Time elapsed _____

1. Cupidity
   a) relating to the Roman god of love
   b) adorableness, state of being lovable
   c) inordinate longing or desire to attain possessions
   d) containing traces of copper
   e) sailing in a direction contrary to the wind
2. Enormity
   a) extreme largeness incapable of being measured
   b) monstrous wickedness
   c) extreme volume too loud to be endured
   d) exaggerated rhetoric
   e) state of extreme anger

3. Progenitor
   a) a descendant in the collateral line
   b) someone who is in favor of a particular law
   c) an ancestor or originator
   d) a biological term relating to descent in the male line
   e) a speaker on behalf of a candidate
4. Careen
   a) to run at full speed
   b) a type of tropical fruit
   c) to turn a ship over on one side for cleaning, etc.
   d) an Arabic name
   e) a peal of bells in a tower
5. Nefarious
   a) related to a queen of an Egyptian dynasty
   b) relating to a new form of travel, undertaken for the first time
   c) wicked or villainous
   d) neglectful of assigned duties
   e) a stall holder at a street fair
6. Risible
   a) capable of rising (said of bread dough or cake dough)
   b) motive power for a balloon
   c) having grown to full height, as a plant
   d) capable of producing laughter, laughable
   e) a variety of rice cultivation practiced without water fields
7. Aperient
   a) a type of before-dinner drink
   b) something perceived

    c) an opening in a wall for looking through
    d) laxative
    e) something that appears to be other than it actually is

8. Diaconate
    a) a poison related to belladonna
    b) a learner
    c) a large crown or wreath of leaves
    d) pertaining to the office or rank of deacon, or time when one is a deacon
    e) a type of earth that readily absorbs liquid

9. Obiter
    a) a laudatory description of someone, written after his or her death
    b) an overbite that must be corrected by an orthodontist
    c) by the way, in passing, incidentally
    d) a legal decision against a plaintiff
    e) the file in a newspaper office where obituaries are kept

10. Eponym
    a) one who gives, or is said to give, his or her name to a people, place, or thing
    b) a synonym
    c) the chief officer of an antique Greek state
    d) a variety of restaurant specializing in horse-meat
    e) a mathematical formula for determining liquidity

11. Gibbet
    a) a form of speech that is almost unintelligible
    b) any long-armed ape of the genus *Hylobate*

    c) convex, rounded, protuberant

    d) a gallows

    e) a gibe or taunt

12. Equinoctial
    a) pertaining to horses
    b) pertaining to a state of equal day and night
    c) pertaining to heavy rains
    d) equitable, fair, just
    e) meaning one thing and expressing another

13. Autonomic
    a) a self-propelled automobile
    b) pertaining to a robot
    c) pertaining to a self-regulating calculator
    d) named after oneself
    e) self-governing

14. Erudite
    a) belching
    b) learned, full of knowledge
    c) a form of ornamental stitching
    d) a winding path
    e) of written, as opposed to oral, learning

15. Dour
    a) a variety of tropical fruit
    b) hard or stern, sometimes obstinate
    c) a variety of rock formed under pressure
    d) a Spanish coin of the later Middle Ages, worth about 25¢
    e) virtuous, valiant

16. Mendacious
    a) begging
    b) lying, untruthful, false

c) capable of being mended or repaired
d) of high quality, superior in choice
e) generous, giving freely to beggars

*"Prolix Prose": These familiar sayings and proverbs have been recast in extremely verbose form. Give the original for each.*

17. Individuals who habitually or commonly domicile themselves in habitats containing side portions or roof coverings made of a silicaceous material would be well advised to refrain from casting any size of hard mineral pellets (other than metal).
18. One who habitually seeks repose in the arms of Morpheus at an hour somewhat before that usually considered, and who equally bids farewell to said repose in an equally prompt manner, is reputed to acquire an excellent bodily condition, not to mention an accumulation of pelf and a substantial store of sapience.
19. An individual who possesses neither sapience nor the knowledge to be aware of this lack will rapidly find that his stock of worldly goods, chiefly in the form of coin of the realm, has vanished.
20. It is considered to be extremely injudicious to attempt the feat of transferring from one member of the genus *Equus* to another member of the same genus while engaged in the process of being transported through or over a moving body of $H_2O$.

# 3
# LOGIC,

J 31, A 31,

S 30, O 31,

N 30, ?

# REASONING, &
# MATHEMATICS

# Warm-Ups

1. If 8-22-5-22-13 equates to seven, and 7-4-12 makes two, how would you write ten?

2. The following word square makes a fractured proverb. If you start at the correct letter and proceed in any direction, one letter at a time, using each letter only once, you will find the fractured proverb. (Hint: Start with the first letter of the alphabet.)

```
N  E  L  O  A
S  S  T  L  L
T  E  G  T  H
R  S  I  L  A
E  T  T  G  T
```

3. Back in the days when there were maidens around who could see unicorns, two of the young ladies passed a field in which some unicorns and some rams were prancing about. One young lady

remarked that she could see a total of forty-four
horns. The other young lady remarked that there
were twice as many unicorns as rams. How many
unicorns and how many rams were there?

4. All gloops have hard skins; all slooms have soft
pits; all slurps are juicy. Some gloops are blue;
some slooms are red; all slurps are yellow. Some
gloops are yellow, and some slooms are yellow.
Which of the following do I know about a sloom,
based on the above information?
a) It is red.
b) It is juicy.
c) It has a hard skin.
d) It has a soft pit.
e) none of the above

5. Which of the lettered objects comes next in the
following series?

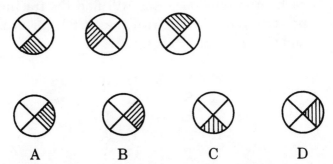

A       B       C       D

6. Mary won't eat fish or spinach; Sally won't eat
fish or green beans; Steve won't eat shrimp or
potatoes; Alice won't eat beef or tomatoes; Jim
won't eat fish or tomatoes. If you are willing to
give such a bunch of fussy eaters a dinner party,

which items from the following list can you serve?

green beans   creamed codfish   roast beef
roast chicken   celery   lettuce

7. A girl decides to take a long walk in the country and visit a friend on the way. She walks at a steady pace of 2½ miles per hour. She spends 4 hours walking over to her friend's house; she has a cup of coffee and a sandwich and talks to her friend, all of which occupies an hour, and then her friend runs her home in the car, over some rough road, at 20 miles per hour. She gets home at 2:30 in the afternoon. When did she leave her house in the morning?

8. The same five letters, if rearranged, can be used to fill in both sets of blanks in the following sentence, to make a sensible sentence:
Each bank - - - - - that it has the very best plan for each - - - - -.

9. What is the opposite of the following scrambled word?
RUECTLY

10. Jake's jalopy uses 10 gallons of gas for a trip of 150 miles. Sam's speedster gets half the mileage that Jake's does. Hal's heap uses 10 gallons for two-thirds the distance that Jake can go with his jalopy. How many gallons does Hal need to go 250 miles?

11. Under certain special circumstances, a peach

costs 20¢, a banana costs 30¢, and a grapefruit costs 40¢. How much will a pear cost under the same circumstances?

12. "A bird in the hand is worth two in the bush" means approximately the same as:
    a) If you go hunting and shoot nothing, you have wasted your day.
    b) Better a small gain you are certain of than a larger gain that you may not be able to obtain.
    c) If you raise chickens, you will always have one to cook for dinner.
    d) It is extremely difficult to catch a bird by hand, so you should be very careful with one when you do catch it.
    e) Be careful what you do with birds; they can be dangerous.

13. If *through* and *threw* are pronounced the same, cross out all of the even numbers in the line below. If they are not, cross out all of the odd numbers. If Albany is the capital of New York State, add all of the numbers that are left. If it is not, multiply all of the numbers left. Your answer?

    1 2 3 1 2 3 1 2 3 1 2 3

14. What comes next in the following series?
    J 31  A 31  S 30  O 31  N 30  _____

15. Which of the numbered figures best completes the following series?

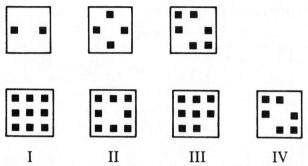

I  II  III  IV

16. You are an employment manager in that mythical land where there are only liars and truthtellers. An applicant comes in to see you and appears to be sincere. He tells you that the next interviewee has admitted to him that she is a liar. Is he lying or telling the truth?

17. If forty pizza bakers can bake twenty pizzas in two hours, how many hours will it take two pizza bakers to make ten pizzas?

18. What is the next letter in the following sequence?
A D G K O T _____

*Rebuses: Mensa members have recently taken up the type of puzzle known as a rebus. These are pictures that suggest a familiar word or phrase. They are not always what they seem, sometimes contain puns, and are usually best solved by wiping your mind clear and thinking of the exact description of the drawing. Try these for practice:*

Practice rebus:

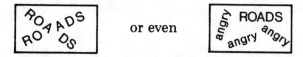     or even     

The answer, of course, is crossroads. Now try the next two.

19.

20.

# It's Only Logical

Many people confuse education and intelligence. "He must be pretty smart; look at all the degrees he has!" In fact, the multidegreed "genius" may be clever only at avoiding honest work by extending his education.

An education is nothing more than a set of tools, equipment with which to accomplish whatever one needs or wants to do. Intelligence, on the other hand, is the ability to select from those tools the ones that can help perform a task with the greatest efficacy. When it comes to practical problem solving, education isn't much good without intelligence, and vice versa.

In a sense, logical thinking can be defined as taking a set of known facts, adding some other known facts, and arraying them in such a way as to come to some inevitable conclusion. It's what computer and management types refer to as the "if-then" technique. Mathematics represents the ultimate in logical thinking because, except in its most obscure and abstract forms, mathematics is always the inevitable result of a logical sequence of events.

Admittedly, virtually all of the stories in this book that show how Mensans use their intelligence in real problem-solving situations can be classified as logical thinking (except for those in the epilogue, which are obviously illogical thinking). The ones in this section, however, seemed to be particularly fine examples of how relatively simple logic—the combining of facts from existing circumstances and from "stored" information—can find solutions to problems. "Reasoning" is really a logic technique. It involves laying out the available information, mentally or on paper, and arranging it and rearranging it until a workable or "logical" sequence falls into place. Depending upon the individual and the problem, that can sometimes be a matter of seconds—or days.

For example, what do you do when you have to move a giant tree? If you're Phyllis J. Dutrow, of St. Petersburg, Florida, you ponder the situation for a while and determine the facts, and a reasonable solution soon presents itself.

For reasons she does not explain, Phyllis had the need to extricate a cabbage palm from its moorings. The tree in question was, she said, "about as big around as a fat man's thigh and . . . in a hole more than knee-deep." (Those measurements are perhaps a trifle imprecise, but you get the idea.)

"These things," she continued, "have bulbous ends with a multitude of roots, each of which is roughly the diameter of a lead pencil, that extend several feet.

After turning the tree in the hole and reaching under
to sever [the roots] with a left-handed tomato knife . . .
I determined that the palm no longer was glued,
screwed, and through-bolted to the far side of the
earth. Problem: how to get it out of the hole, which
was alongside the sidewalk." (Somewhere in that
paragraph, Phyllis mentioned that the left-handed tomato knife had cut far more palm and palmetto roots
than it had left-handed tomatoes, but I decided not to
include that information because it's irrelevant.)

First she shoved the tree to one side. Then she
shoveled a few inches of sandy soil into the gap on the
other side. Next she shoved the tree over to the side
with the soil, which was now four inches higher, leaving a gap on the first side, which she promptly filled
with more soil, and then pushed the tree onto *it*. "Alternately fighting the palm from side to side as I re-
filled the hole a few inches at a time, I got the mon-
strosity to sidewalk level. I tipped it flat on the walk
and rolled it more than a hundred feet to the dump-
ster. I didn't want to tarry among the fire ants to
figure how to get it in there," she said, so once again
she resorted to quick thinking and logic: "I had a couple of neighbors lift it in. . . . "

(Phyllis's problem—and her clever solution—bears
an uncanny resemblance to the dilemma faced by the
good people of Pisa, whose famous tower, they believed, was beginning to lean a little more than somewhat and was in danger of eventually rendering itself
horizontal. A Mensa member not only solved the
problem but was able to reassure the Pisans that

there really was no problem. I've decided that a story about the Leaning Tower of Pisa belongs in the Culture section, where you'll find it.)

The late Jimmy Durante could always count on a laugh with his famous line "Don't raise the bridge, men; lower the water." Perry Oliver, of St. Joseph, Missouri, used simple logic to apply that basic principle to an annoying, and seemingly insoluble, difficulty.

"When Wavalea [Mrs. Oliver] and I first moved here, I had a problem with her about a clothesline," Perry wrote. "She kept complaining about it sagging. I kept tightening it, and it kept sagging. She wouldn't believe that a clothesline couldn't be straight." The fact is, however, that it couldn't because the weight of the wet clothes would invariably stretch the line and cause it to sag, despite the fact that it was, according to Perry, "as high on the poles as it would go."

"She wanted taller poles, which I didn't have," he continued. Perry's personality and life-style do not lend themselves to acquiring new things when the old things are still serviceable, so new, longer poles were never a serious consideration. "My tractor and grader blade were handy," he said with his usual practical succinctness, "so I lowered the ground between the poles."

Perhaps nowhere does the combination of quick thinking and a little knowledge of basic science prove more effective than in combating the elements. The tale is reported by Jerry Salny:

"When I attended the Massachusetts Institute of Technology," Jerry writes, "I lived in a fraternity house. . . . Six of us, on double-decker beds, slept in each room. The rooms were kept dark and quiet, and with the windows open." Unfortunately, the climate of Boston is given to sudden changes, with what Jerry describes as "horizontal rain, snow, and sleet." Also unfortunately, such changes tend to occur in the middle of the night, wreaking havoc on a frat dormitory with an open window and a half-dozen students, each feigning sleep in the hope that someone else would get up and shut the window. Soon, however, one of the occupants hit upon a solution.

"First," relates Jerry, "he cut the sash cords so the window would fall by itself. Then he propped open the window with a stick. Next he put a sugar cube under the bottom end of the stick. When the rains came, the sugar cube melted away, the stick fell out, and down came the window." Of course, the stick was tied to a string to prevent its plummeting four stories to the ground.

"Now," concludes Jerry, "in my opinion, the fact that Dr. Richard P. Feynman [the perpetrator of the just-described ingenuity], Tolman Professor of theoretical physics at Caltech, later won the Nobel Prize in physics, simply pales into insignificance compared to his having figured out how to close a window on a cold Boston night without getting out of a warm bed."

If that is so, then there is no telling to what heights Morris Berwick, of New Orleans, may yet ascend. His tale of logical thinking is my personal favorite among all the stories sent in by Mensans. Let him tell it in his own words:

"I spent a year in Wichita, Kansas, in a mobile

home. During my tenure, I got to see both trees. I also got to see nineteen degrees below zero, with thirty-mile-an-hour winds.

"The aluminum awning attached to the end of the trailer had tried valiantly to resist the wind, but to no avail. Finally, it separated, all the way along one edge, and became a battering ram that tried to destroy its own now-useless mounting.

"This happened in late evening. Since it was adjacent to our bedroom window, sleeping was fitful, at best. I had considered going outside to pop-rivet it together, but just opening the door was enough to convince me that my hands wouldn't last long enough.

"After a very light and troubled sleep, I awoke at 1 A.M. with the solution. I took a bath towel and soaked it with water. I then ran outside and threw the towel across the break. The towel froze solid. Fiberglass and resin could not have made a better patch.

"Two quiet weeks later, when the temperature rose above freezing, the patch fell off. I then made a permanent repair in relative comfort."

And eventually got the hell out of Kansas and moved to New Orleans.

In each of these instances, the problem solvers examined the circumstances, matched them up with appropriate bits of information, and logically arrived at a conclusion. Now it's your turn to do the same. On to the next quiz.

# Match Wits with Mensa

## LOGIC, REASONING, AND MATHEMATICS TEST

Time started _____

Time elapsed _____

1. All of my grandchildren are under eighteen. All of my granddaughters are very beautiful. All of my grandchildren have red hair and blue eyes. My oldest grandchild has very long red hair. The legal voting age is twenty-one. Which of the following statement(s) can be proved by the information given?
   a) My oldest grandchild may not yet vote.
   b) My oldest grandchild is a beautiful girl.
   c) My youngest grandchild may not yet drive legally.
   d) My youngest grandchild has short red hair.

2. The following word square is a takeoff on a well-known proverb. If you start at the correct letter and move in any direction, one letter at a time, you will find the slightly fractured proverb. Each letter may be used only once. There is a dash in the sentence, which is included also. (Hint: The sentence starts with THE.)

| N | R | A | E | E | T |
|---|---|---|---|---|---|
| E | L | T | E | G | S |
| T | Y | H | R | M | W |
| A | E | W | O | A | H |
| S | — | E | S | T | I |
| E | V | R | E | D | T |

3. You have twenty-four socks in a drawer, six each of brown, black, white, and red. How many socks must you take out of the drawer, without looking, to be sure of having a matched pair (of any color)?

4. A man walks to his friend's house at 2 miles per hour. He spends an hour eating lunch, and then rides home on his friend's bicycle, five times faster than he walked. The distance to his friend's house is 10 miles. At what time must he leave home in order to complete the round trip and return home by 4 P.M.?

5. Which of the lettered words could logically come next in the following sequence?

APE BIRD CAN DIG EAT
a) MAN b) HAT c) CAR d) SEA
e) FIG

6. Sally goes out on a shopping expedition for some new clothes. She buys a coat, a skirt, and a scarf. The coat costs twice as much as the skirt, and ten times as much as the scarf. She starts out with $180 and comes back with $20. What was the cost of each item of clothing?

7. The same five letters, if rearranged, will make two different words to fill in the blanks in the following sentence:

Those who wish to be good - - - - -, it is said, must have excellent memories, otherwise their stories run off the - - - - -.

8. "Birds of a feather flock together" means approximately the same as:
   a) All songbirds stick together.
   b) Feathered birds get along well.
   c) People tend to congregate with others like themselves.
   d) If you see a lot of birds together, they will probably be the same color.
   e) Birds without feathers are not accepted by birds with feathers.

9. In the square at the left below, a rule of arithmetic has been followed which applies both across and down. Find the rule and supply the missing number to the square at the right.

| 15 | 3 | 5 | 24 | 4 | 6 |
|----|---|---|----|---|---|
| 5  | 1 | 5 | 6  | 1 | — |
| 3  | 3 | 1 | 4  | 4 | 1 |

10. Which lettered figure best completes the following series?

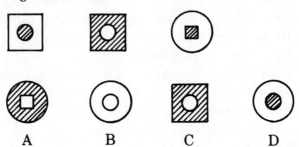

A          B          C          D

11. So you're good at Roman numerals. Here's a different use for them:
CXV = SIX; CMLMI = SEVEN.
What does LMXI equal?

12. Each of the letters in the puzzle below represents a number. The answer will be the same numbers, reversed, as shown. Fill in the numbers.

ABCD
×9
————
DCBA

13. What word is the opposite of the following scrambled word?
CWCADORIE

14. Which number in the following series of numbers is least like the others?
1  3  5  7  11  13  15

15. Which of the following scrambled words is the

"odd man out" when the words are unscrambled?
CGHICOA TTOOORN IMMIA
CPOEHNANGE

16. Four couples are going to the movies. Each row holds eight seats. Betty and Jim don't want to sit next to Alice and Tom, and Alice and Tom don't want to sit next to Gertrude and Bill. On the other hand, Sally and Bob don't want to sit next to Betty and Jim. How can the couples arrange themselves so that they all sit where they would like?

17. Which of the lettered designs best completes the sequence in the first row?

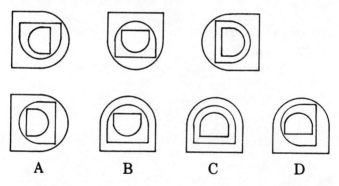

|   |   |   |   |
|---|---|---|---|
| A | B | C | D |

18. If *diaphanous* and *sheer* do not have the same meaning, cross out all the 9's in the line below. If they do, cross out all the 6's. If *slough* and *cough* are pronounced the same, multiply the number of 4's by 6. If not, add up all of the non-crossed-out numbers and multiply by 4.

9 4 6 4 9 4 6 9 4 6 9

19. The price of an article is cut 40% for a sale. When

the sale is over, the store owner wants to bring the price back up to the original selling price. What percentage of the sale price must be added to that sale price to bring the price back up to the original selling price?

20. All readers of this book are clever. Some readers of this book are Mensa members or will join Mensa. Some readers of this book like to solve puzzles. Therefore, which of the following statements can be justified by the information just given?

   a) All readers of this book like to solve puzzles; otherwise they wouldn't be reading this puzzle.

   b) All clever readers will join Mensa.

   c) Some Mensa members like to solve puzzles.

   d) none of these from the information given

4

# ANALOGIES

# Warm-Ups

1. The Panama Canal is to the Atlantic and Pacific as the Suez Canal is to _____ and _____ .

2. *p* and *q* are to *g* as *b* and *d* are to:
   a) *y*  b) *g*  c) *j*  d) *a*

3. *Bankrupt* is to *solvent* as *grouped* is to:
   a) discrete  b) assembled  c) massed
   d) schooled

4. D. W. Griffith is to the motion picture as Henry Fielding is to the:
   a) opera  b) story novel  c) stage play
   d) epic poetry

5. The Empire State Building is to New York City as the Sears Tower is to _____ .

6. Lockheed is to airplanes as Stutz is to _____ .

7. Paul Bunyan is to Babe as Don Quixote is to _____ .

8.
   is to as is to:

A      B      C      D

9. President William Howard Taft is to Senator Robert A. Taft as President John Adams is to _____ .

10. Piccard is to ballooning as Cousteau is to _____ .

11. *Humoresque* is to Dvořák as *Minute Waltz* is to _____ .

12. William H. Porter is to O. Henry as Eric Blair is to _____ .

13. The Underground is to London as the Metropolitain is to _____ .

14. Trenton is to New Jersey as Pierre is to _____ .

15. Leo Durocher is to baseball as Knute Rockne is to _____ .

16.

is to as is to:

A      B      C      D

17. A scepter is to a king as a mitre is to a _____ .

18. The Packers are to Green Bay as the Chiefs are to _____ .

19. The Ilyushin is to Russia as the Hawker-Siddeley 748 is to _____ .

20. The telephone is to Alexander Graham Bell as the mercury thermometer is to _____ .
21. The Japanese language is to Japan as Tagalog is to _____ .
22. Chosen is to Korea as the Gold Coast is to _____ .
23. The Nile is to Egypt as the Volga is to _____ .
24. The New York Cosmos are to soccer as the Toronto Maple Leafs are to _____ .
25. Henry Fonda is to *On Golden Pond* as Rex Harrison is to _____ .

# Look at It This Way...

Solving analogy puzzles involves the ability to see relationships between sets of situations that may not be immediately obvious. To be sure, that often requires some special knowledge, such as a nodding acquaintance with, say, history or botany. (Nothing heavy; any good shopper probably knows enough about botany—which is to say, fruits and vegetables—to handle such questions on a typical analogy quiz.)

But apart from the usual and acknowledged fun and diversion in working such questions, is there any real value to them? Would I be asking that question if the answer were no?

The ability to understand that a given situation is analogous to some other situation, and, in so doing, to solve a problem, is something of a talent, but it is also a skill that can be developed with practice. Rather than lecture you on how using analogies can enhance your understanding as it frees your thinking, let's attempt to prove it by example.

This is a true story, but I won't use real names, to avoid the risk of offending someone—particularly someone who authorizes the issuance of a check to me on a regular basis. I write a column, for a fortnightly international business publication, on computers and telecommunications. For the most part, I'm expected to generate my own stories; technology being what it is these days, there's hardly a scarcity of material. The catch, however, is that in every case, there has to be a direct tie-in with international trade and/or transportation.

One day, I received a press release in the mail, sent to me not by the public relations firm promoting the company, but by the associate editor with whom I've been dealing these many months. It described a computer service that made it possible to settle automobile collision claims more promptly and fairly through computerized analyses of the damages as recorded by inspectors. Normally, it might merit half a column in some other context; to me, it was worthless. Nevertheless, attached to the press release was a note from the associate editor, whom I'll call Denise: "Call me when you get this."

I dutifully followed instructions. "A so-so story," I said, "but not for me."

"Harold wants you to write it up for your column," Denise said. Harold is the executive editor. My "column" runs a minimum of 1,500 words. "That's idiotic," I replied. "What does this have to do with international trade and transportation?"

"I asked Harold that same question," she said.

"What did he say?"

"He said they have automobile collisions in Europe, too."

"That's ridiculous," I replied, trying desperately— and not succeeding—to maintain a modicum of composure. "We're talking export-import here; we're talking international banking here; we're talking cargo ships and planes and ports and piers and marine insurance here. We're not talking European automobile collisions!"

"Harold wants the story," she said, through what I was certain were clenched teeth. The conversation was over.

For the next three days, that press release sat on my desk. Approximately once every hour, I picked it up, read it through, and angrily tossed it aside.

Then, literally in the middle of the night, inspiration struck. On the fourth day, I telephoned the public relations man who had issued the release and said, "I have two questions for your client. Their answers will determine whether I do this story. One: If your system works for damaged cars, can it be adapted to work for damaged ships, trucks, and cargo containers? Two: If the answer to the first question is yes, would your client entertain offering to license the system to overseas computer service organizations?" Happily, he came back with the right answers, resulting in a highly successful 2,000-word story that made everybody happy, especially the public relations man and Harold. I think even the readers enjoyed it.

They don't call me the King of Transitions for nothing.

Norris Swan, of Hastings, Nebraska, can also claim

credit for being able to turn over a situation in his mind and look at it from different angles. One evening, he arrived late for a meeting of a church carpet committee to which he belonged. His colleagues had determined that the carpeted center aisle of the church had to be widened. Norris explains:

"The seats consisted of benches, arranged in five sections, with a center aisle, two middle aisles, and two outside aisles. The benches were curved as necessary for the arch. Those in the front were short, and the benches got progressively longer toward the back.

"The committee was in the process of arranging to have the two center sections of benches taken to a millworks to have one-foot sections taken out of each end and then have the end arms reattached. (Two-foot sections could not be taken from one end because that would destroy the curvature of the benches.)

" . . . I asked why we didn't simply take out the back row of benches and move all the other benches back one row. If we needed the additional seating of the lost row in front, we could make a small section for these front seats from one or two of the back benches. It was decided we could use the space up front for a better purpose than seating, so that is what we did." To the never-ending gratitude, probably, of the budget committee.

I have no doubt that somewhere in this world, a group of financially concerned citizens are equally grateful to James A. Harris, of Redondo Beach, California. His story is reproduced here verbatim:

"Working under an oil derrick with a ten-ton rating, I was asked to calculate the safety margin when lifting an eight-ton load. While drawing vector-force diagrams for each cable (like they teach us in school) it became obvious that the strain on the derrick was simply the weight of the load plus the strain on the line that went to the hoisting drum. The hoist was rigged by block-and-tackle to give a mechanical advantage of 4:1, so the derrick load was 8 + (8/4) or no margin at all. We rerigged to give the hoist drum a 6:1 advantage, thereby reducing the strain to 9.33 tons."

I sincerely hope that's all perfectly clear to you, because it makes no sense to me whatsoever. If you have any questions, you can send them to me. I'll forward them to Harris.

When I was a kid, a popular expression was "If the mountain will not come to Mohammed, then Mohammed must go to the mountain." As a schoolteacher, James T. Hart, of Napa, California, applied that simple notion in a masterful manner.

"I was faced with the problem of teaching math to intermediate-grade children who were at varying levels of proficiency in mastering their basic facts as well as the algorithms, fractions, decimals, etcetera," Jim told us. Traditionally, a teacher presents a mathematical concept to the entire class, and all the students work on the accompanying exercises, whether they're capable of doing them or not. That encourages, as some of us know all too well, a sink-or-swim situation, which in turn leads to disruptive behavior and other discipline problems.

"I set out to develop an individualized prescriptive math program that allowed me to chart each student's programs at whatever proficiency level he could achieve. . . . I admittedly spent a lot of hours and used a lot of other people's creations to put my program together. When I was finished, each child had an individual contract assignment spanning a week or so of work, which was self-corrected. Upon completion of each contract, the child would take a self-corrected posttest. If the child passed that test with 80 percent or higher, I would administer the final posttest that I corrected. . . .

"Some of the more motivated students were doing trigonometry by the time they were out of the sixth grade, and almost without exception, my students scored well above state and national averages on the standardized tests the district required all schools to administer."

Unless you've been a math student in California, you may not have benefited from Jim Hart's innovative teaching methods. But if you've ever had a tooth drilled, you certainly have benefited from John F. Johnson's ability to draw an analogy between an automobile factory and the human mouth.

"In 1947," writes Dr. Johnson (you knew he'd turn out to be a dentist, didn't you?), "I worked on drill presses for the Ford Motor Co. and found it was essential to keep the coolant flowing on the drills or they would get hot and be ruined.

"In 1948, as a junior in the School of Dentistry, University of Michigan, I started drilling on the teeth of live people, in the required way, with no coolant. A former dean had convinced the world of dentistry that drilling should be done dry. But here the drill got hot, too, and it hurt," he said, in a masterpiece of understatement.

Shortly after graduation, the Korean "conflict" began, and Dr. Johnson wound up practicing dentistry at Fort Knox, Kentucky. "A friend of mine was in charge of the machine shop," Dr. Johnson recalls, so he had the friend rig a dental drill that would use diamond burrs instead of steel, and at very high speeds—cooled by water. A tank-type vacuum cleaner was adapted to suck up the overflow.

By 1958, a former professor whom Dr. Johnson identifies only as "Dr. Peyton" promoted the teaching of the water-cooled method, and soon, he claims, "high-speed dentistry became the hot issue." (I refuse to believe the pun is unintentional.) "Within about ten more years," he adds, "practically all dentists were using high-speed techniques and high-volume suction, and patients were beginning to realize that dentistry had gotten out of the dark ages. . . ."

I was intrigued by the notion that if the young John Johnson had not worked in an automobile plant, we would still be screaming in terror every time we looked at a dentist, so I asked him, pointblank: "Are you, in fact, the 'inventor' of water-cooled dental drilling?"

His reply: "It is possible somebody would contest the statement that I am the 'inventor' of water-cooled drilling. People still disagree as to who should be named the inventor of the airplane, and evolution, and the telephone. But the chance that anyone will dispute the sequence I gave as to the development of water cooling is slim. . . . I used it exclusively from the day I started practice, at Fort Knox, Kentucky, and about sixty dentists there had it used on them. They were from all over the country, and it was new. I doubt if there will be any real disagreement on the start of the use of the system." That's good enough for me. And for my dentist. And it should be for you, too.

It has long been my contention that being able to see how things are somewhat the same makes it possible to see the same things a little differently. Betty Kubicek, of Milwaukee, helped prove the point. One Sunday morning, her father had undertaken the task of repairing his favorite clock at the kitchen table. "The morning ended," she wrote, "with the clock's successful dismantling, and by late afternoon, he had it all put together again and ticking perfectly." She was, therefore, somewhat surprised, when preparing to set the table for dinner, to find Dad still at it and, as she described it, "the clock being prepped for open-heart surgery once again. 'I thought it was fixed,' I said. 'It is,' he muttered. 'Only thing is, the damned thing only runs upside-down!' "

At this point, Betty did a terrible thing. She picked up the clock and turned the printed-paper clock face a full 180 degrees so that the 6 was where the 12 had been and vice versa.

"I'm not sure it was really so clever of me," she now

says. "The clock worked great, but Dad didn't speak to me all through dinner."

Apparently, the ability to stretch one's mind by making analogies works best when accompanied by a healthy portion of diplomacy.

You won't need any diplomacy for the next quiz. Nobody's looking; go ahead and show yourself how good you are.

# Match Wits with Mensa

## ANALOGIES TEST

Time started _____
Time elapsed _____

Analogies are relationships. Some relationships are obvious and some are more subtle. Each of the following questions gives one set of relationships and asks you to fill in the missing relationship of the second pair.

1. Roquefort is to France as Liederkranz is to _____ .

2. Triskaedekophobia is to the fear of the number 13 as photophobia is to _____ .
   (Hint: It is *not* the fear of being snapped by a photographer in a less-than-desirable situation.)

3. Florentine is to spinach as Parmentier is to _____ .

4. LAX is to Los Angeles, California, as EWR is to _____ .

5. Drawer is to reward as Anna is to _____ .
6. Wolves are to pack as whales are to _____ .
7. The musical *Oklahoma!* is to *Green Grow the Lilacs* as *My Fair Lady* is to _____ .
8. Mary Ann Evans is to George Eliot as Charles L. Dodgson is to _____ .
9. Cape Horn is to South America as Cape of Good Hope is to _____ .
10. Conforming is to orthodox as nonconforming is to _____ .
11. Enervate is to weaken as energize is to:
    a) strengthen   b) weaken   c) improve
    d) add new batteries
12. Franc is to France as dirham is to _____ .
13.

A          B          C          D

14. Profitable is to remunerative as fallacious is to:
    a) fraudulent   b) reward   c) possible
    d) proverbial   e) carnivorous
15. Concealed is to secret as overt is to:
    a) occult   b) science   c) ancient
    d) revealed   e) none of these

16.

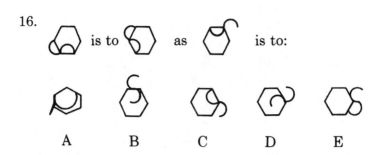

    A        B        C        D        E

17. Romeo is to Juliet as Tristan is to _____ .

18. Watergate is to Nixon as Teapot Dome is to:
    a) Harding  b) Wilson  c) Truman
    d) Jackson  e) Pierce

19. Golden Gate Bridge is to San Francisco Bay as Bridge of Sighs is to:
    a) Venice  b) Paris  c) London
    d) New York  e) Istanbul

20. Linen is to flax as glass is to:
    a) acrylic  b) polyester  c) sand  d) water
    e) stone

21. McKinley is to Roosevelt as Roosevelt is to:
    a) Carter  b) Taft  c) Truman  d) Garner
    e) Barkley

22. Constantinople is to Istanbul as Ceylon is to:
    a) Zimbabwe  b) Sri Lanka  c) Malagasi
    d) Malawi  e) Papeete

23. Narcissus is to flower as Arethusa is to:
    a) tree  b) rose  c) stone  d) fountain
    e) mountain

24. Gray is to anatomy as Ali-Bab is to:
    a) dressmaking  b) cooking  c) grammar
    d) history  e) newswriting

25. 3 is to 5, 8, 9 as 4 is to:
   a) 1, 11, 14   b) 2, 3, 6   c) 1, 13, 16
   d) 16, 15, 9   e) 1, 3, 6

5

CULTURE

# Warm-Ups

## ART

1. Many people know that the world-famous paintings of Michelangelo, including *The Last Judgment,* are in the Sistine Chapel at the Vatican. Why is it called the Sistine Chapel?
2. The series of famous Japanese pictures called *The Floating World* is about a specific subject. What aspect of Japanese life is depicted?
3. François Auguste René Rodin was a famous French artist. For what field of art is he best known?
4. Raphael (Raffaello Sanzio) was best known as a painter, but he had another artistic talent. What was it?
5. Anyone who takes a tour of St. Paul's Cathedral in London, or of many English country houses, will hear the name Grinling Gibbons. Who was he?

## MUSIC

1. Why were the Gilbert and Sullivan operetta players known as Savoyards?
2. What is the national anthem of France?
3. In what country does the opera *Aida* take place?
4. Have any famous waltzes come down to us from Elizabethan days?
5. In what city in the United States is jazz supposed to have originated?

## GREEK AND ROMAN CULTURE

1. They were known as Jupiter and Juno in Rome. What were they called in Greece?
2. Who were the twins that were popularly believed to have founded Rome?
3. What was the famous device used to enter the city of Troy by trickery?
4. Sappho was a famous Greek poet whose name is specifically associated with the island where she lived. What was the island?
5. What was the usual occupation of the Fates?

## LITERATURE

1. What was the chief characteristic of female roles on the stage in Shakespeare's time?
2. What are the collected works of the great early Norse poets and writers called?
3. John Milton suffered from a major handicap for a

large portion of his adult life. He refers to it in many of his works. What was it?

4. What was Dante (Durante) Alighieri's greatest work?

5. What is the subject of Tennyson's series of poems, *Idylls of the King*?

## ETIQUETTE

1. What shape of glass is preferred by many connoisseurs for champagne?

2. If you are introducing an old man to a young woman, who is introduced to whom?

3. When does a lady take off her gloves to shake hands?

4. What should be printed on a thank-you card for wedding presents?

5. When may you eat lamb chop bones (after the meat is trimmed) with your fingers?

# More Than Yogurt

One person's "culture" is easily another's boredom, which makes Culture with a capital *C* nearly as difficult to define as intelligence. Even my favorite dictionary, the *Oxford American,* noted for its terseness, lists five definitions for the word, ending with "a quantity of bacteria grown for study." (Yogurt is a cultured milk product.)

And, as with the definition for intelligence, the first dictionary entry, while seemingly clear and direct, raises several unanswerable questions: "the appreciation and understanding of literature, arts, music, etc." Fine. Now all we have to do is define *appreciation, understanding, literature, arts,* and *music,* and it becomes crystal-clear.

Let's see . . . music. I love Mozart and abhor Wagner. I can't stand any of the composers who follow Tchaikovsky—except for Rachmaninoff. (Within seconds after that last sentence was written, *Rhapsody in*

*Blue* began issuing forth from the radio. Add Gershwin.) I can listen to Dixieland far into the night (and have), but I can't tolerate acid rock. Disco gives me a headache, but reggae is strangely soothing—almost hypnotic. Indian music hurts my ears; Greek music makes me passionate.

There's more, but by now you're probably bored to stupefaction, so I won't burden you with my views on "arts," which would have to begin with categories— what kind of "arts" do we mean? Performing? "Fine"? Graphic? Conversational? Medical? Why list literature separately? Isn't that one of the "arts"?

As for the "etc." in that definition, it's a prime example of a lexicographical cop-out. But we can't really blame the dictionary writers; they used the "etc." catchall because "culture" is in itself a catchall; in terms of appreciation and understanding of the so-called finer things in life, it can mean virtually anything you want it to mean. (In Mensa, for example, it often means the understanding and appreciation of food and drink.)

The vague definition of culture presented some problems, as you can well imagine, in selecting questions for the quiz that follows and in choosing anecdotes to describe how Mensans apply their intelligence to solving problems within a cultural context. We decided to cop out, too: The questions have to do with the traditional concepts of culture, which may differ a little from yours and mine, but which most people tend to associate with the word. As for the anecdotes, their inclusion in this section is somewhat arbitrary, but so are all the other selections and placements in this book.

One of the best places to observe Mensans' notions of culture is a kind of convention called a Regional Gathering (or, more familiarly, RG, perhaps because that's so easy to pronounce as "orgy"). In 1982 there were over thirty-five RGs, all over the country.

RG workshops and activities can range from lessons in massage to discussions of the criminal justice system, from exhibitions of art by Mensans to regional history, from trivia contests to classical and X-rated films, and on and on. RG hospitality suites are always filled to capacity with people actively engaged in conversations as varied as the participants themselves. Those conversations tend to be liberally lubricated with many gallons of free-flowing domestic wine and beer (yet another tribute to Mensans' eclectic notion of "culture") and snacks. Not everyone, however, partakes of the free refreshments.

Ann-Marie Dobbs, American Mensa's groups officer (whose responsibility is overseeing national special-interest groups), likes a little wine as well as the next RG devotee, but she also likes a change occasionally.

"A friend and I took our own champagne to an RG because we were tired of hospitality-suite Chablis," she writes. "Once we got the wine chilled, we realized we couldn't walk around with glasses of champagne unless we were prepared to share. Since we had brought only a half-dozen bottles, and they had to last an entire weekend, that was out of the question. My friend dug two empty beer cans out of a trash can. We washed them out, filled them with champagne, and aroused no more comment than 'I didn't know you were a beer drinker.'"

For many Mensans, the aforementioned "appreciation and understanding" begins at an early age, so it's not surprising that they encourage a love of "culture" in their children. Linda Kelso, of Portland, Oregon, uses her spare time to edit *Interloc,* a kind of "house organ" for Mensa officers and others involved in the inner workings of the society. Several years ago, she solved a parent-child problem with a little culture.

"My second child was born when the first was just eighteen months old," Linda relates. "What to do with child No. 1 while child No. 2 nursed presented a dilemma because No. 1 already had the how-to-get-attention routine down pretty well.

"No. 1 loved to have books read to him, so nursing time became reading time. No. 1 would sit quietly beside me with no jealousy or interruption."

She added that the older child is now a National Merit Scholarship winner and a Mensan—no small feat for a kid who has to go through life with a name like No. 1.

Clare Neuman, of Allendale, New Jersey, recognizes that among the attributes of a "cultured" person is the ability to be a good host. "People say entertaining is difficult. They're wrong," she insists. "All it takes is some smarts. When people ask what they can bring [to a dinner party], don't decline; instead, have them bring their specialty. Mom's chopped liver,

Aunt Shirley's carrot cake . . . they're all on the table as part of the feast. Everyone admires the fantastic food and enjoys the dinner because they've contributed to it. And they say, 'You're a perfect hostess—so relaxed!' "

Clare offers another cultural tip, if one considers "culture" in the ethnic sense. To adapt as a new member in "a warm, extended Jewish family," she advises: "First observe, and then *kiss!* Everybody—great aunts, second cousins, friends of friends. . . . Saying good-bye at family gatherings, kiss everyone twice—it's great fun, and you're a success!"

Well, listen, if it works for Clare, it may work for you. I know from firsthand experience that (a) the technique is not restricted to extended Jewish families and (b) it can sometimes require more intestinal fortitude than may be available under the circumstances. A suggested variation is the almost-official greeting at RGs and that has become so popular that it is now commonplace wherever and whenever Mensans gather: the hug. Some RGs even hold "hugging competitions," in which secret judges present awards in categories they invent themselves. I have, on more than one occasion, been the recipient of such awards, and while I am grateful for them, it's a little discouraging that they all tend to range from the avuncular to the ursine. (My size makes me a natural for great bear hugs.) The sexy awards always go to other people.

Nevertheless, hugging is a well-proven icebreaker and, when it comes to "friends of friends," considerably easier to perpetrate than kissing. It's also more sanitary.

A couple of years ago, the damnable Rubik's Cube became an ingrained part of American culture, to the delight of the Ideal Toy Company and to the consternation of Marvin A. Silbermintz, of Kew Gardens Hills, New York, who works for Ideal as a game designer and was charged with the task of coming up with saleable variations of Erno Rubik's little torture device. (You may have gathered by now that I have neither the patience nor the skill to "solve" the cube. I am convinced that the several people who gave me versions of it as birthday gifts had nothing but pure malice in their hearts.)

Ideal received thousands of unsolicited suggestions for Rubik variations, but, as Marvin says, "most of these ideas merely changed the material or superficial design of the cube."

Marvin's first response to this challenge was Rubik's Race, an ingenious combination of the basic elements of the cube and those "15" puzzles that consist of fifteen sliding tiles in sixteen spaces; the object is to arrange the tiles in some sort of sequence. (For the record, I hate those, too—and for the same reasons.) Marvin's description of how he developed the Race is too long to include here; besides, Ideal might not appreciate publicizing such things, which are, I suppose, properly regarded as industrial secrets. Suffice it to say, therefore, that he laid out the procedure for me, and it is a classical example of logical thinking in a commercial-cum-cultural context.

Marvin then solved the problem of the Rubik's Cube Perpetual Calendar by drawing on one of his cultural attributes: He was an artist before he became a game designer. His familiarity with graphics no doubt led him to such solutions as designing certain letters so that they could be used in the names of months either right-side-up or upside-down. (According to the advertising copy, "it takes only a few minutes—maybe" to come up with the right day and date every morning. I guess it's sort of a daily fix in the office for Rubik's addicts.)

Among my all-time favorite problem solvers is Harry Brown, of San Antonio, Texas, whom I described in a magazine article as "your ordinary, garden-variety genius with an uncommon appetite for problems and an uncanny ability to solve them." Harry, a true Renaissance man, became aware of a serious problem worrying the culture mavens of the world, not to mention the Italian tourist authorities. When Bonanno Pisano began construction in 1174 on what was supposed to have been a bell tower, he expected it to stand up straight. It didn't. It leaned. Furthermore, over the centuries, it continued to lean. In the mid-1970s, Italian engineers concluded that if something were not done soon, the Leaning Tower of Pisa would become the Horizontal Tower of Pisa. Here's the story, in part, as I wrote it for the magazine*:

"A call went out for the engineer . . . who could develop a practical method for keeping the familiar

*Cavalier, February 1976; used with permission.

233

phallic symbol from collapsing like a spent lover. Harry Brown read about the contest and decided to have a go at it. He went to the library, which is how he begins solving all his problems, read a few books and came up with a solution so simple that only a genius could have devised it.

" 'The tower is sinking more on the south than on the north,' he explains, 'giving the effect of rotating on an imaginary axis. The problem is to stop or reverse the rotation. . . . What they have to do is pour a circular foundation around the tower, a concrete disc a hundred feet in diameter. . . . Increasing the area . . . would reduce the pressure to about 4,100 pounds per square foot. The disc should be off center. . . . The resulting differential in pressure would reverse, although very minutely, the direction of rotation.'

"So Harry drew up his blueprints and he and his wife went off to Pisa. There he received a shock. His calculations and solutions were based on the premise that the tower was set on a concrete foundation, but according to local legend, the foundation consisted of rubble. A search through Bonanno's original drawings confirmed the legend. It occurred to Harry that with that kind of foundation, the damned thing should have toppled centuries ago, but he had to set that aside to cope with the newer and more immediate problem. Installing the concrete disc would require digging away the earth around the tower's base. A foundation made of rubble would never withstand the digging. . . ."

Harry bought himself some drafting equipment,

locked himself in his hotel room for five days, and came up with a set of drawings for a plan that resembles—but with more complexity and grandeur—the method described earlier for extracting a palm tree from a hole in the sidewalk.

"It turned out, however, that Harry's original calculations had been correct. Over the centuries, underground water and seepage from rainfall had changed the rubble to concrete. He had been right all along.

"He had been right about something else, too: In Rome, he had told the Minister of Public Works that the government's fears were—well, without foundation. The tower might lean a little more, but according to his calculations, it was good for another couple of centuries at least. That prediction was [later] confirmed by an official scientific pronouncement . . . the Leaning Tower of Pisa would remain diagonally erect for another 200 to 500 years. . . ."

It should be remembered that Harry, whose checkered career runs from devising a space capsule for the first monkey to achieve orbit to designing, making, and installing stained-glass windows (his work, along with his iron sculptures, has been exhibited in museums), is self-taught. His chief attributes, in addition to his IQ, are an insatiable curiosity and the inability to resist a challenge.

Perhaps Harry Brown will inspire you as you attack the next quiz. And however you come out, remember that when you're finished, there's a symbolic Mensa hug waiting for you. Even though it may be a bear hug.

# Match Wits with Mensa

## CULTURE TEST

Time started _____
Time elapsed _____

### GREEK AND ROMAN CULTURE

1. There is a famous river in Greek mythology which the dead had to cross by ferry. The ferryman was Charon. What was the name of the river?
2. Who was the Roman god of wine and drinking?
3. Name any of the nine Muses; take double credit if you can give the Muse's specialty.
4. Who was the individual who admired his reflection in a fountain so much that he jumped in to try to reach that beautiful person, and drowned?
5. *The Odyssey* is one of the most famous works of literature ever written. What is its main theme?

## ART

1. There is a world-famous painting showing a young woman on a shell apparently rising from the sea. What is the name of the painting, for one credit? You get another point if you can name the painter, and one more if you can give his full name.
2. Most people have heard of Leonardo's famous painting called the *Mona Lisa*. What else is it called?
3. Who painted the picture of George Washington that appears on American dollar bills and on some postage stamps?
4. Which French artist is best known for his paintings and sculptures of ballet subjects?
5. There is a famous art museum in New York City that created a stir when it was built because of its unusual architecture—a spiral ramp as the main display gallery. What's the name of the building?

## LITERATURE

1. Chaucer is best known for a collection of stories about the people and the life of his times. What is the book?
2. Rudyard Kipling's most famous books were chiefly about one country. Which one?
3. Name any two winners of Pulitzer Prizes for fiction since 1960. Take an extra point for each one

if you can name the book that won the prize.

4. What is generally considered to be Marcel Proust's most important work, in seven volumes? (English or French title will do.)

5. *Winnie the Pooh* has become famous in this country based largely on the later development of characters from the original books. Who was the author?

## ETIQUETTE

1. How do you write a letter of regret to the White House declining an invitation to dinner?

2. Among your grandmother's possessions, you find a small tray, about 3½ by 8 inches, with a slightly raised edge. It's obviously not a candy dish. What is it?

3. What is the traditional twenty-fifth wedding anniversary title (and gift)?

4. What is the official, or approved, way of addressing a former U.S. president?

5. At a formal dinner, who is served first?

## MUSIC

1. How many complete symphonies did Beethoven compose?

2. What does *a cappella* mean in relation to music?

3. Georg Friedrich Handel was born in Germany but

became famous in another country. What was his adopted country?

4. What is generally considered Wagner's most important work (or series of works)?

5. Gilbert and Sullivan wrote many operettas together. Who wrote the music?

# Epilogue: Turn of the Table

*Most of this chapter was drawn from several of Marvin Grosswirth's columns, "Views & Reviews" (considered a highly imaginative title when it was first begun over eleven years ago), in the Mensa Bulletin. The revival of Elstob's Foibles, as explained below, eventually led to another column, devoted to gaffes among the top 2 percent and overseen by Orville Brandes, a lady with a gravel-crusher voice, a machetelike wit, and a marshmallow heart. While working on this book, we learned, in January 1983, of Orville's death in a New Orleans hospital. This epilogue is dedicated to her, in memory of a beloved and gifted friend. Mensa, you'll recall, is Latin for "table." Orville's column was called, appropriately, "Turn of the Table."*

"Boy, for someone who's supposed to be smart . . . "

Which of us has not heard, with dread, that opening of a sentence that, when concluded, revealed to all within earshot that we have managed to perpetrate an act of grandiose stupidity? We have heard it from parents, teachers, employers, lovers, spouses, and, perhaps most cruelly, from children. Anyone who has reached the age of seventeen who claims never to have heard it either is lying or simply isn't supposed to be smart. Basically, it is a case of intelligence running ahead of itself, of literally "outsmarting" itself.

There's no need to dwell on analysis. Having called your attention throughout this book to examples of how Mensans use their intelligence to solve problems, it seems only fitting that we now have a look at what happens when Mensans "oversolve."

It also seems only fitting that I begin with a tale about a garment bag. I had returned from a trip, unpacked, and proceeded to restore the garment bag to its proper resting place—the top shelf of a clothes closet. I rolled it up, tossed it on high, and watched in disbelief as it slid down again. I caught it in midair, rolled it again, and once more lofted it onto its shelf. The damnable bag sprang back at me like a thing alive, with what can only be described as naked hostility. Two or three more attempts seemed only to strengthen the bag's resolve not to stay on the shelf and to cause me physical damage at the same time.

Viciously, I grabbed the rebellious sack. I rolled it yet another time, but now I clutched it in a viselike stranglehold with one hand as I reached for a wire coat hanger with the other. Once more I flung the bag onto its shelf, and before it had a chance to unfurl, I stabbed it with the coat hanger, pinning it against the wall. My intention was to hold the bag on the shelf with the hanger while, with my other hand, I sort of stuffed the bag into position. As I did so, however, my trousers, unaccustomed to the lack of tension around my equator that resulted from so much arm-stretching, slid gently to the floor.

For a second or two, I simply froze, my arms on high and my pants bunched ignominiously around my ankles. (Mercifully, my wife was already asleep and witnessed none of this.) Finally, I looked down at my pants. In so doing, I discovered that behind the shoe rack on the floor of the closet was a perfectly good space for the garment bag. I stepped out of my trousers, kicked them aside, and held out my arms to catch the villain. I swept aside the tangle of wire coat hangers that had fallen during the fray, and I dumped the garment bag in the space, where it now permanently resides. I hung up my pants and went to watch television.

At such moments, I gain some solace from remembering a British Mensan named Peter Elstob who, some years ago, regaled readers of the *International* (Mensa) *Journal* with a tale about a padlock. Mr. Elstob had purchased what he described as "an expensive little padlock with a beautiful brass key." After the lock had served the purpose (unnamed) for which it had been bought, he decided that the most efficient thing he could do would be to store both lock and key so that he could find them easily, should the need arise to do so. "Carefully threading the U of the lock through the hole in the end of the key," he wrote, "[I] snapped it shut in order, of course, for them to remain together. They still are."

That little tale gave rise to similar stories, which soon became known, in honor of the inspirer, as Elstob's Foibles. One writer told how, before he began painting a floor, he had made certain that he had an escape route. He planned the job so that he would finish at a door in the room. It never occurred to him to check whether the door was unlocked. You know the rest. Another told how he had prepared frozen daiquiris, only to discover that some of the "finely granulated ice" would not melt. A little later, he also discovered that a shot glass was missing and developed new respect for his blender.

One particularly creative Mensan needed to make holes in a mailbox to mount a name plate. He got out his rifle and shot the holes through the mailbox. He also shot up the name plate, which he had put into the box for safekeeping.

When I related the sad, frustrating tale of the garment bag in my *Bulletin* column, I revived Elstob's Foibles and invited readers to contribute. The response was extremely gratifying.

One correspondent found it necessary to move a television antenna from one end of his one-story house to the other. Upon moving the cable, along with the stepladder that got him on and off the roof, he discovered that the line was too short. So, of course, he immediately bought additional cable. He carefully described (but I will spare you the details) the difficult and tedious task of splicing coaxial cable, involving stripping, unbraiding, soldering, insulating, re-braiding, all the while trying to keep the blood from punctured fingers from interfering with his work.

"Since I'm an engineer," he explains, "I did all that quicker than you could write three novels. So . . . I grab antenna and climb to roof only to find the co-ax cable is threaded through the stepladder treads. How can I restore my wife's faith in Mensa?"

There were others: There was the woman who left her kitchen and headed for the back porch, with a cup of cocoa in each hand and cookie in her mouth. Her sweater got caught on a splinter in the door frame. With both hands occupied, she was unable to extricate herself. With her mouth likewise occupied, she could not call for help. She stood there, saying "Mfff" as loudly as she could, hoping someone would come. Someone did, freeing her while asking why she hadn't either chewed or dropped the cookie. "Mfff," she replied. There was the navy photographer's mate who left a photo darkroom carrying a stack of carefully exposed—but undeveloped—photographic printing paper under his arm, completely ruining the latent images waiting for chemical baths. There was the woman who astonished a friend who had come home with her by plopping her car keys into a teacup while simultaneously pouring boiling water into her open handbag.

Of all the foibles, my favorite is the Tale of the Ant Killer, reported in a local-group newsletter. The hero of the tale discovered ants in the kitchen and devised an ingenious plan for summarily dispatching them:

He swooped them up with a vacuum cleaner. Quickly realizing that the ants were probably still alive inside the machine, he decided to asphyxiate them by holding the end of the vacuum cleaner hose over an open, unlit gas jet. Vacuum cleaners have electrical motors. Electrical motors give off sparks. Sparks from electrical motors and gas from kitchen stoves tend to be incompatible. The vacuum cleaner blew up. Fortunately, no one was hurt, except for the ants, who are presumed dead (but may only be missing in action).

The fact that Mensans are capable of such foibles should in no way detract from the realization that we do, on occasion, come up with solutions to problems that seem insoluble to others. For example, I once protested the fact that there seemed to be an inordinate number of car alarms going off early in the morning. I am referring to those horrible sirens that are supposed to scare off anyone tampering with the hardware of a parked automobile. Maybe they accomplish their goal, but they also destroy sleep and engender a sense of irritation that persists through the day. My solution for doing away with this problem was to do away with the time during which it occurred.

I was less tolerant in those days than I am now, so I pointed out that the only people abroad between the hours of 4:30 and 5:30 A.M. were hunters, fishermen, people waiting for the golf courses to open, muggers working overtime, and car thieves, and I characterized them all as undesirable. I then urged everyone to write to his or her government representative, demanding that the hour in question be abolished. "When those noxious sixty minutes cease to exist, the undesirables whose time it is will be unable to function," I said.

But Stan Bercovitch, a long-time friend and now head of the Mensa local group in Fort Myers, Florida, said: "I have always felt that the morning was much too close to the night. By abolishing the hour between 4:30 and 5:30, you are bringing the two even closer together."

He was quite right. The solution, however, is beautiful in its simplicity. Rather than being discarded, those minutes should be inserted between 6:00 and 7:00 A.M., making a 120-minute hour. Everything else is being recycled; why not time? Just think what it would mean to have 120 minutes to spend between six and seven o'clock in the morning. The longer you think about it, the more plausible the idea will become, especially when you are getting ready to go to work.

Another solution to a long-standing problem was published in several local newsletters and is offered here with the permission of its author, John H. David, of St. Louis. It is included here not to draw ridicule; on the contrary, it is such an elegant piece of logical thinking that it is an eminently appropriate note on which to conclude this book.

Jack David proposes the abolition of presidential elections, on the premise that in an ailing economy, with both the Republicans and Democrats making claims and counterclaims, we don't know whom to believe. With a presidential election looming, matters are bound to get worse, with, as he puts it, "the added burden of media coverage of every nose twitch of every possible candidate.

"I think I have a solution for both of these situations, although there are a few bugs left to be worked out in the system," he admits.

"Reduced to its essentials, the system posits that we would dispense with the presidential election and put the government out for bids. The winning party can decide for itself who should be president.

"Of course we would have bidding specifications, such as: (1) a top limit for the national debt, (2) a guarantee that unemployment would not go beyond a certain percentage, (3) adequate defense against invasions by foreign powers, (4) the maintenance of the Social Security system at a specified level.

"I imagine we would have thirty or forty such items.

"Congress would meet just once every four years to set up the specifications. The results should be reasonable, since each side would want to be able to meet them.

"Control of the government would go to the lowest bidder. Since our tax structure would be based on the low bid, this should work out well for the taxpayer. Think of all the money we could save in the electoral process alone, not to mention all the other dollars that the present procedure costs.

"And, perhaps best of all, we could require a performance bond, something we've never had before."

Sounds good to me, Jack. Now all we have to do is convince Congress.

When you write to your congressperson in support of Jack's proposal, why not mention the 120-minute hour, too?

# ANSWERS

# TRIVIA WARM-UP ANSWERS

1. The word *piccadil* was applied to the slashed collar worn by dandies who strolled in the area that is now Piccadilly. A house called Pickadilly Hall, built by a tailor named Higgins who made a fortune selling these collars, was built on the street, according to a 1656 citation.

2. Percy Bysshe Shelley was the husband of Mary Wollstonecraft Shelley, who wrote *Frankenstein*. (The monster himself is never named, incidentally; Frankenstein is his creator.)

3. Sandhurst.

4. Wine grapes.

5. A baronetess. She is addressed as "Lady"—for example, Lady Jones. (A baroness is the wife of a baron.)

6. A woman, under the applicable British law, takes her husband's rank. Queen Elizabeth II holds her title in her own name. A husband does not take his wife's rank under the same circumstances.

7. A morganatic marriage, in which the wife and children do not take the husband's rank or right to succession.

8. Switzerland. It's the abbreviation for Confederation Helvetia. Helvetia is the country's Latin name.

9. O'Hare Airport, Chicago, Illinois.

10. John Harvard and Harvard University.

11. English. There had been English fishing boats

along the New England coast for many years, and fairly good evidence indicates he had been to England, taken there by one of the fishing boats.

12. From *planta genesta,* the broom plant. Geoffrey, Count of Anjou, adopted the use of a sprig of this plant as a symbol during a pilgrimage. His descendants used it as a family name and ruled England from 1154 to 1485.

13. The color titian, a brownish orange, was named after Titian (1477–1576).

14. Verona, Italy. Although the lovers of Shakespeare's play did not really exist, their "homes" are on the standard tourist route.

15. Pocahontas.

16. Arabia. (Don't confuse him with the writer D. H. Lawrence of *Lady Chatterley's Lover* fame.)

17. Saturday's child must work for a living.

18. In Mr. McGregor's garden.

19. The Ninth Symphony.

20. Queen Elizabeth I.

21. *"To Anacreon in Heaven."*

22. In Dublin's fair city.

23. Chile.

24. The Boer War.

25. In Agra, India.

# TRIVIA TEST ANSWERS

The figure following each answer is the percentage of Mensa members who got the correct answer. Nobody got them all right. The average number of right answers was fourteen; the average time taken to complete the test was nine minutes. The highest score was nineteen correct.

1. In the pancreas. (Credit is also given to the British member who said, "Near St. Pancras Station," which is a railway station in London.) (57%)
2. Mata Hari. (More than 14% thought it was Gertrude Stein, who would probably have been amused. "Name is a name is a name.") (11%)
3. Rhodesia. (68%)
4. A novel that uses real people, thinly disguised, under other names. The French term means "novel with a key." (25%)
5. One example is *Cakes and Ale* by Somerset Maugham, in which, it is believed, Thomas Hardy and Hugh Walpole were satirized. There have been a good many novels in the last few years that appeared to be fictionalized, thinly disguised lives of personages such as movie or stage stars and Greek shipping tycoons. (21%)
6. (a) a shoe. (55%)
7. A garden in Kashmir. (7%)
8. Janus, the two-faced Roman god of gates and doorways. (89%)
9. Fishing. (61%)
10. Printing. (82%)
11. Peanut. It is also sometimes called a monkey nut. (71%)
12. Northeast, to the Atlantic. (79%)

13. They are all spas, locations where hot or mineral springs exist and are used. (93%)
14. *Life with Father.* (36%)
15. Probably from the Clink Prison, on Clink Street in Southwark, London. The street still exists, and there is a sign indicating the former site of the prison. (There is some question whether the street was named for the prison or vice versa; another possible derivation is from *clinch*, an old English or Dutch word meaning "lock up" or "fasten securely.") (4%)
16. (b) (91%)
17. Perennial. An annual may reseed, but perennials are supposed to come up every year. (79%)
18. From Nimes in France. The cloth was originally known as "de Nimes" or "from Nimes." (58%)
19. Athos, Porthos, and Aramis, and D'Artagnan (no credit lost for spelling the names incorrectly). (39%)
20. Village smithy. Not so incidentally, if your answer was *blacksmith*, you were not correct. Smithy is the building, blacksmith is the person, and the poem says very clearly that it was the building standing under the tree. (50%)
21. In the Southern Hemisphere sky. (Credit is also given for answering that it is found on certain flags.) (86%)
22. Mauritius. (21%)
23. Louis Daguerre, of daguerreotype fame. The moral of this question may be that if you are going into partnership with anyone, make sure *you*

have the more pronounceable name. (11%)

24. March 15. (Several people also included 44 B.C., but there were Ides every March. It should also be noted that the Ides occur on the 15th only in March, May, July, and October. The other months of the year have their Ides on the 13th.) (71%)

25. The Trylon and Perisphere. (32%)

# VOCABULARY WARM-UP ANSWERS

1. (c) The dinner was a *medley* of recipes from around the world.
2. (d) The guest who insulted his host was *injudicious*, to say the least.
3. (e) A *deputation* from a group of workers in the plant visited the management office.
4. (d) Garlic is reputedly an *antidote* for werewolves.
5. (d) She volunteered for the dangerous mission entirely of her own *volition*.
6. (b) There are many sports that seem to be *hazardous* to the participants.
7. (c) When I asked for a logical explanation, all I got was a *rigmarole*.
8. (a) The rules of the boarding school tend to *circumscribe* the conduct of the students.
9. (b) *Empirical* judgment is often sound, but a little study helps, too.

10. (d) To refuse to shake hands with someone is a direct *affront*.
11. (a) The child who was refused permission to play outside became *petulant*.
12. (c) The courtier was *assiduous* in his attentions to the new king.
13. (a) The actress's *sardonic* smile showed her disbelief of the story told to her.
14. (b) When the usually shy, sedate young lady became a go-go dancer, her behavior was totally *incongruous*.
15. (b) Many science fiction stories and novels relate to *chronal* discrepancies.
16. (c) Religious meetings are often opened with an *invocation*.
17. (b) The butterfly was particularly colorful, with *iridescent* gleams on its wings.
18. Don't look a gift horse in the mouth.
19. A stitch in time saves nine.
20. Too many cooks spoil the broth.

# VOCABULARY TEST ANSWERS

The average number of correct answers was fifteen. The highest correct score was nineteen. (That person missed *obiter*.) The average time was six minutes. The figure in parentheses following each answer is the percentage of Mensa test takers who got it right (rounded off).

1. (c) The miser had an inordinate amount of *cupidity*. (75%)
2. (b) The *enormity* of the mass murder shocked the nation. (There is almost unanimous agreement, among standard authorities that *enormity* does *not* mean "very large" and should not be used in that sense.) (40%)
3. (c) *Progenitor* can be used literally or figuratively, to refer either to a person who is the source of an idea or to an actual ancestor. (100%)
4. (c) You may *careen* a ship by turning it over, or a wagon may *careen* from side to side, figuratively showing the underside; but a car that is speeding out of control is *careering*. (33%)
5. (c) The *nefarious* criminal was stopped in his tracks by the hero, who was wearing a white hat, of course. (92%)
6. (d) Many of the scenes in television situation comedies are intended to be *risible*. (92%)
7. (d) Many herbal products and chemical irritants have been used to produce *aperient* products. (25%)
8. (d) The *diaconate* of the church was occupied alternately by a man and a woman. (50%)
9. (c) An *obiter* (or *obiter dictum*) is an opinion expressed in passing and, if given by a judge, has no effect on a ruling. (33%)
10. (a) A restaurant named Sam's Place uses the owner's name as an *eponym*. (75%)
11. (d) Executed pirates, as described in old stories, are usually said to be hanged from a *gibbet*. (50%)

12. (b) Anything occurring during the period of the equinoxes, which is when the days and nights are of equal length, can be described as *equinoctial*. (75%)
13. (e) Many bodily functions are considered to be *autonomic*. (60%)
14. (b) A specialist in a field is generally *erudite* in that particular subject. (100%)
15. (b) A *dour* person is usually not pleasant company. (100%)
16. (b) The forger was *mendacious*, as well as criminal, in his actions. (56%)
17. People who live in glass houses shouldn't throw stones. (100%)
18. Early to bed and early to rise, makes a man healthy, wealthy, and wise. (96%)
19. A fool and his money are soon parted. (96%)
20. Don't change horses in the middle of a stream. (75%)

# LOGIC, REASONING, AND MATHEMATICS WARM-UP ANSWERS

1. 7-22-13. This is a simple substitution cryptogram in which you substitute letters for numbers: 8 = S, 22 = E, 7 = T, etc.
2. ALL THAT GLITTERS GETS STOLEN.

3. Twenty-two unicorns with 1 horn each; eleven rams with 2 horns each.
4. (d)
5. B
6. Lettuce, celery, and roast chicken.
7. 9 A.M.
8. Avers; Saver.
9. *Kindness* or its equivalent; the word is CRUELTY.
10. 25 gallons.
11. 20¢ (10¢ per vowel).
12. (b)
13. 16
14. D 31 (December 31; the series started with July 31).
15. II
16. Lying—because no liar would admit to being a liar.
17. 20 hours.
18. Y
19. Small change.
20. One-way (one-weigh).

# LOGIC, REASONING, AND MATHEMATICS TEST ANSWERS

The figure in parentheses following each answer represents the percentage (rounded off) of Mensa members who got that question right. The highest number correct was nineteen, and that individual finished in ten minutes. The average number right was almost fifteen (a small fraction under), and the average time was thirteen minutes, with the exception of problem 12. Many people took more than an hour to work that one out, if they did not know how to do it initially. An explanation of how to solve puzzles of this type is included with the answer, as requested by many people.

1. (a) All of the others may or may not be true, but you cannot tell from the information given. The oldest grandchild could be a boy, for example. (65%)
2. THE EARLY WORM GETS WHAT IT DESERVES—EATEN. (50%)
3. Five—one more than the number of colors. (80%)
4. 9 A.M. (84%)
5. (e) FIG (alphabetical order). (88%)
6. Coat, $100; skirt, $50; scarf, $10. (96%)
7. Liars; rails. (36%)
8. (c) (92%)
9. 6 (84%)
10. A (100%)
11. VEIN. It's a simple substitution cryptogram. (44%)
12. $1089 \times 9 = 9801$. (24%)
   The puzzle and explanation were provided by Warren Sears, of Beachwood, Ohio.

```
1089        ABCD
 ×9          ×9
9801        DCBA
```

It is reasoned out as follows: 9 × A must equal a one-digit number. So A can only be a 1 or a 0. Trial and error prove that A = 1; 9 × D must equal a number ending in 1. The same trial and error demonstrate that D = 9; 9 × B must equal a one-digit number, but 1 has already been used. Therefore, B = 0. Next, 9 × C (+ 8 carried from 9 × 9) must equal a number ending in 0. By the same trial-and-error method, it is possible to demonstrate that C = 8.

13. Bravery (scrambled word is COWARDICE). (24%) (Take credit for *courage* also.)

14. 15. It is the only one of the numbers shown that is not a prime. (48%)

15. COPENHAGEN. It is the only city not on the North American continent. (44%)

16. Alice and Tom, Sally and Bob, Gertrude and Bill, Betty and Jim (or, of course, the same lineup in reverse order). (44%)

17. D (60%)

18. 208 (32%)

19. 66⅔% (52%)

20. (d) (56%)

# ANALOGIES WARM-UP ANSWERS

1. Red Sea and Mediterranean Sea.
2. (d) *a*. It is the only letter that is above the line, as *p*, *q*, and *g* are below the line.
3. (a) discrete.
4. (b) story novel.
5. Chicago.
6. Automobiles.
7. Rosinante (the animal to which the folk hero is linked).
8. A
9. President John Quincy Adams (father and son).
10. Underwater exploration.
11. Chopin.
12. George Orwell (pen name).
13. Paris—both are what we call the subway. In England, a subway is an underground walkway below a street, usually used for getting across a dangerous intersection.
14. South Dakota (state capital).
15. Football.
16. D
17. Bishop.
18. Kansas City.
19. Great Britain.
20. Gabriel D. Fahrenheit.
21. The Philippines.
22. Ghana.

23. Russia.
24. Hockey.
25. *My Fair Lady* (Oscar winners).

# ANALOGIES TEST ANSWERS

The average number of correct answers was fourteen. The highest score was eighteen. The average time was ten minutes. The figure in parentheses following each answer is the percentage of Mensa members who achieved a correct score on that question.

1. The United States. Liederkranz cheese was developed by Emil Frey in the 1890s and named for his singing group (*Liederkranz* is German for "wreath of song"). It is a U.S. trade name. (4%)
2. Fear of light. Photophobia is often due to illness or unusual sensitivity. (80%)
3. Potatoes. Parmentier introduced potatoes to French cuisine, so if you don't like potatoes, don't order anything à la Parmentier. (8%)
4. Newark, New Jersey. Those are the initials used for the airports. (64%)
5. Anna (the word reversed). (64%)
6. Pod (or small school or herd, but *pod* is the technical word). (40%)
7. *Pygmalion* (the source of the musical comedy). (36%)
8. Lewis Carroll (pen name). (36%)

9. Africa. (92%)
10. Heterodox (the exact opposite; but *unorthodox* is also an acceptable answer). (44%)
11. (a) strengthen. (68%)
12. Morocco. (4%)
13. D (96%)
14. (a) fraudulent. (92%)
15. (d) revealed. (84%)
16. C (52%)
17. Isolde or Iseult (or any variant of the same name). (92%)
18. (a) Harding. (64%)
19. (a) Venice. (So called because condemned prisoners crossed it after sentencing.) (56%)
20. (c) sand. (72%)
21. (c) Truman. The first Roosevelt (Theodore) succeeded McKinley and became president on McKinley's death, as Harry S Truman did after the second Roosevelt's (Franklin Delano's) death. Note: There is no period after the S in Truman's name because he had no middle name, and the S is not an abbreviation. (16%)
22. (b) Sri Lanka. (68%)
23. (d) fountain. (16%)
24. (b) cooking. (8%)
25. (a) 1, 11, 14. This is comparable to warm-up analogy question 2. Here, the first set of numerals (3, 5, 8, 9) are considered as curved lines, so the only set that would match 4 would be the numerals written with straight lines. The warm-up question used letters similarly, but it is the same general idea. (12%)

# CULTURE WARM-UP
# ANSWERS

## ART

1. The chapel was named after Pope Sixtus IV and was built as a papal private chapel in 1473. There are many other famous paintings in it besides those of Michelangelo.
2. The pictures depict the life of the upper-class courtesans who were an important part of Japanese male social life of the time.
3. Sculpture.
4. Raphael was also an architect. He designed, among other buildings, the Palazzo Pandolfi in Florence, Italy.
5. Gibbons was a sculptor and woodcarver who did a tremendous amount of work at St. Paul's Cathedral and many other places.

## MUSIC

1. D'Oyley Carte presented the operettas at the Savoy Theatre in London.
2. *La Marseillaise.* Claude Joseph Rouget de Lisle composed the words and music, but it was originally written as a war song for the Army of the Rhine. On well-documented evidence, on July 30, 1792, a troop of volunteers from Marseilles entered Paris singing the song, which was thereafter called by its current name.

3. Egypt.
4. No, because the waltz wasn't invented until almost two hundred years later.
5. New Orleans.

## GREEK AND ROMAN CULTURE

1. Zeus and Hera.
2. Romulus and Remus.
3. The Wooden (or Trojan) Horse.
4. Lesbos.
5. Spinning thread. Clotho held the distaff, Lachesis spun the thread (of life), and Atropos cut off the thread when life was finished.

## LITERATURE

1. They were played by boys.
2. Eddas (the Poetic Edda and the Prose Edda).
3. Blindness.
4. *The Divine Comedy.*
5. The Arthurian legends—the life and death or disappearance of King Arthur.

## ETIQUETTE

1. The flute-shaped glass, since the bubbles dissipate more slowly. Of course, the champagne "saucer" is also correct.
2. The gentleman is always presented to the lady, unless the gentleman is the president of the United

States, the recognized head of another country, royalty, or a high church dignitary.

3. Never. According to etiquette books which cover the subject, a woman does not take off her gloves to shake hands, and does not apologize for them.
4. Nothing. It is considered more courteous to write the message, even if it is only a few words.
5. According to most authorities, at home at the family dinner table, or at a picnic.

# CULTURE TEST ANSWERS

The average number of correct answers by Mensa members was just under eighteen out of a possible thirty. (Some questions have several parts.) The average time was twelve minutes, with a low of eight minutes and a high of thirty-nine minutes. The figure in parentheses following each answer is the percentage (rounded off) of Mensa members who got that answer correct. There was one question, number 4, on Greek and Roman Culture, that everybody got right.

GREEK AND ROMAN CULTURE

1. River Styx. (80%)
2. Bacchus. (85%)
3. Calliope, Muse of epic poetry; Clio, Muse of history; Erato, Muse of love poetry; Euterpe, Muse

of lyric poetry; Melpomene, Muse of tragedy; Polyhymnia, Muse of sacred poetry; Terpsichore, Muse of choral song and dance; Thalia, Muse of comedy and idyllic poetry; Urania, Muse of astronomy. (50% named one or more; 45% were able to give the Muse's specialty. Among Mensans the best known Muse was Terpsichore.

4. Narcissus. (100%)
5. The adventures of Odysseus (Ulysses) on his long and epic journey home from Troy. (60%) (Two other answers given were *Greece on $5 a Day,* and *You CAN Go Home Again.*)

## ART

1. *The Birth of Venus* (the usually accepted title) by Sandro Botticelli (a.k.a. Alessandro di Mariano Filipepi). (60% knew the name of the painting; 45% knew the painter; 5% knew the painter's first name.)
2. *La Gioconda* (Italian) or *La Belle Joconde* (French). (40%)
3. Gilbert Stuart. (35%)
4. Edgar Degas. (60%)
5. The (Solomon R.) Guggenheim Museum, designed by Frank Lloyd Wright. (70%)

## LITERATURE

1. *Canterbury Tales.* (90%)
2. India. (90%)
3. 1960, *Advise and Consent* by Allen Drury; 1961,

*To Kill a Mockingbird* by Harper Lee; 1962, *The Edge of Sadness* by Edwin O'Connor; 1963, *The Reivers* by William Faulkner; 1964, none; 1965, *The Keepers of the House* by Shirley Ann Grau; 1966, *Collected Short Stories* by Katherine Anne Porter; 1967, *The Fixer* by Bernard Malamud; 1968, *The Confessions of Nat Turner* by William Styron; 1969, *House Made of Dawn* by M. Scott Momaday; 1970, *Collected Stories* by Jean Stafford; 1971, none; 1972, *Angel of Repose* by Wallace Stegner; 1973, *The Optimist's Daughter* by Eudora Welty; 1974, none; 1975, *The Killer Angels* by Michael Shaara; 1976, *Humboldt's Gift* by Saul Bellow; 1977, none; 1978, *Elbow Room* by James Allan McPherson; 1979, *The Stories of John Cheever* by John Cheever; 1980, *The Executioner's Song* by Norman Mailer; 1981, *A Confederacy of Dunces* by John Kennedy Toole; 1982, *Rabbit Is Rich* by John Updike. (And, of course, any added to the list since then.) (70% could name two authors, 20% could name the book of one author, 5% could name both authors and both books.)

4. *Remembrance of Things Past,* or *À la Recherche du temps perdu.* (35%)
5. A. A. Milne. (65%)

## ETIQUETTE

1. You don't—it's a command performance except for an absolutely major reason, such as your own wedding or funeral. (35%)

2. It is most probably a visiting-card tray, for calling cards. (50%)
3. Silver. (95%)
4. Officially, just plain "Mr." Usually, out of courtesy, "Mr. President," when you speak to him. (He is spoken of as "the former president.") (50%)
5. Woman guest of honor, to the host's right. The host used to be served first, according to some texts, to prove to his guests that the food was not tainted or poisoned. At present, service is as given, except for certain circumstances, such as a single hostess. (50%)

## MUSIC

1. Nine. (95%)
2. Voice alone, without accompaniment (literally, "in chapel or church style"). (55%)
3. England, where he became a citizen. (50%)
4. *The Ring Cycle,* or *The Ring of the Nibelungs,* or *Der Ring des Nibelungen.* (75%)
5. Sir Arthur S. Sullivan. (30%) (He also wrote "The Lost Chord," a famous hymn.)

# THE MENSA GENIUS
# QUIZ-A-DAY BOOK

*Dr. Abbie F. Salny and the Members of Mensa*

To Jerry, as always

# To the Reader

This puzzle book is intended to amuse, edify, instruct, but mostly to interest you, the clever reader. The puzzles have been tested on several hundred Mensa members, who racked their brains on the more difficult questions or sneered at what look like easy questions. But be warned! There are tricks in some of the apparently easy puzzles, and even the Mensa members, in many instances, failed to spot the hidden traps.

The puzzles are arranged in chronological order over the course of the year—one for each day and an extra one for Leap Years. The answers can be found in the back of the book, organized by date: the answers for the first day of each month, then the answers for the second day, and so on to the thirty-first. The percentage of Mensa members who solved that puzzle correctly is given with every answer. Most of these percentages have been rounded off to the nearest 5 percent for the sake of convenience.

You may find some old puzzles in new guises. You may find others that are totally new to you. There's even one type of puzzle in this book that I invented myself (see February 8). All the rest were inspired by puzzles that people have been making since one person first passed on the "Riddle of the Sphinx" to another. Magic squares are thousands of years old; number puzzles have existed since the early days of written numbers; paradoxes and logic puzzles were recorded by the early Greeks. Word ladders and alphametics are more recent, having been invented by Lewis Carroll and A. H. Hunter within the last two hundred years. But there is little new under the sun.

One thing which is not new is alternate answers. Try as a puzzle author might, unless a puzzle is the type to which only one answer can possibly be given, there may well be alternate solutions. If you find a clever, more elegant, or more interesting solution, please drop me a note. I'd be glad to hear from you.

All the puzzles were proofed by my nitpicking husband, Jerome Salny, but all errors are my sole responsibility. Happy puzzling!

*Abbie F. Salny*

# What Is Mensa?

First of all, Mensa is not an acronym. It is the Latin word meaning "table," and it indicates that all members are equal. (Remember King Arthur's Round Table?) Of course, some are more equal than others, because those who become involved and participate in the multitude of activities Mensa offers get the most from the society. The sole requirement for membership in Mensa is a score in the top 2 percent of the population on any standard intelligence test or the equivalent (130 on the Wechsler scale, 132 on the Stanford-Binet, 1250 on the Scholastic Aptitude Test after 1977).

Because this is the only criterion for membership, the diversity of human beings in Mensa is immense. Members include authors, executives, carpenters, dancers, physicists, students, and many other kinds of people. You can well imagine the interest and fun generated when Mensans get together at a gathering (the official term). The talk can range over all and any subjects. One has the pleasure of hearing from an intelligent expert in a field other than one's own. There is the delight in recognizing a new idea, a new concept, or a new outlook on an old theme. And there is just plain fun. Mensans love to play games of all kinds—computer games, word games, logic games, silly games. Most groups have a Games Night when those so inclined to this sort of thing (the sort of thing in this book) can participate.

Mensans band together in Special Interest Groups (SIGs) of members with a common fascination or desire. These interests run from the Age of Chivalry SIG to the Feudal Japan SIG, the Scripophily (paper money) SIG, the Skydiving SIG, through M.A.R.I.A.N., a SIG devoted to nurturing and visiting, in person or by letter, the sick and dying, and to the Vacation Network SIG and the Singles Network SIG.

Many Mensans participate in the society exclusively by mail. They get their local newsletter telling them what is going on in their area; they receive the Mensa Bulletin and the *International Journal,* which tell them about national and international Mensa; and they may belong to a SIG which, though it may never meet, ties hundreds of Mensans together in a postal network.

Who are these Mensans, anyway? Mensans tend to be reasonably well educated, but we have plenty of high school dropouts as well as Ph.D.'s. Mensans tend to have above-average incomes—but many do not, preferring to spend their time on avocations of consuming interest. Mensans tend to have a slightly smaller number of children than the national average—but we have a highly active Gifted Children's Program, with a national network of coordinators. The society also publishes a newsletter full of ideas for gifted children. Mensans tend to be ages thirty or over, but there is a very active Young Mensa for people who are twenty-two or younger. Mensans tend to be verbal and fluent, whether on paper or in person. We talk and talk—but we listen, too.

Mensans are just like everyone else, but more so. You meet a lot of intense people in Mensa who throw themselves wholeheartedly into what they do for the society. (All Mensa activity is volunteer and unpaid, except for a small staff at national headquarters in Brooklyn.) Many members help out with the intellectual and scientific activities of the Mensa Education and Research Foundation (MERF). This branch runs the numerous scholarships (to which this book contributes), the *Mensa Research Journal,* the surveys, the Awards for Excellence, and all the other activities that satisfy our intellectual side. MERF raises money for special projects and is limited only by what we can raise and the vision of those who propose projects. MERF also collaborates on the intellectual Colloquium. It is the idealistic, social-service side of Mensa, and contributions to MERF are tax deductible.

But above all, Mensa is friends. Whether in the local chapter or in any of the thirty countries around the world where Mensa exists, it means finding ready-made friends. There is even a group organized to provide hospitality wherever in the world (almost) you might travel. You need to have had the experience of arriving by plane in a strange land at midnight, tired and droopy, to be welcomed by Mensa strangers-who-will-soon-be-friends, to realize what this means.

And that's meeting one or two Mensans at a time. There are large gatherings of anywhere from seventy-five to fifteen hundred Mensans. The joint American-Canadian Annual Gathering at Montreal in 1988 was attended by fifteen hundred Mensans from both countries. For many, it was like being in a room filled with bubbly champagne, full of friendship and good cheer. What did the Mensans do at this gathering? They talked; they took French lessons; they attended lectures on mathematics, on art, on history, on romance, on Montreal; they talked; they ate at the hotel banquets and nibbled in the Mensa hospitality suites, which are always jammed wall to wall with talkers; they went on sightseeing tours; they went to a French-Canadian sugar shack for a party; they talked; and when they finished with all these activities, they talked some more.

There are many such gatherings a year. There are even gathering addicts, who spend their vacations visiting one regional gathering after another, each with its own special flavor, or attending the Colloquium, a biannual event sponsored by both MERF and Mensa with meetings devoted to intellectual topics and renowned speakers. Past themes have included "The Future," "The Arts," and "Man and Science."

Mensa is fun, it is serious, it is intellectually stimulating, it is friendly. In short, Mensa is the sum of fifty-odd thousand bright people, effervescing.

# Acknowledgments

Special thanks to Mensans Bob Buethe, Ron Frederick, Friend Kierstead, Ron Ruemmler, Marilyn Seltzer, and Russ Washburne. They corrected, annotated, criticized, and helped. Thanks also to Lucille Hitchuk and Gene Sheridan for their clerical assistance.

The following list includes those Mensans who helped by taking the various puzzles included in this book. Not all did every puzzle, of course, but I'm grateful to everyone. My apologies to anyone whose name does not appear. I could not read, or find, a few names on the answer sheets. If you will send me your name now, we'll include it in a later printing.

Lois Abel
Charles E. Adams
Micki Ross Adams
Virginia Andrews
N.B. Angelo
Suzanne Armstrong
Warner Ashby
Jean Babcock
John E. Ballinger
Pat Bechlear

Carol Bell-Jesion
Paul Berghold
Jerome Bernstein
Mervin Bierman
H.W. Bodley
W.E. Bowser
Joan K. Boyer
M. Brockhoff
Lorin Browning
Robert A. Buethe

Jerri Burket
Jerry Butler
Shanna Cartwright
Paul D. Cernota
Terri A. Chepregi
Laurence P. Ching
W. Edward Christiansen, Jr.
Elizabeth Claire
Lorilyn Coggins
Seth Cohen
Roy Cornelius
George M. Couch
Joel Cox
Antonia Dailey
Jane Dalton
Evelyn N. Doody
Pat Doody
Judy Dosse
Amby Duncan-Carr
Wendy Ebersberger
Leslie A. Ellis
Sean M. Ferrell
Leslie Fife
Marian Fox
Ron Frederick
Sonia Follett Fuller
Henry Gertzman
R.O. Ginsburg
Vella L. Goebel
Larry Gomberg
Al Greengold
Yale L. Greenspoon
Elaine Gruber
Michael Hanson

Monroe Harden
Patricia A. Hardesty
Charles Harding
Amy Harold
Thomas Henneman
Porter Henry
Dayle Hodge
Jack Howell
Michael Jankowski
Jerry Javine
Bruce W. Jean
Elvin Jensen
John M. Jensen
Kathy Jones
Donna Jones-Cosgrove
Arielle Kagan
Kevin Kauffman
Ted Kelly
Mary Lee Kemper
Friend H. Kierstead, Jr.
Virginia Krenn
Ravi Krishnan
Florence Kuehn
Teri Lacher
Nancy Laine
Eileen Leskovec
Rich Loeffler
Virginia Long
Gene Lucas
M.P. Ludlum
Melinda Maidens
Ward Mardfin
Teresa MarQuand

Stuart Maudlin
Lois McDonley
Vernon McFarlin
Ernest McLain
Barbara H. Miller
Phyllis Miller
Jean Moffett
Caroline Monks
Barbara A. Moore
Dennis B. Moore
Mildred Morgan and family
Rosalie Moscovitch
Kathy Mullholland
Warren Murphy
Diane Nagel
Edward J. Nasipak
Caryn Neumann
Everett Newton
Ruby V. North
Kathleen E. O'Malley
Florence Otis
D. June Owen
Howard S. Passel
Kyle J. Perun
Thomas M. Phelps
Sharon Pidgeon
Heather L. Preston
Dimitri Raftopolous
Bill Raiford
Gloria Reiser
Kate Retzlaff
Cecilia M. Roberts
Mary Lou Robinson

Wm. Ridgway, Jr.
Mary Lou Robinson
Diane Rozek
Pat Rudy-Baese
Ron Ruemmler
Charlie Runtz
Minerva A. Russell
Vicki P. Samples
Danika Lea Sanders
Jules Savan
Sharon Scanlin
Kenneth Schwartz
Marilyn Seltzer
Dave Senner
Terri Shaw
Kenneth M. Silver
William M. Sloane
Donald J. Strand
Ray Suhles
Merrilee Tanner
Colleen J. Theusch
Elaine Thompson
Hank Trent
N. Trigobotti
Barbara R. Tysinger
Tony C. Vaca
Alden Vaitulis
Stanley Veyitl
Alice Volkert
Roger Volkert
Charles R. Voracek
Mary Washburn
Russ Washburne

Shirley Washburne
G.H. Waxter
A. Weiss
Frank Wershing
Hugh White and family
Ray Wilbur

Sherie J. Winslow
Cynthia Wolford
Jeanne R. Wood
Mark A. Yezzi
Joe Zanca
Carl Zimmerman

# January

The calendar as we know it is the result of a great deal of work by the Romans. Even the word *calendar* derives from the Latin *kalends,* a system of reckoning.

The Roman calendar originally started with what we now call March, which had 31 days, followed by April (30 days), May (31), June (29), Quintilis (31), Sextilis (29), September (29), October (31), November and December (29 each). There were a good many extra days in this system, and January and February appeared more or less at whim. This calendar became a political football when the pontifex maximus, the highest priest of Roman religion, was given the power to regulate the empty dates. By extending or shortening the final periods, for example, an unpopular politician could be pushed out of office early, or a popular one kept in long past his elected term. By the time of Julius Caesar, January was falling in the fall, and the entire system was obviously in need of a major overhaul.

Caesar enlisted the aid of astronomers and set up a system much like that of the ancient Egyptians, who had the year figured out to within a few hours. During 46 B.C., the 445-day "Year of Confusion," Caesar added days, made January and February settled months, and gave every fourth February an extra day for Leap Year.

## January 1

Janus was the Roman god who was represented with two bearded heads placed back to back so that he could look forward and backward at the same time. A palindrome is a word, phrase, or sentence that reads the same forward and backward, so it seems especially appropriate for Janus's month, January. Try to come up with palindromes from the following clues, in which the word division is given. (Example: First man introduces himself to first woman—Madam, I'm Adam.)

Query by rodent-phobic person:

— — —  — —  —  — — —  —
— — — ?

Comment by cake- and pie-loving overweight person about meal habits:

— — — — — — — —  —
— — — — — — — — .

## January 2

At my favorite fruit stand in Puzzleland, an orange costs 18¢, a pineapple costs 27¢, and a grape costs 15¢. Using the same logic, can you tell how much a mango costs?

## January 3

Even if you don't like cats, you should be able to determine the following words. Each of these includes the word CAT. (Example: grape—mus*cat*)

A dreadful event:

— — — — — — — — — — —

A robber who climbs walls:

— — —    — — — — — — —

A systematized list:

— — — — — — — — —

## January 4

Margot likes knights but not battlers; she likes writing but not typing; she likes to listen but not to sing. Does she like an unknown or a famous author?

## January 5

My husband and I can't seem to get our watches to work properly. His consistently runs one minute per hour fast, and mine runs two minutes per hour slow. This morning we nearly missed a wedding because our watches were an hour apart and we looked at the slower one. How many hours had elapsed since we set both of them properly?

## January 6

Cressida didn't like to tell her age, so when she was asked, her mother answered for her. Her mother said, "I'm just seven times as old as she is now. In twenty years, she'll be just half the age that I will be then." How old is clever little Cressida?

## January 7

This type of puzzle used to be very popular among puzzlers who thought they were poets, and poets who thought they were puzzlers. The verse spells out a word letter by letter, and often defines that word as well. "My first" refers to the word's first letter, and so on. Can you discover the word that this verse describes?

> My first is in fish but not in snail
> My second in rabbit but not in tail
> My third in up but not in down
> My fourth in tiara not in crown
> My fifth in tree you plainly see
> My whole a food for you and me

## January 8

All the vowels (A, E, I, O, and U, but not Y) have been removed from the following proverb, and the remaining letters broken into groups of three letters each. Replace the vowels to find the proverb.

BRD SFF THR FLC KTG THR.

## January 9

One letter—a different letter for each word—has been removed from each of the following words. At least three of that letter are missing in each one. Replace the missing letters to find the words.

ILIN  HAERAN  ILLOARE

## January 10

What is the four-digit number in which the first digit is one-third the second, the third is the sum of the first and second, and the last is three times the second?

## January 11

If six winkles and three wonkles cost 15¢, and you can buy nine wonkles and three winkles for the same 15¢, what will it cost to buy one hundred wonkles?

## January 12

The names of three famous cheeses are "interlettered" in the following line. All the letters are in the correct order for each word. Unscramble your cheeses:

R L C O I M H Q B E U U D E R D F O G E R R A T R

## January 13

The same seven letters, if rearranged, will make two different words. These words will make the following sentences (more or less) complete. Fill in the missing letters.

The job they were doing was long and
— — — — — — — .  Every few hours,
the workmen put down their tools to go
— — — — — — — .

## January 14

It's hard to go back to school after vacation, but you have to get to work sometime. Go from FAIL to PASS in only four steps, changing one letter at a time and making a good English word at each step.

F   A   I   L
—   —   —   —
—   —   —   —
P   A   S   S

## January 15

Since it is January, thoughts often turn, fondly or not, to snowflakes. Each shape of snowflake in the boxes below has a numerical value. The sum of each line and column has been given for all but one line. Fill in the missing sum.

| ❄ | ❄ | ☆ | ✳ | ? |
|---|---|---|---|---|
| ❄ | ✿ | ☆ | ✿ | 85 |
| ✳ | ☆ | ❄ | ✳ | 87 |
| ✿ | ✳ | ☆ | ✳ | 82 |
| 87 | 86 | 93 | 79 | |

## January 16

Rearrange these six matchsticks to make "nothing." No matchsticks may be bent, broken, or placed over each other.

## January 17

This simple substitution cryptogram is a warning. (A substitution cryptogram is one in which each letter is replaced by another letter, number, or symbol; CAT becomes DBU when the next letter of the alphabet is used.) Can you solve the cipher?

S V   D S L   R H   G L L
H S Z I K   H L N V G R N V H
X F G H   S R N H V O U

## January 18

Using all the digits from 1 to 9, you can construct many different additions (for example, 317 + 628 = 945). There are four such examples which have a total of 468. Find the missing numbers. You *may not* simply reverse the top and bottom numbers; new combinations must be found.

| 1 x x | x x 5 | x 9 x | x x x |
|-------|-------|-------|-------|
| x x x | x x x | x x x | x 7 x |
| 4 6 8 | 4 6 8 | 4 6 8 | 4 6 8 |

## January 19

How many common English words can you make from the letters DRIBA? Use all the letters each time.

## January 20

You have decided to take your morning run in preparation for the local marathon at an average speed of 6 miles per hour. Unfortunately, you are not in as good shape as you thought, and you are running uphill. You find that you complete a half of the run, all uphill, at an average speed of only 3 miles per hour. How fast must you run to make the return trip—all downhill—at an average speed for the entire round trip of 6 miles per hour?

## January 21

In that same marathon, which you watched from the sidewalk, Sam was faster than Jack. Denise beat Jim, but lost to Jack. Who came in last?

## January 22

After paying all your holiday bills, you're very short of cash. You have a total of $9.60 in your pocket. The money is composed of equal numbers of quarters, dimes, and nickels, but no other coins. How many of each of those three coins do you have?

## January 23

Each of the following words except one can be rearranged to spell the name of a person or city. Unscramble the words to find the one that cannot be unscrambled. Both parts must be done correctly for full credit.

ANIMAL    BUTCHERS    PASTURE
PANELS    VIKING

## January 24

Here are two more palindromes—phrases reading the same in both directions (Madam, I'm Adam). Word division is given for each.

Consumed a Greek delicacy:

— — —    — — — —

Where Napoleon dined:

— — — —    — — — — —

## January 25

Entire countries are hidden in the sentences below—at least their names are. One or more names appear in each statement. Find the countries.

> Don't reach in a crack in the rocks, there might be snakes there.
> While I was on the highway called the Alcan, a daily occurrence was car breakdown.
> The top social class, as defined by many investigators, is the upper-upper.

## January 26

Harper and Rose Lee were debating the major purchase of some candy. They found out, by looking at the prices, that they could get three tiny bags of jellybeans and two tiny bags of chocolate chips for 24¢, which was under their limit of a quarter. They could also get four tiny bags of chocolates and two tiny bags of jellybeans for the same 24¢. How much did each tiny bag of chocolates cost?

## January 27

The following quotation, from a famous author born on this date in 1832, has had all its vowels removed and has been broken into groups of three letters. (There's one null letter at the end.) Put back the vowels to read the quotation.

| | | | | | |
|---|---|---|---|---|---|
| THT | MHS | CMT | HWL | RSS | DTT |
| LKF | MNY | THN | GSF | SHS | NDS |
| HPS | NDS | LNG | WXF | CBB | GSN |
| DKN | GSX. | | | | |

## January 28

The following coiled sentence contains an idea that every motorist agrees with. Start at the right spot and move, letter by letter, in any direction to find the sentence.

```
V  E  O  E  T
E  U  Y  L  P
R  Y  S  L  A
H  T  R  O  M
I  N  A  A  D
G  E  X  R  T
E  C  O  E  I
P  O  T  F  D
T  H  W  O  L
```

## January 29

One letter can replace the first letter of each word pair shown below so that two new English words are formed. Place the letter you have used for both words on the line between the words. (Example: RAIN _____ DARK = MAIN __M__ MARK). When you have finished, the new letters will spell out a new English word.

| MAIL | _____ | PINK |
| CART | _____ | SAID |
| GRID | _____ | RIMLESS |
| LINK | _____ | BOUND |
| ROWED | _____ | RIPPLE |

# January 30

At the top below is a box that has been unfolded. Next to it are six folded boxes. Which of these folded boxes *cannot* be made from the unfolded box? (There may be more than one.)

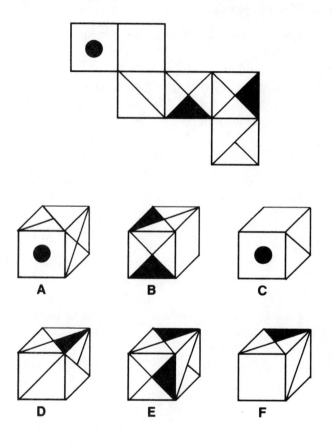

# January 31

Each of the following words includes the letters JAN in order. (They may contain another J or A or N, which does not appear in the lines shown.) The definition for each word is given. Find the words.

A variety of semiprecious stone, a color either blue
or orangy:                J A __ __ N __ __

A type of soldier:      J A N __ __ __ __ __ __

Pertaining, now, to the Democratic party of the U.S.,
but originally with a slightly different meaning.
Adjectival form of politician's name:

      J __ __ __ __ __ __ __ __ __ A N

# February

B ecause February fell at the end of the Roman year, it was assigned fewer days than the rest of the months. According to legends, Julius Caesar and Augustus each took one day from February to add to the month named after him. They seem to have covered their thefts successfully, however, as these legends cannot be verified.

If you think cold February days are hard now, you would not have liked being around a few centuries ago. Average temperatures in Europe dropped during the thirteenth century, and they remained lower than they are now through the 1700s. The Vikings had to abandon their settlement on Greenland when this "Little Ice Age" began. Canals in Holland froze. The wine industry in England, which had flourished under the Romans, disappeared.

In London, February often produced a "Frost Fair" on the Thames. The river was frozen so solid for several weeks that a whole country fair could be held on the ice. We are indebted to English diary keepers and writers for our knowledge of this lost tradition. The last such fair occurred in 1814, the approximate beginning date of the current warming trend.

## February 1

A palindrome is a word or phrase that reads the same backward as forward, such as "Madam, I'm Adam." The following two palindromes are more difficult, but not impossible. Word divisions are shown:

> A zookeeper announces that he has captured two fewer than a dozen beasts by hitting them hard with a reticulated object and putting them inside it.

— — —  — — — — — —  —
— — — —  — —  —  — — — .

Spoiled children of performing luminaries:

— — — —  — — — —

## February 2

The following puzzle consists of a proverb with all its vowels removed. The remaining letters have been broken into groups of four. Put back the vowels to find the proverb.

FLND    HSMN    YRSN    PRTD.

## February 3

The coiled sentence below will complete a rhyme with the first line "Murphy's Law is very fine." Move from the correct starting letter in any direction, letter by letter.

```
T  K  K  O  E
I  E  C  F  N
P  E  E  F  I
S  Y  N  T  L
O  U  R  H  E
```

## February 4

You can often place a word between a pair of other words to form an entirely new word or phrase with each of them (example: SCHOOL *BOOK* BAG). In fact, one four-letter word will fit in all three pairs below. What is it?

| | | |
|---|---|---|
| BACK | _____ | SOME |
| LEFT | _____ | WORK |
| FORE | _____ | SHAKE |

## February 5

If six puzzle makers can compose nine puzzles in a day and a half, how many puzzle makers does it take to compose 270 puzzles in thirty days?

## February 6

It is nice in real life, but it's much easier on paper. Can you go from POOR to RICH in seven steps, changing one letter at a time, and making a good English word each time? (There are several solutions.)

| P | O | O | R |
|---|---|---|---|
| — | — | — | — |
| — | — | — | — |
| — | — | — | — |
| — | — | — | — |
| — | — | — | — |
| — | — | — | — |
| R | I | C | H |

## February 7

Two youngsters were running as hard as they could. They averaged 6 miles per hour, and then had to rest. On the way back, they averaged only 4 miles per hour for the same distance. Not counting resting time, what was their average speed?

## February 8

If Brazil is east of New York, cross out all the W's and X's. If not, cross out all the A's. If Henry VIII lived in the same century as Columbus, cross out all the Y's. If not, cross out the M's and N's. If Golden Gate Bridge is the longest suspension bridge in the world, cross out all the S's and E's. If not, cross out all the I's and Z's. What word do you have left?

M X Y E Z W N X Y Z S I I X Y A Z W X I

## February 9

The following addition example uses letters instead of numbers. Each letter must be replaced with a number—the same number each time the letter appears. The puzzle will then be correct mathematically.

$$
\begin{array}{r}
OH \\
OH \\
OH \\
\underline{OH} \\
NO!
\end{array}
$$

## February 10

All the vowels have been removed from a popular proverb and the remaining letters broken up into groups of four (with three nulls). Replace the vowels to read the proverb.

LLTH    TGLT    TRSS    NTGL    DXXX

## February 11

Each of the following words contains the letters FEB. Fill in the missing letters. (Additional F, E, B letters may appear but not be shown.)

Feverish:                          F E B __ __ __ __
Untenable; that cannot be excused or justified:
                    __ __ __ __ F E __ __ __ B __ __
Not strong:                       F E __ B __ __

## February 12

You've had a tough time lately. Birthdays, weddings, what-all, have just about brought your finances down to your household piggy bank. With your trusty broad blade knife, you manage to extract quite a few coins, for a total of $16. To your surprise, you have exactly the same number of half dollars, quarters, and nickels. How many of each do you have?

## February 13

If Susan is 10, Arabella is 20, and Jim and Neal are both 5, but Richard is 10, how much is Jennifer by the same system?

## February 14

Valentine's Day has its roots in the tradition that Saint Valentine provided dowries for unmarried poor girls. His feast day thus became a celebration of love and marriage, and young men sent tokens of affection to young women of their choice. Now Valentine's Day seems to have gotten a little out of hand, with people sending wishes to their mothers-in-law, aunts, teachers, all their third-grade classmates, and many others. Given this crush of cards, if seven valentine makers can make seven valentines in one hour and forty minutes, how long does it take fourteen valentine makers to make fourteen valentines?

## February 15

The office team is out racing at the skating rink during a long lunch hour. Samantha beat Jim. Louise was not last. Dennis was beaten by Jack and Louise, in that order. Jim was not first. Jack lost to Jim. Who won?

## February 16

How many common English words can you make from the letters AEKL? (All the letters must be used for each word.)

## February 17

You bought two antique lamps for $50 each. Later, you were offered $60 for one and sold it, changed your mind when you saw its duplicate being sold for more, and bought it back for $70. You then sold it for $80. The first one didn't sell at all so you reduced it 10% below what you originally paid and managed to get rid of it. Did you make or lose money on the deal, and how much?

## February 18

When Jim was taking a stroll one day, he met his father-in-law's only daughter's mother-in-law. What did he call her?

## February 19

A sentence was dropped into the grid below, but the letters dropped out. The letters all appear underneath the squares where they belong, but they have been arranged in their columns alphabetically. A black box in the grid shows a space between words; a dash at the end of a line means that a word continues onto the next line. Can you reassemble the sentence? (Hint: Asking friends to help may be more trouble than it's worth.)

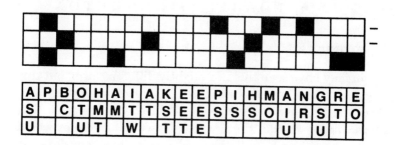

## February 20

The following line consists of three countries whose names have been "interlettered." The letters are in the correct order for each country. Unscramble the three countries.

ALUHRUXNGEMEBNOUTRIGNGARAY

## February 21

Billy had a coin purse with fifty coins, totaling exactly $1.00. Unfortunately, while counting them, he dropped one coin behind the radiator. What is the probability that it was a penny?

## February 22

George Washington was born on February 22, 1732, so we now celebrate President's Day around this date. Each of the following three lines contains three presidents' names. Unscramble them to find the chief executives.

R T O K O E S N E R V N E U L E M D T A N Y
J J T E O F Y F H L E N E R S R O S O N N
T C A O W F O A S T L H I I D N G G E T O N

## February 23

(You may have seen this in a slightly different form, but this version has an unusual twist to it.) It was a bring-your-own-food party, but not everybody could contribute food. The agreement was that those who couldn't bring edibles would chip in some cash. Sally brought a certain number of pies, Jane brought one more than Sally, and Hector brought one more than Jane. William brought nothing, but asked them to divide the nice little pies equally, and he would pay. The four split the pies evenly. There was a total of a dozen pies, each worth $1.00. How much should each of them get or pay?

## February 24

How many common English words can you make from the letters LGNEA? (There are at least three.) Use all the letters for each word.

## February 25

The following silly palindromes—a word, phrase, or sentence reading the same backward as forward as in "Rise to vote, sir"—have the word divisions given. Can you find them?

Debutante is sleeping:  _ _ _   _ _ _ _
Edna and Delia weren't feeling too well:

_ _ _ _ _   _ _ _   _ _ _ _

_ _ _ _ _ .

## February 26

Each of the following four words has had the *same* vowel removed. At least three of that vowel are missing from each word. What are the reconstructed words?

PRMAT     RHARS     TNAGR     FORSR

## February 27

If 9 is twice 5, how will you write 6 times 5 in the same system of notation? (This type of puzzle dates back to the early Middle Ages, so don't say it isn't logic.)

## February 28

What is the highest four-digit number, with no zeros, in which the first digit is one-quarter of the third digit, the second digit is three times the first digit, and the third and last digits are the same?

## February 29

Colonel Cholomondely-Snaithwirth-Jones was very proud indeed of his big-game hunting exploits. He had published several monographs about his life among the pygmies, his exploits during the Boer War, and his single-handed capture of an entire tribe of blow-dart hunting natives in Borneo. He had even brought home a poisoned blow dart as evidence, and, as he told friends, he was going to use it to start a collection for the Victoria and Albert Museum. This particular day, dressed in his usual explorer clothes, he was sitting comfortably in an armchair, being interviewed by the Explorers Club membership committee.

"As I said," he continued, "my reputation had spread before me, and these poor chappies sent word via the drums that they needed me desperately. Two of their babies, one of the women, and two warriors had been snatched right out of the village by this man-eating tiger. They were desperately short of warriors, the drums said." He nodded affirmatively. "So I assembled my bearers, my full set of guns, and set off for the village. It was at the headwaters of the Nile, in territory so remote no white man had ever been there. I learned all I could from my bearers about the habits of nocturnal hunters like that tiger—" At this point, each of the four committee members seized one limb of the hapless colonel and threw him down the club's magnificent flight of twenty-two marble steps and onto the street. Why?

# March

March was named after Mars, the god of war, by the Romans, who valued military prowess highly. Mars was also the father of Romulus and Remus, the twins who founded Rome.

On March 15, the Ides of March, in 44 B.C., Julius Caesar was assassinated. The senators who stabbed him had grown fearful and jealous of his power; Plutarch reports that some people viewed even his calendar reforms as dictatorial. Incidentally, the Ides usually fell on the thirteenth of the month—only in March, May, July, and October was it the fifteenth. To make that date even less auspicious, United States income tax payments used to be due on the Ides of March. The postponement of tax day to April 15 removed a source of great inspiration for financial writers. *Et tu,* Uncle Sam!

March also brings the vernal equinox for the northern hemisphere, about the twenty-second of the month. The spring and fall equinoxes are the only two dates during the year when day and night are each exactly twelve hours long. The words *spring* and *fall* derive from what leaves do during those seasons: spring from their buds and fall to the ground.

## March 1

Which set of numbers would most logically come next in the following sequence?

10 1 9 2 8 3 7 4 6 5 5 6 4 7 3 8 2
(a) 9 1   (b) 9 3   (c) 8 5   (d) 6 7

## March 2

The spy was captured easily, and his message proved to be so simple that the lieutenant saw its importance immediately. Here it is. What does it say?

Alice: Tom told Ann Carter Killy and Ted, David Atwood was not moving out now. David awaiting you.

## March 3

Rearrange these matchsticks, by touching only *two,* to make a correct equation. (There may be several solutions.)

## March 4

The happy couple had decided what to name their expected baby, even though they didn't know whether it would be a boy or a girl. Both their family names contained the letters ODLYL, and names for both sexes could be made from those letters. What were the two names?

## March 5

A palindrome is a word or a group of words that reads the same backward and forward. (TENET, for example.) What is the nine-letter palindrome with which the very shy person admitted shyness?

— — — — —  — —  — — .

## March 6

Although Jim and Barbara had to buy four presents for various weddings, they found they could not agree on four identical presents. They bought four separate gifts; and the first one cost $5.00 more than the second. The second was half the cost of the first, plus one-third the cost of the first. The third cost two-thirds of the first, and the last cost double the third. They spent a total of $115. What did each of the four cost?

## March 7

The names of three foods are mixed up on each of the following lines. The words are given with their letters in correct order, but each word is "interlettered" with the others. Unscramble the foods.

C F H R M E U E E I A S E T T
A P E P P A R L E P L S S U M S

## March 8

Using all the letters each time, how many words can you make from the letters REIAMN?

## March 9

How many squares of any size are in the diagram below?

## March 10

On this date in 1876, Alexander Graham Bell, having spilled acid on himself as motivation, succeeded in sending the first telephone message: "Mr. Watson, come here, I want you." It's a good thing Watson had the only other telephone and Bell didn't have to call Directory Assistance for the number. If three operators can answer 120 calls in half an hour, how many operators does it take to handle 560 calls in one hour?

## March 11

Grandma looked up from her rocking chair and said, "As far as I can determine, there is only one anagram of the word TRINKET. What is it?"

## March 12

The Puzzleland toy store may go out of business soon because of the owner's idea of pricing. He charges $6 for a doll, $7.50 for a train, $4.50 for a top, and $12 for a paint set. By the same rules, what does he charge for a bicycle?

## March 13

People who are afraid of the number 13 are said to have triskaidekaphobia. What are the names for each of the following phobias?

Fear of cats
Fear of foreigners
Fear of open spaces (or of leaving an enclosed space)

## March 14

Homonyms are words that sound alike, though they are spelled differently. (Example: to, two, too) One pair of homonyms has meanings that are precisely opposite, and need not be stretched. What are the two spellings of this homonym?

## March 15

Which is more, seconds in 100 hours or inches in 100 yards?

## March 16

Each of the following words contains the letters MAR. Using the definitions, fill in the blanks:

More insane; colloquially, more angry—also a paint color:                         M A __ __ __ R
A shopping area; colloquially, anywhere goods are sold:             MAR __ __ __ __ __ __ __ __
Scanty:                                   M __ A __ __ R

## March 17

For Saint Patrick's Day, the letters ERIN have been placed in the box below. Fill in each line so that those four letters are in each row, across, down, and on the long diagonals. No two letters may be the same in any line, nor may two identical letters be next to each other.

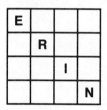

## March 18

What relationship to you is your father's only brother's wife's only brother-in-law?

## March 19

Each of the following groups of letters can be anagrammed into at least two words. Unscramble the letters.

EFIRSSU    EEMPRSU    EENPRST

## March 20

High finance in the kindergarten: Sheree and Tyler's playstore was doing well. Sheree, the more successful shopkeeper, had 75¢ in play money plus 75 percent of what Tyler had. The poor unsuccessful salesman had 50¢ in play money plus half of what Sheree had. How much did each have?

## March 21

If three salesmen can sell three stoves in seven minutes, how many stoves can six salesmen sell in seventy minutes?

## March 22

> This is an Izaak Walton tale.
> As the fish hung by its tail,
> The angler proudly had it weighed.
> "Three-fourths of its total," he then said,
> "Plus three-fourths of three-fourths of a pound
> Will give the whole, exact, not round."

## March 23

How many words can you make from the letters *CEEIPR*, using all the letters each time?

## March 24

You can substitute one letter for the first letter of each word in the following pairs and make two new words (Example: RACE __P__ CLAY = PACE—PLAY). Then insert the new letter on the line between the words, and you will spell a new word reading down.

| | | |
|---:|:---:|:---|
| TALL | _____ | LABEL |
| SOUND | _____ | COUGH |
| SLIT | _____ | HIM |
| ALL | _____ | ARE |
| ROSE | _____ | TETHER |

## March 25

You would really like to stay longer at the party, because you are having such a good time. Unfortunately, it's getting very late. You realize that if it were one hour later, it would be twice as long past midnight as it would be if it were only right now. When you start thinking like that, you've been up too long. What time is it now?

## March 26

Each of the following words includes the letters MAR. Using the definitions, fill in the words.

An unusual type of boat:

$$\_\ \_\ \_\ \_\ \text{M A R} \_\ \_$$

An Italian seafood:  $\_\ \_\ \_\ \_\ \text{M A R} \_$

A title of nobility:

$$\text{M A R} \_\ \_\ \_\ \_\ \_\ \_\ \_\ \_$$

## March 27

Only one word can be anagrammed from SPRINGIEST. What is it?

## March 28

March usually brings warmer weather. Can you go from COLD to WARM on paper in only four steps? Change one letter each time, forming a new word each time.

| C | O | L | D |
|---|---|---|---|
| — | — | — | — |
| — | — | — | — |
| — | — | — | — |
| W | A | R | M |

## March 29

The following diagram has eight sections. Each of them contains four letters, with a question mark in the middle showing that one letter is missing. Your job is to find the one letter that is missing and then rearrange the letters in each section to form eight words. You may find the same letters in two sets of boxes. This merely means that two words can be made from the same letters. Find them both, in that case.

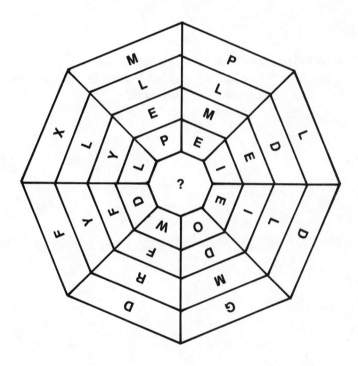

## March 30

Your brother is color blind and, since he has four different colors of socks in his drawer, he usually just pulls out the first two and wears a mismatched pair. He has blue, brown, black, and blue-and-white-striped socks in the drawer in the ratio of 8 blue to 6 brown, to 6 black, to 8 blue-and-white. How many socks would he have to pull out before he could be certain of having a matched pair?

## March 31

Tony likes indigo but not blue. He likes onions but not turnips; he likes forms but not shapes. According to the same rule does he like tomatoes or avocados?

# April

There is some evidence that the Romans named their month *Aphrilis* after Aphrodite, the Greek goddess of love. Aphrodite metamorphosed into the Roman goddess Venus, just as Zeus became Jupiter, Ares became Mars, and other foreign deities adapted to the new culture. The Romans considered the month of April sacred to Venus. In the *Odyssey,* Homer tells how Ares and Aphrodite fell in love with each other, so perhaps it is fitting that they are so close together in the calendar.

April 1 has been the day for "fooling" since sometime in the seventeenth century. The French say *poisson d'Avril,* "April fish," for the poor soul who is the victim of such a joke. One favorite stunt used to be to phone somebody who was out of the office, leave a message to call Mr. Fox, and give the number of the zoo. The Bronx Zoo, and many others, have stopped taking calls for Mr. Fox on April 1.

## April 1

Here's one to try on April Fools. What would you call your ex-spouse's former daughter-in-law's first husband's daughter?

## April 2

The same five letters, rearranged to make two different words, can fill in the blanks below. Complete the sentences.

"I had to fire that nincompoop," said the boss. "Our company _ _ _ _ _ somebody a lot less _ _ _ _ _ ."

## April 3

The names of three mammals are hidden in the following sentences. Find them. All the letters are in the correct order.

The large crowd at the flea market came looking for bargains.
I took off the peel and ate the banana.
He has no judgment, no sense altogether.

## April 4

If TEN = 20 − 5 − 14; and MEN = 13 − 5 − 14; what do WOMEN equal by the same logic?

## April 5

You are working out some estimates for your boss. You can come up with a very good package for your nice little widgets, but the packaging may be too expensive. The cost of the widget and the packaging is $1.10, and the widget is $1.00 more than the package. How much will you have to tell your boss that the package for each widget will cost?

## April 6

You've been standing at a bus stop in the April rain. The transportation system in your town is not very effective. You waited fifteen minutes and then a group of buses came along together. The first was too crowded, so you took the last. There was one bus ahead of another bus, one bus behind another bus, one bus behind two buses, and one bus with two ahead of it. What is the smallest number of buses there could have been in that bunch?

## April 7

You are decorating for spring, and you've found a bargain: a huge box of beautiful decorated tiles, enough to provide a border in two rooms. You really can't figure out how to arrange them, however. If you set a border of two tiles all around, there's one left over; if you set three tiles all around, or four, or five, or six, there's still one tile left over. Finally, you try a block of seven tiles for each corner, and you come out even. What is the smallest number of tiles you could have to get this result?

## April 8

One four-letter word will fit on all three lines below to make new words with the word preceding and the word following. (Example: IN __(DOOR)__ STOP) The same 4-letter word must be used for all 3 lines. What's the word?

| BACK | _____ | SOME |
| FREE | _____ | MADE |
| SECOND | _____ | BAG |

## April 9

If today is Monday, what is the day after the day before the day before tomorrow?

## April 10

Mensaman flew to Puzzleland at the fantastic speed of 1000 miles per hour. There he picked up his ever faithful friend and flew back, burdened by the extra weight, at only 500 miles per hour. What was his average speed?

## April 11

In this type of verse, "first" and "second" and so on refer to the individual letters of a word. Find the correct letter for each definition or explanation, and complete the word.

> My first is in sugar but not in tea
> My second in swim but not in sea
> My third in apple and also pear
> My fourth in ring and also hare
> My last in ten but not in herd
> My whole a very complimentary word.

## April 12

The following multiplication example uses every digit from 0 to 9 once (not counting the intermediate steps). Fill in the missing numbers.

$$
\begin{array}{r}
7\ x\ x \\
4\ x \\
\hline
x\ x\ x\ x\ x
\end{array}
$$

## April 13

The same five letters can be anagrammed into four different words to fill in the blanks in the sentence to make (somewhat) good sense. What are missing words?

The farmer with hundreds of _ _ _ _ _ , deeply _ _ _ _ _ about the amount of rainfall, and _ _ _ _ _ around with artificial watering systems when the ground is dry enough to _ _ _ _ _ him about the possibility of crop failure.

## April 14

Which set of numbers would most logically fill in the blanks in the following series?

101 99 102 98 103 97 _ _ 105 95 104 94
(a) 101 98      (b) 104 96      (c) 106 99
            (d) none of these

## April 15

An aphorism is indicated below. All the vowels have been removed and the remaining letters broken into groups of four letters each. Replace the vowels to read the saying.

NFFC    NTBS    NSSW    MNWH    FNDM
CHNT    HTWL    DDHL    FHRW    RKBG
HTTW.

## April 16

It was time to send the kids to camp, and Sally and Jim were shopping for supplies. They spent half the money they had plus $4.00 on socks for the kids; half of what was then left plus $3.00 on name tapes; and half of what was then left plus $2.00 on a small wallet for each child. They found themselves with $3.00 left over, so they treated themselves to a glass of iced tea each. How much did they start with? (Hint—work backward.)

## April 17

What is the five-digit number, no zeroes, in which the second digit is three times the first, the third is one more than the second, the fourth is four times the first, and the last is one-half more than the second?

## April 18

When the two met, one was half the other's age plus seven years. Ten years later, when they married, the bride was thirty, but this time one was nine-tenths the age of the other. How old was the groom? (No fractions, no partial years—whole numbers only)

## April 19

The engineering department was arranging for a rather expensive catered lunch to bid farewell to their retiring colleague. They calculated that it would cost each person $30. One good mathematician remarked, "It's lucky that there aren't five fewer of us to split the bill, or it would be $10 more from each." How many engineers split the bill, and how much did it cost?

## April 20

There are many English words to which you can add one *s* to make plural nouns. There are very few that become singular again if you add another *s*. Can you name two?

## April 21

Complete the last square of letters, using the same system as followed in the previous four squares.

| T H | U Z | I S | E O | U A |
|-----|-----|-----|-----|-----|
| P | E | D | Q | ? |
| S I | L Z | A M | S F | E R |

## April 22

If Boston is east of New York, cross out all the A's. If not, cross out the R's. If Paris is south of New York, cross out all the O's. If not, cross out the I's. If Sri Lanka is in Asia, cross out the B's and U's. If not, cross out the C's. The remaining letters will tell you whether you've found the right answer.

C A A O I I A B U R R I A U E I B B C I A U T

## April 23

The Order of the Garter, a prestigious award for English knights, was founded this day in 1349. (It's the day of Saint George, patron saint of England and fabled dragon slayer.) See if you deserve an award by unscrambling the following thirteen letters into a common English word.

A T C S D R I E I N O N O

## April 24

Mother was very proud of her lace tablecloth, which was an heirloom. She was most upset when the children came home from school and put their dirty school books on it. She said (start at the correct letter, and move in any direction to a touching letter):

```
T  I  P  S  S
L  O  O  O  K
T  H  O  O  B
E  L  T  M  Y
C  O  H  A  N
```

## April 25

You can replace the letters below with numbers, so that the addition will be correct numerically. (Hint: K = 9)

```
    M O M
    M O M
  _____N O
  B O O K
```

## April 26

The logic professor posted a notice on his class door: "Class is canceled today on account of spring. We will meet again at 1:00 P.M. three days after two days before the day before tomorrow." What day does the class meet?

## April 27

Dot likes pots and pans but not cooks. She likes straw but not hay; she likes sagas but not poems. Does she like a star or a planet?

## April 28

The lovely but not-terribly-bright contessa was swindled of her jewels. She knew that her beautiful diamond pin had nine diamonds down each side, and nine across the top and bottom, clustered as shown below, but she had never really examined the arrangement closely. A clever thief had figured out a way to steal four of the magnificent diamonds so that the contessa never missed them. He had reset the diamonds so that there were still nine diamonds on each side of the pin, but only twenty diamonds in all. How did he reset the jewels to get away with four of them?

## April 29

Each of the following words contains the letters APR somewhere. Using the definitions, fill in the words.

A fruit:                A P R __ __ __ __
Took by force:          __ A P __ __ R __ __
Sign of the zodiac:     __ A P R __ __ __ __ __

## April 30

It's hard to keep within a budget, Maura discovered as she prepared her class's May Day party. She had been assigned money from the common fund, and she spent half of it plus $2.00 for a nice cake. Then she spent half of what she had left plus $2.00 for baskets and flowers. Then she spent half of what she had left plus $1.00 for candy. At that point she was out of money. How much had she started with?

# May

There are two different theories about how May got its name. Some experts say it was named for the goddess Maia, the mother of Hermes. Others say that Caesar named the month to honor the *Major,* the senior branch of the Roman Senate, and that he named June not for Juno, but for the *Junior* branch of the Senate. You can take your pick—there isn't anyone around today who remembers just why those names were chosen.

May Day, before it acquired its present connotation as a worker's holiday, had far more rural roots. For centuries it was a British, and then American, custom to gather flowers on the first of May and hang baskets of freshly picked blooms on the doorknobs of friends' houses. Louisa May Alcott mentions this custom several times in her books. Dancing around the Maypole is another time-honored ritual. For anyone who didn't go through teacher-training classes forty or more years ago, this is the procedure. A tall pole is set up with long ribbons of different colors attached to the top. Each ribbon is taken by a separate dancer, who weaves in and out among the other dancers around the pole. Eventually the pole is wrapped in many colors, and the dancers are left standing right at the pole with a few inches of ribbon in their hands. It isn't as easy as it sounds!

## May 1

To start the month right, figure out the word concealed in the following poem. (First, second, etc., refer to letters of a word.) By selecting the right letter you will come up with an appropriate word.

> My first is in silly but not in fool
> My second in pupil but not in school
> My third in read and also write
> My fourth in glimpse and also light
> My fifth in ten but not in three
> My last in glad and also glee
> My whole a season of the year
> That's clue enough to solve it here.

## May 2

Why are 1980 pennies worth more than 1979 pennies?

## May 3

The following three lines contain the names of U.S. cities, one city per line. Find the hidden cities.

We were no longer interested in returning there because of the bad weather.

"I am sorry to tell you that you have injured your lumbar region," said the doctor.

I would be happy to join you, but temporary problems keep me away.

## May 4

If SIX is TEN, ONE is HIS, and FIVE is LEGS, what is SEVEN?

## May 5

What is the word coiled inside this circle?

```
        T  P
    I         U
    A         N
        L  S
```

## May 6

The same five letters can be rearranged into two separate words to fill in the blanks.

The caveman shook a primitive sort of _ _ _ _ _ . It was too heavy to use against some of the faster animals, but it seemed to work against _ _ _ _ _ .

## May 7

You have one of those fancy double boilers whose lid fits either pot. They aren't very heavy pots, either. The bigger pot weighs 12 ounces by itself; with the lid on, it weighs twice as much as the little pot without the cover. The little pot, with the lid on, weighs one-third more than the big pot all by itself. What does the pot lid weigh by itself?

## May 8

Each of the following words contains the letters MAY. Using the definitions, fill in the missing letters and complete the word.

A creamy dressing made with eggs and oil:

M A Y _ _ _ _ _ _ _

Astonishingly:       _ M A _ _ _ _ _ Y

## May 9

Back at the Puzzleland toy store, the proprietor has priced a game at 14¢, a doll at 21¢, a koala bear at 28¢, and a top at 14¢. Using the same logic (or lack of it), how much does he charge for a pinwheel?

## May 10

Andy likes orange but not purple. He likes torches but not chandeliers. He eats berries but not fruits. Following the same rules, does he like Byron or Keats?

## May 11

Ages seem to be perennially fascinating to puzzle writers, so why fight it? Of three sisters named April, May, and June, none is yet twenty-one. April is now as old as June was fourteen years ago, and two-thirds of May's age. May, on the other hand, will be June's age when May is twice as old as she is now plus two years. Three years ago, May was as old as April is now. How old are April, May, and June?

## May 12

The first word of the following word square (the words read the same down and across) has been filled in for you. Fill in the remaining words so that you use three E's; two each S, L, O, G, R, and A; and one T in total for the whole square.

```
O G R E
G
R
E
```

## May 13

Take the number of states before Alaska and Hawaii were added. Double that and add the number of "winds." Then subtract the number of Ali Baba's thieves, not counting Ali Baba. Divide by the number of days in May minus 1. Cube the result. What do you get?

## May 14

You have fifty coins totaling $1.00. You drop one down an open drain while tossing the coins in your hand. What is the chance that you have lost a quarter?

## May 15

A "Tom Swifty" is a pun based on Tom's extraordinary expressiveness: "Hand me the eggbeater," said Tom stirringly. A "Tom Swifty" punning sentence is encoded below. All the vowels, including Y, have been removed, and the letters broken into groups of three. Reconstitute the sentence.

THR    SNW    TRS    DTM    DRL.

## May 16

Four of the words below have one significant feature in common which distinguishes them from the fifth word. Which is the odd man out?

REACT    TRACE    CARTE
CATER    SCARE

## May 17

A definition was dropped into the boxes below. Each of the letters shown is in its proper column, but they have been arranged alphabetically. The black boxes show the spaces between words; a dash at the end of a line shows where a word has been broken. Fill in the definition.

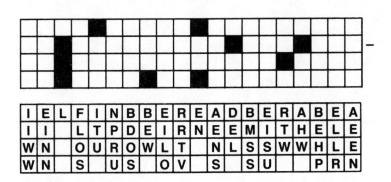

## May 18

The alleged perpetrator was trying to get even with his foe. This all happened in Puzzleland, so it was easy for him to obtain a sack of magic gunpowder to carry off to his enemy's fort. He did not realize, however, that the powder was self-igniting, and it had been leaking since he stole it. He had been running at his usual magic speed of 14 miles per hour over the 28-mile distance, but had to hide for a while when he reached his enemy's fort. Meanwhile, that magic gunpowder was burning itself up along his trail at the rate of 12 miles per hour. How long could he hide without making a spectacle of himself?

## May 19

Somehow or other I got talked into buying something on the installment plan. I'm not sure I got a good deal. The payments to date, according to my checkbook, have reached $96. The second year cost $2.00 more than the first year; the third year cost $3.00 more than the second; and the fourth year cost me $4.00 more than the third. What were my payments the first year?

## May 20

The following coiled sentence, when you find the proper starting letter and move in any direction to a touching letter, will finish the quatrain below. There is one null letter. Each letter is used once only. (Hint: A common problem in labs)

> The head of the research lab said one day,
> Looking solemn and sad and grave,

```
T E A T R O E E X
O H D A P V M V A
N L Y T O E R S T
E R A T H G I O N
T H O S E I D I D
```

## May 21

One letter, a different one for each line, has been removed from each of the words below. The missing letters appear at least three times (and sometimes more) in each word. Fill in the missing letter for each word and reconstruct the words. The letters are also scrambled, just to make it a little harder.

FILPRT     PSVRR

**May 22**

The following cryptogram has been done in a simple substitution cipher: each number represents a letter, and the same number always represents the same letter. What does it say?

```
14 26 23 26 14 22    24 6 9 18 22
24 26 15 15 22 23.    8 26 18 23    8 19 22
4 26 8    20 22 7 7 18 13 20
20 15 12 4 18 13 20    9 22 11 12 9 7 8
12 13    19 22 9    4 12 9 16.
```

**May 23**

In this addition alphametic, you can replace each letter with a number (the same number for each letter), to find a correct arithmetical solution. (Hint: A = 1)

```
        H A N G
        H A N G
        H A N G
      ─────────
      G A N G S
```

**May 24**

In the puzzle below, change the first letter of each word on either side of the blank to make a new word. Use the same letter for both words on one line. Then fill in the new letter on the line between the two words. When you have finished, you will have a new word, reading down.

| | | |
|---|---|---|
| MART | _____ | HARD |
| ROUND | _____ | WERE |
| FASTER | _____ | WITHER |
| PLASTIC | _____ | FAST |
| BOLES | _____ | AIMLESS |

## May 25

Six seamstresses could sew six seams in twenty minutes. How many seamstresses would be needed to sew thirty-six seams in two hours?

## May 26

The following circle contains all the letters except one of six words, one in each pie-shaped section. The letters have been scrambled. When you unscramble them, you will find that the missing letter, which will complete each word properly, is quite clear. Find the missing letter and the words.

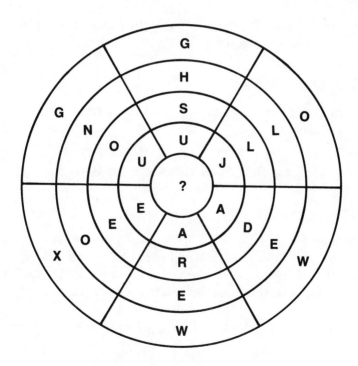

## May 27

You've bought your weekly egg supply at the local farm store. The first morning you have company for breakfast and use half the eggs plus one-half an egg. The next morning you use one-half of what's left plus one-half an egg. The third morning you use one-half of what's left plus one-half an egg, and on the fourth morning, you're down to one solitary egg, so you make French toast. In all this cooking, you've never had one-half an egg to carry over to the next day. How many eggs did you buy originally?

## May 28

You are female. What relationship to you is your father's only son-in-law's mother-in-law's only daughter?

## May 29

Which set of letters would logically come next in the following sequence?

A Y D V G S J P M M P J ? ?
(a) R K (b) S G (c) R S (d) S I

## May 30

My quiz for this day, May 30, is most unusual. As is this paragraph. What is so unusual about it? If you look hard, you should find what it is without too much difficulty. Try hard to spot it. How long did you think about it?

## May 31

As you may recall, a palindrome is a word or group of words that reads the same backward as forward (Madam I'm Adam). Definitions for two palindromes are given below, as well as the number of letters. Complete the palindromes.

Unselfish mother, says caring child.

‒ ‒   ‒ ‒   ‒ ‒

‒ ‒ ‒ ‒ ‒ ‒ ‒ ‒   ‒ ‒   ‒

‒ ‒ .

A scarlet alcoholic beverage is homicide, politely.

‒ ‒ ‒   ‒ ‒ ‒   ‒ ‒ ‒   ‒ ‒

‒ ‒ ‒ ‒ ‒ ‒

# June

June is now a popular month for weddings, but it was not always so. September used to be the favored month and, in farm communities, marrying after the harvest was still more popular. But way back, the Romans considered June the luckiest month for marriages, and May the unluckiest.

One interesting June custom dates from the Middle Ages, when, in the English village of Dunmow, a flitch of bacon was awarded to any husband and wife who could swear that they would marry each other again, had not quarreled for a year, and had never regretted their marriage. There are only a few records of couples bringing home the bacon. Married life was probably similar to its current state, and village life provided little privacy, hence not much opportunity for false swearing.

Around the twenty-first of June comes the summer solstice—the date on which the sun reaches the most northerly point in the zodiac. It is also the longest day of the year, and the beginning of summer—at least for the northern hemisphere. The earth is farther from the sun in June than it is in December, but the sun's rays strike the northern hemisphere more directly, and thus provide more heat.

# June 1

There seems to be only one other word that can be made from the letters in the word IMPORTUNATE. Find it.

# June 2

All its vowels have been removed from the following rather cynical statement, and the remaining letters have been broken into groups of three letters each. Reconstruct the sentence.

PDS    TRN    SCM    NTW    SRT    STH
QCK    NDT    HDD

# June 3

The following cryptogram is simple substitution of an unusual sort. Each letter or symbol represents one letter, the same one each time. Decipher the sentence.

JS$\frac{11}{44}$OMRDD    OD    S    DYPVL    YJSY
D$\frac{1}{4}$;OYD    YJTRR    GPT    PMR    YJR
FSU    SGYRT    UPI    NIU    OY.

# June 4

By using all the digits 1 through 9, it is possible to construct four addition examples with the sum 873. Reversing the top and bottom numbers is not permitted. Each combination must be different. One number in each set has been filled in to give you a head start.

```
  x x 4      x x 9      x 5 x      x x x
  x x x      x x x      x x x      6 x x
  -----      -----      -----      -----
  8 7 3      8 7 3      8 7 3      8 7 3
```

## June 5

One of the most famous puzzles in the math world is "How Old Is Ann?" Here's another variation. Ann is now exactly two-fifths of her older sister's age, and two years from now she will be one-half of her older sister's age. Conversely, two years ago, Ann was only one-fourth the age of her older sister's age at that time. How old is Ann now? (She's a fairly young child, by the way.)

## June 6

You have stealthily raided your small child's piggy bank. You feel slightly guilty as you count the money. You have the same number of dimes and quarters, totaling exactly $2.45. When you turn honest and put it back, how many of each coin will you need to replace? (Your child keeps a record of how much she puts in and in what denomination, of course.)

## June 7

When Maria went to get a passport, she had to give her real date of birth, but under all other circumstances she refused. When somebody asked how old she was, she said she was twenty-one, mentally omitting all Sundays. Sundays she didn't work, so naturally she didn't get any older. How old was Maria really?

## June 8

What would logically come next in this sequence?

S30    031    N30

## June 9

The following sentence has two blanks. The same six letters, rearranged, can be used to make two different words which will fill the blanks appropriately. Find the words.

> The little woodland _ _ _ _ _ _ was having a wonderful time playing with all the animals in the woods; unfortunately, she had no previous knowledge of the pretty furry little animal with the peculiar _ _ _ _ _ _ , but soon was sadder and wiser.

## June 10

Barbara is a young lady with decided tastes. She likes khaki but not brown; she likes rendezvous but not meetings; she likes mousses but not jellies. Does she like jodhpurs or riding pants?

## June 11

This slightly jumbled version of a nursery rhyme has had all its vowels removed and the words have been broken up (or down) into groups of three letters each. Replace the vowels to decipher the sentence.

> JCK     BNM     BLJ     CKB     QCK     FRT
> HLG     HTJ     STC     HNG     DND     THR
> DSS     LCK.

## June 12

Which would you rather have, half a dozen dozen dimes or a dozen and a half dimes?

## June 13

Two of the four boxes *cannot* be made from the unfolded cube shown below. Which ones are they?

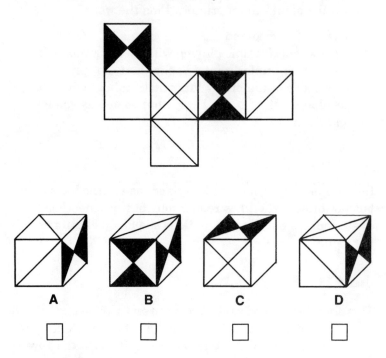

| A | B | C | D |
|---|---|---|---|
| ☐ | ☐ | ☐ | ☐ |

## June 14

If you reverse the digits of my age, you have the age of my son. A year ago, I was twice his age. How old are we both now?

## June 15

You're so desperate to find a job that you're even looking in Liar and Truthteller Town. That's a special part of Puzzleland where half the people always tell the truth, half the people always lie, and outsiders have no way to tell them apart by sight.

You're waiting in the reception room for your interview, feeling nervous. An attractive young lady next to you whispers she is sure that the previous applicant won't get the job because she heard him admit that he was a Liar, and obviously unemployable. Then the interviewer calls you in.

"I'm wearing a blue suit," he says, and indeed he is, so you know that he's a Truthteller. "I need to test your logical reasoning for the position we now have open. What can you tell me about the young lady who talked to you outside?"

The job depends on your answer. What have you decided about the woman in the reception room?

## June 16

It's not easy having a mathematics professor as a new friend. When she invites you to her house she says, "All the houses on my side of the street are numbered consecutively in even numbers. There are six houses on my side of my block and the sum of their numbers is 9870. You don't know which block I live on, and it's a long, long street, but I will tell you that I live in the lowest number on my side of the block. What's the number? Or are you just going to ring the first even-numbered doorbell for twenty blocks?

## June 17

The following brief message has been broken into letters.
Each letter has been placed below its proper position in the
diagram, but the letters have been put in alphabetical order.
The black spaces show word divisions. Fill in the saying.

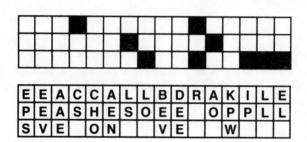

## June 18

In Puzzleland's silly grocery store down the block, the proprietor has decided to price his produce a certain way. A daf-
fodil (he sells flowers too) is worth 10¢; a carrot is worth 8¢;
a peach is worth 5¢; a zucchini is worth 10¢. What is a plum
worth?

## June 19

You have ten coins totaling 49¢. By an odd coincidence, so
does your friend Henry with whom you are walking. One of
you accidentally loses a coin through a hole in a pocket.
What is the chance it is a dime?

## June 20

While Isabelle was out walking one day with her husband, Ferdinand, she met Cristoforo, who was her only sister's mother-in-law's only son's grandfather-in-law. What was his relationship to Ferdinand and Isabelle?

## June 21

Each of the following jumbled words has had at least three of the same letter removed from it, a different letter from each word. Find the missing letters to reconstruct the words.

YTHLNM    AEEHNRU    DEINNOI

## June 22

You've finally decided to clean under the chair and sofa cushions. To your great pleasure you find you have $1.80 in all, the same number of nickels and quarters. How many of each have you found?

## June 23

All the following words contain the letters JUN somewhere. (Those letters may in fact appear more than once.) Using the definitions, fill in the words.

A lower professorial rank; also an addition to:
$$\_\ \_\ J\ U\ N\ \_\ \_$$
A person not legally an adult:
$$J\ U\ \_\ \_\ N\ \_\ \_\ \_$$
A kind of berry or shrub:    $$J\ U\ N\ \_\ \_\ \_\ \_$$
A diary, a record of daily events:
$$J\ \_\ U\ \_\ N\ \_\ \_$$

## June 24

After escaping from the earthquake, flood, and tornado which had afflicted his city, all the poor shopkeeper could dig out of the rubble of his store was four pairs of weights and a balance scale. Fortunately, he was good at math, and found that he could weigh anything from one pound to 170 pounds with the four pairs (please note: pairs, not individual weights). What were the four pairs of weights?

## June 25

How many common English words can you make from the letters EHISTTW? All letters must be used each time.

## June 26

The names of three countries appear in the paragraph below. All the letters of each country are in the proper order. Can you discover the names?

> Interpol and the FBI were working on the same case. "How can a daily routine be so varied?" asked the chief. "Oh, just watch the lady decked in diamonds," Agent Hobart replied. "She changes her route every day."

## June 27

Darlene likes 225 but not 224; she likes 900 but not 800; she likes 144 but not 145. Does she like 1600 or 1700?

## June 28

You just dumped a bag of fruit into the deepest end of the fruit bin, and now you can't see what you have. They're all smooth skinned, and about the same size, so you can't tell by touch either. You know you have five large plums, five nectarines, and five small smooth-skinned peaches. How many pieces of fruit must you take out to be absolutely sure of getting a plum?

## June 29

So far as we can determine, only one other word can be made from the letters of INSATIABLE. Find it.

## June 30

Each of the following three sets of letters has been made up of items relating to June weddings. Unscramble the three items in each set. All the letters are in their proper order.

B B O R U V I Q D U E E E S T M A I I D L

G R H I O R N N E O G Y O M O M O N

M F L O W E T D H O E W R E D I I N N R G
L G M A A I W R R C L H

# July

J uly had a bad reputation in classical times. Because of the heat, and the illnesses the heat caused, the Romans felt it was under the influence of the unfriendly star Canicula, the "Little Dog." They called the days from July 3 to August 11, which then corresponded to the rising and setting of this star, the "Dog Days."

Three western countries celebrate their national holidays in July: Canada on the first, the United States on the fourth, and France on the fourteenth. Perhaps the July heat makes people dissatisfied enough with their governments to revolt. More likely it just makes them want a holiday. Canada became independent peacefully in 1867. The American Revolution had been going on for over a year when the Declaration of Independence was signed on July 4, 1776. And the storming of the Bastille in Paris on July 14, 1789, was just the start of a series of revolutions in France. Since then, France has had five republics, four kings, and two emperors.

## July 1

Tom is younger than Rose, but older than Will and Jack, in that order. Rose is younger than Susie, but older than Jack.

Jack is younger than Jim. Susie is older than Rose, but younger than Jim. Jim is older than Tom. Who is the oldest?

## July 2

Jemima has the same number of brothers as she has sisters, but her brother Roland has twice as many sisters as he has brothers. How many boys and girls are there in the family?

## July 3

The following multiplication example uses all the digits from 0 to 9 once and once only (not counting the intermediate steps). Finish the problem. One number has been filled in to get you started.

$$
\begin{array}{r}
\text{x x x} \\
\underline{\text{x } 5} \\
\text{x x x x x}
\end{array}
$$

## July 4

If King George IV was ruler of England during the American Revolution, cross out all the N's, I's, and D's. If not, cross out all the O's, U's, and B's. If Paul Revere was not a real person, cross out all the E's and P's. If he was real, cross out the W's, R's, and S's. If General Lafayette fought on the side of the Colonies, cross out the X's, F's, and T's. If not, cross out all the C's. Well?

I B O N U U D W E R P S E S N S D X E X N F C T E T

## July 5

You leave your job interview in Liar and Truthteller Town with two other candidates, who seem to know each other. The interviewer has told you that one of them is a Liar and one is a Truthteller, but you were so nervous you didn't ask him which was which.

Out on the sidewalk the three of you find the local Witch selling apples from a booth. Wicked witches are notorious for making apples that will put you to sleep for one hundred years, and you have a train to catch. But those apples look delicious. So you turn to the other candidates and randomly ask one for advice. Her answer tells you all you need to know about the local Witch's apples. What was your question?

## July 6

The coiled sentence below contains the lines that will complete the following rhyme. By starting at the correct spot and moving letter by letter in any direction—up, down, sideways, and diagonally—you can work it out. (The square contains two null letters that don't appear in the lines.)

> As Hans was walking up the Alps,
> A vision turned his head.
> With Mother on his handlebars
> Along the road Fritz sped.
> They hit a curve!

```
H  E  O  K  E  J  U
S  P  O  L  E  T  S
A  H  K  O  C  N  O
N  S  N  O  M  A  H
B  B  D  I  A  S  E
```

## July 7

There is a very odd zoo on the planet XzyQE. It houses animals with two heads and three legs and animals with two heads and two legs. A count reveals that there are 102 heads and 134 legs in all. How many of each kind of animal are there?

## July 8

The brilliant but not entirely sensible inventor had discovered three separate ways to save fuel while driving. Each one saved approximately 30 percent on fuel consumption. "Aha," said the brilliant inventor, "I will use only 10 percent of the fuel I now use and save a great deal of money." Unfortunately, it didn't work out that way. How much fuel did he save, assuming that all the savings were independent and cumulative?

## July 9

Jack and Jill were racing, but it was no contest. Jack beat Jill by 10 yards on a 100-yard course. Jill suggested that for the second race, Jack should start 10 yards behind the starting line—she figured that would give her a fair chance, since he had won by 10 yards. Who won, and by how much?

## July 10

The young fellow was extremely eager to join his girlfriend for dinner. It was a 24-mile run upstream to visit her. His boat's speed would be 14 miles per hour but the current is running 4 miles an hour against him. He just filled his tank and he knows he has 20 gallons, but he uses up 6 gallons per hour. Will he make it or will he run out of gas?

## July 11

Each of the following four words is the name of a bird, but most of the letters have been removed. Fill in the blanks to get the names of the birds.

L _ _ W I _ _
P _ _ _ E _
_ R _ B _
_ A _ _ I _ A _

## July 12

As an antiques dealer located, of course, in Puzzleland, you are used to taking a loss now and then. The genuine Louis XIV TV set you bought has proved very difficult to sell. You priced it originally at $100. Then you marked it down to $80. Then you marked it down to $64. Following your same rules, how much will its price be after the next markdown? (You realize, of course, that Louis XIV TV sets are hard to sell; they aren't state of the art.)

## July 13

Another Tom Swifty. Follow the rules and trace from letter to letter in any direction. One null letter to fill in a space.

```
I  L  I  P  S
K  T  Y  L  I
E  H  X  R  C
E  S  S  A  M
E  C  S  I  O
H  I  P  D  T
```

## July 14

Today is Bastille Day, the French national holiday, so this question is in honor of the French people's love of good food.

Pierre stopped at his favorite wine shop to buy a bottle of Sauternes for the celebration. He spent half of what he had plus $2.00 for a very special bottle of Château d'Yquem. Then he spent half of what he had left plus $3.00 for a small tin of foie gras. Then he stopped at his favorite bakery and bought brioches to spread the foie gras on, and spent half of what he had left, plus $4.00. At that point, he had $2.00 left, with which he bought a small bottle of digestive medicine, just in case. How much did he have to begin with?

## July 15

The same four-letter word can be added to each of the following words to make a new word or a common phrase. What is the word?

BOUND    PROOF    TREE    LESS    BIRD

## July 16

The Great Detective is hot on the trail of the guilty party who has perpetrated some atrocious puns. "Intent to deceive" is the charge, and he is now interrogating three suspects. George says, "I'm innocent—Jane is too." Jane says, "Sally did it, and George is innocent." Sally says, "I'm innocent and Jane did it." The guilty one lied, and the innocent both told the truth. Who is the perpetrator?

## July 17

A particular plan has been followed to determine the middle number in each diagram. Fill in the missing number.

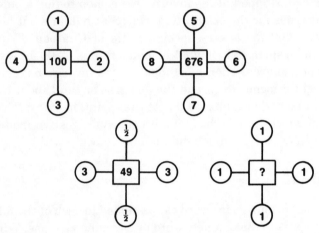

## July 18

Simon Walton was an inveterate fisherman, and his wife an inveterate objector—especially to cleaning fish. This time, he cut off her objections before they started by announcing that he had sold his fish to another fisherman. "And it was a fairly large one, too," he said. "The fish weighed ten pounds plus half its own weight." How many pounds of fish had he sold?

## July 19

Your solar clock isn't working perfectly. Each day, in broad sunlight, it picks up half a minute, and each night, in the darkness, it loses one-third of a minute. In how many days, starting at sunrise on the first day, will it be five minutes fast? (Assuming that daylight and darkness are constant, of course, or the puzzle won't work.)

## July 20

Each of the following words contains the letters JUL. The letters may appear in the word more than once but are only shown once. Using the definitions given, fill in the words.

One of Shakespeare's heroines:   J U L _ _ _
A flower:                          J _ _ _ U _ L
Extremely happy, shouting for joy:
                               J U _ _ L _ _ _

## July 21

Palindromes read the same forward and backward (Otto or Madam, I'm Adam), and can be words or phrases or whole sentences. Here are some definitions.

What you do when the walls of your apartment are
   no longer fresh:   _ _ _ _ _ _ _
First appearance on television:

   _ _ _ _    _ _ _ _ _

## July 22

How many triangles are in this drawing?

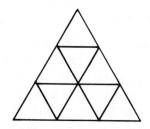

## July 23

There was a fabric sale going on at Caveat Emptor Yard Goods. True to his store's name, the owner had a slightly short yardstick—3 inches short, to be exact, which he wasn't. However, to make up for this, and so he wouldn't lose too many customers, he added 5 percent to whatever yard goods he gave, which was usually enough. This time, however, Sally ordered 5 yards of curtain material, having measured her windows very, very exactly. Was she short or over? (When you figure, remember that he gave the additional 5 percent on his short yard measure, not on a regular yard!)

## July 24

I personally don't care for health fiends. I refuse to do what is good for me. I stroll daily at 2 miles per hour. One of my jogger friends said, "Why don't you jog? You'd cover the same distance—12 miles—and save a lot of time." I found out that he jogs exactly three times as fast as I stroll. How much time would I save if I jogged alongside him?

## July 25

The same seven letters, rearranged into two different words, can be used to fill in the blanks below. Fill in the blanks to complete the sentences.

"What happened to your constant
__ __ __ __ __ __ __ ?" asked the lady with
the parasol, having the driver stop her carriage
to ask this most indiscreet question. "Well," said
the lady in the bustle gown who had just returned
to town for a visit, "Didn't you hear? We
__ __ __ __ __ __ __ ."

## July 26

If you have a good memory and a big vocabulary, you may be able to come up with at least three words containing all five vowels, A, E, I, O, and U. The vowels don't have to appear in order (though they can be), and you don't have to include Y (though you can).

## July 27

The local recycling plant had a contract requiring anyone who obtained recycled bottles for storage from them, to bring them back to be recycled again. The plant could make one new bottle from every seven bottles returned. One week, on Monday, they got 343 bottles to recycle. Assuming that everybody brought back all the empties, how many could they eventually remake from the 343?

## July 28

The following word square is a little more complicated than the previous ones. It has five letters, not four, across and down. Fill it in so that it contains, in addition to the letters shown, one each, R and I; two each, T, O, and L; three E's; and five S's.

```
H A B I T
A
B
I
T
```

## July 29

Your boss has gone out of town. Her secretary is angry at you for some reason, so he tells you, "She wants to see you in her office at 8:30 A.M. two days after the day before the day after tomorrow." What day will you show up half an hour early to see your boss? Today is Tuesday.

## July 30

You can buy four chocolate bars and three peanut butter cups for 50¢, and three chocolate bars and four peanut butter cups for 48¢. What is the most candy (the greatest number of pieces) you can buy for exactly 50¢?

## July 31

The digits from 0 to 9 have been used in the multiplication example below (excluding intermediate steps). Fill in the missing numbers.

$$
\begin{array}{r}
\text{x } 0\ 2 \\
\text{x } 9 \\
\hline
1\ \text{x x x } 8
\end{array}
$$

# August

The month the Romans originally called Sextilis was renamed August in 27 B.C. for Julius Caesar's adopted son, the first Roman emperor. He was originally named Octavian, but a grateful Senate renamed him Augustus, "revered," after he had managed to kill or defeat all his rivals, including many senators. In a monumental display of modesty, Augustus did not accept the gift until the year 8 B.C.

Try to be outside on clear nights around August 10, the approximate date of a meteor shower that occurs every year. This celestial phenomenon, called the Shower of the Perseids, was noted by the Chaldeans as early as 2700 B.C. The meteors seem to follow the path of a comet through space. Only when they enter our atmosphere do they start to burn up and become visible. It's a beautiful sight!

## August 1

Each of these boy's names *except one* can be anagrammed into a common English noun. Which name cannot be made into another word?

CORNELIUS     DANIEL     CAMERON

THOMAS     BOSWELL

## August 2

Patty doesn't feel she is really a child anymore. Ten years ago, her mother was five times her age. Now she is three-sevenths of her mother's age, and in five years she will be half her mother's age. How old will she be when she is half her mother's age?

## August 3

Shopping can present a terrible dilemma, the new couple discovered. Three pounds of potatoes and two pounds of eggplants cost $2.25. Or they could just buy eggplants for the same amount of money and make a casserole out of all those eggplants. But potatoes are cheaper than eggplants. How much did potatoes cost per pound?

## August 4

Can you go from PINK to ROSE in four steps, changing one letter at a time and making a new English word each time?

| P | I | N | K |
|---|---|---|---|
| — | — | — | — |
| — | — | — | — |
| R | O | S | E |

## August 5

Here a common proverb has been dressed up in multisyllabic guise. Dress it down to its normal language.

> A totality of numerous objects that coruscate or are refulgent are not necessarily composed entirely of auriferous substances.

## August 6

Find the two anagrams of the same nine letters that make sense in the following statement.

The delegates at the international conference were extremely _ _ _ _ _ _ _ _ _ .
They had completed the first
_ _ _ _ _ _ _ _ _ agreement in a very important area, and even though it was not finalized, it was a good start.

## August 7

Each of the following sets of letters has three or more related words interlettered. Unscramble the words, in which all the letters appear in their proper order. (Hint: think food.)

B P K I A I N N P E W E A A A I N P F C A P R L U E I T H

P S P M I E A A Z G H T Z E B T A A T L I L S

C P C A U R K E A D E M D P I U N F G F S

## August 8

Mehitabel operated on a peculiar shopping system. She wouldn't allow herself to spend all her money in one place to start, as she had been warned not to do. Therefore, last Saturday she spent half of what she had plus $3.00 at Jones's clothing store, for a blouse; then she spent half of what she had left plus $1.00 at Smith's, and trotted off for stockings to Brown's, where she spent half of what she had left plus $4.00. She was then out of money. How much had she started with?

## August 9

These are the dog days of the year. Each of the following words contains the word DOG somewhere. Fill in the missing words.

Persistent, sticking to a goal: _ _ _ _ _ _

A religious theory or belief: _ _ _ _ _

Slang for an old sailor: _ _ _ _ _ _

## August 10

The following multiplication example uses all the digits from 0 to 9. Three numbers have been filled in to get you started. Complete the example. (You can use the digits more than once in the intervening steps, but not in the answer.)

$$
\begin{array}{r}
\text{x x x} \\
\times\ 3 \\
\hline
5\ \text{x x}\ 0\ \text{x}
\end{array}
$$

## August 11

The following puzzle is based on the Tom Swifty form, as in, "We lost one of the girls," said Tom ruthlessly. Start at any letter and move up, down, diagonally, or sideways to spell out the message (two null letters to fill up space).

```
H S Y P A R
W O O A P E
R U L L N T
M T O E L Y
M O M W B B
```

## August 12

Each of these words can be changed into something edible by scrambling the letters and making a new word. How much of a meal can you produce from these anagrams?

PLAYERS SANDIER ASSUAGE BARELY

## August 13

On August 13, 1929, a Mr. Perrey crossed the English Channel from Dover to Calais in seven hours and twenty-five minutes on a motorbike equipped with special flotation devices. Can you cross from DAWN to DUSK in only five steps, changing one letter at a time and using a good English word each time?

  D  A  W  N
  —  —  —  —
  —  —  —  —
  —  —  —  —
  —  —  —  —
  D  U  S  K

## August 14

Each of the following words contains the letters AUG. Fill in the words.

How we tell the world—and the official—he's on
 the job:    _ _ A U G _ _ _ _ _
A female offspring:  _ A U G _ _ _ _
Unduly proud, rude to the point of arrogance:
        _ A U G _ _ _
Was visibly and probably audibly amused:
        _ A U G _ _ _

## August 15

The following box will remind you of the weather (at least in the northern hemisphere). Fill in the letters HEAT so that those four letters are in each row, across, down, and on the long diagonal, but no two letters may be the same in any line, nor may two identical letters be next to each other. One line is filled in to get you started.

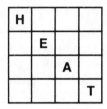

## August 16

Our hero the brave knight, is trying to rescue the beautiful Princess of Puzzleland. The maiden has slipped him a message. She will be able to stand at the stable gate from 12:30 to 12:40—but no more than those ten minutes—on the following day. If he arrives promptly, she will elope with him. If not, she will be married later that same evening to his hated rival. The castle is 12 miles away. The first third is uphill, and his horse can make 4 miles per hour uphill; the second third is level, at 8 miles per hour, and the last part, one-third, is downhill, at 12 miles per hour. He figures that that averages out to 8 miles per hour, so if he leaves at 10:55 to give himself five minutes' leeway, he should arrive exactly within the 10 minutes. Of course, he can't get there too early, or he'll be caught hanging around. Does he make it in time? Why or why not?

## August 17

The following is an easy type of substitution cryptogram (each letter standing for a different letter—the same substitution each time).

UR   UA   NYXG   RII   GIR   RI   SI
RGWAW   RGUBFA   EUFGR   BIQ

## August 18

How many common four-letter English words can you make from the letters EANM using all the letters in each word? Give the words.

## August 19

It may look like playing with blocks, but this is a visual puzzle. How many different ways can you form the word COLD? You can use each letter more than once, but you can't use the same combination of letters in a different order. (Letters need not be adjacent.)

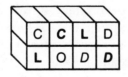

## August 20

What number is two-thirds of one-half of one-fourth of 240?

## August 21

"See," said the richest man in the world to his secretary as he bought up another country, "money talks." The secretary sighed. "He's right," she said. (The rest is cryptic—a simple substitution.)

"13 15 14 5 25    20 1 12 11 19,    2 21 20
20 15    13 5    9 20    19 1 25 19
7 15 15 4 2 25 5."

## August 22

The two youngsters were playing with pennies. Neither of them had many. They did figure out that if you squared the number of Abe's pennies and added Lizzy's pennies, you'd have 62; but if you squared Lizzy's pennies and then added Abe's, you'd have 176 pennies. Since they didn't have either amount, they gave up, but how many pennies did each one actually have?

## August 23

All the vowels have been removed from the following statement, and the remaining letters have been broken into groups of three letters each. Replace the vowels and reconstruct the words to read the sentence.

| THN | LYT | HNG | WRS | THN | HSB |
|-----|-----|-----|-----|-----|-----|
| NDW | HNV | RNT | CSW | HTY | CKR |
| WHT | YWR | SHS | BND | WHL | WYS |
| NTC | SWH | TYC | KND | WHT | YWR. |

## August 24

The name of a country is hidden in each of the following sentences. Find the country.

> If you are adventurous, you want a fast boat, but if you just want to be out on the water, a sloop or tug alike will do.
> He lost the rally because he got lost on the way, not seeing a semihidden marker.
> He opened the window, and, with a loud buzz, air entered the room along with a wasp!

## August 25

One word among the following is the odd man out. Which one, and why?

CORSET    COSTER    SECTOR
ESCORT    COURTS

## August 26

Sallie Lou likes sequoia trees but not evergreens. She doesn't want either disease, but she'd rather have pneumonia than influenza. She jokes facetiously but not humorously. Does Sallie Lou shop stingily or abstemiously?

## August 27

Grandpa was feeling generous, so he gave a total of $100 to his five grandchildren. Starting with the youngest, each got $2.00 more than the next younger one. In other words, the youngest got one sum, the next got $2.00 more, and so on. How much did the youngest grandchild get?

## August 28

Jack and John had been friends for a long time—a very long time, it seemed to them. Jack was six years older, but it hadn't made any difference when they met, and it didn't on the day they were talking about their long friendship. "It's twenty-two years this week since we met at Bill's wedding," said John. "Yes, and our ages now, added together, are exactly double what they were then. That makes me feel old," said Jack, but they really were not—not even fifty. How old were they now?

## August 29

In each of the word pairs that follows, a different word can be placed between the two words on the line to make two new words. The number of letters is indicated by the dashes. What are the four words?

BACK _ _ _ _ ROBE
DOOR _ _ _ STONE
PAD _ _ _ _ STEP
SAW _ _ _ _ WHEEL

## August 30

What is the five-digit number, with no zeros and no repeated numbers, in which the second digit is two times the first, the third is three times the second, the fourth is four times the first, and the last is one-half more than the second?

## August 31

The quotation has been placed in the boxes below and the letters have been put in alphabetical order in the "drop-in" boxes. Word divisions are shown. Fill in the boxes to read the saying. (A dash at the end of a line indicates a broken word.)

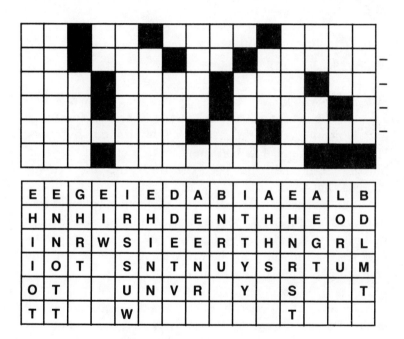

# September

Anyone who knows Latin recognizes that the root of September is *septem,* "seven," just as October, November, and December take their names from Roman numbers. However, September is not the seventh month of the year, but the ninth, and it has been the ninth since the Romans decreed that their civic year would start in January in 153 B.C. It did not occur to them that this discrepancy would lead to confusion. After all, people who calculated with Roman numerals would hardly be fazed by such a petty problem. Just try multiplying CVII by XXIV someday when you find yourself with a great deal of time.

The major U.S. holiday in September is Labor Day, the first Monday of the month. It traditionally signals the end of the summer season, as Memorial Day in May signals the beginning. Beaches often close on Labor Day even though swimming can still be very enjoyable. Water changes temperature more slowly than air, so it takes longer to warm up but stays warm longer. Anyone who has swum in the Atlantic in June and September knows that the water is appreciably warmer after Labor Day.

## September 1

A palindrome (like Madam I'm Adam) can be words, phrases, or even whole sentences that read the same forward and backward. Work out the following three palindromes.

Legal or illegal ways to obtain something:

_ _ _ _ _ _ _ _ _ _ _

A description of an Eskimo who has fallen out of his boat: _ _ _ _ _ _ _ _ _

Look at lots of judges on the sports scene:

_ _ _ _ _ _ _ _ _ _

## September 2

If you stack the words that match these definitions, you will have a word square that reads the same across and down.

1. Geometric shape
2. Not shut
3. Lack or want
4. Brings to a conclusion, polishes off, finishes

## September 3

The following coiled sentence can be unscrambled by finding the right letter for a start, and then tracing letter by letter up, down, sideways, or diagonally to find a statement. (There are two null letters.)

```
I H E W I D R A
T T E R I T L Y
D N H S A O N G
F O U I M S K I
E V I K N H O C
```

## September 4

Here is a drawing of an unfolded cube, plus six constructed cubes. Which of the drawings *cannot* be made from the unfolded cube at the top?

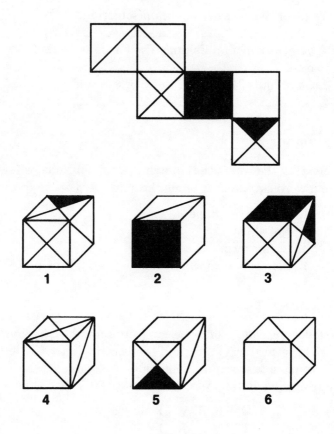

## September 5

All the vowels have been removed from the following sentence. (Y is not counted as a vowel.) Put back the vowels to find the sentence. The letters have been broken into groups of 5.

THRSN     TMSCN     NTHSW     HLPLC
SDTHC     NDCTR     TNLSS     LYXXX.

## September 6

The new teacher thought she'd get the children to drink the milk at recess more cheerfully by offering cookies with it. A lot of the children had illnesses and were out, causing various numbers of children to be present each day. One day the teacher noted that if there were five fewer children the next day, they would each get two cookies more if she brought the same number she had that day. However, the absentee list was low the next day, and she had four more children instead of five fewer. This meant that each received one cookie less than each child had received the day before. How many cookies did the children get the second day?

## September 7

The name of a country is hidden in each of the sentences below. Find the countries.

> The doorbell sign said, "Don't touch. In a real emergency, pull the cord."
> They got married secretly, but no one is wed entirely alone, so there were witnesses.
> We needed to visit a health resort, so we went to a spa in another country.

## September 8

The circle below contains a word of eight letters with one letter missing. Replace the letter to read the word. It may read counterclockwise, but the letters are in the proper order.

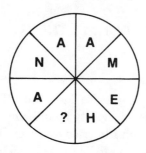

## September 9

This problem *must not,* I repeat, *must not* be solved by looking at the telephone. It is a test of your visual memory and your logical ability. Find the sum of all the numbers on a telephone dial and multiply that sum by all the numbers on the telephone dial. What is your answer? (The average time is thirty seconds. Can you beat it?)

## September 10

Two names of people are hidden in each sentence below. The letters are in their proper order and are not separated by intervening letters. No name has fewer than three letters. Find the names.

> Oh, call the cab, I'll be ready.
> That tie is all yours, I hate it.
> Get me an orange or get me a lemon, quickly.

## September 11

Soon the only trees left with leaves will be pine trees. Can you complete this word square so that the same words can be read across and down? (There can be several answers.)

```
P I N E
I
N
E
```

## September 12

There are many words which have the same pair of letters at the beginning and the end, like ONION. Here are four words with only the middle of each one showing. The number of dashes indicates the number of letters that must be placed before and after—the same letters for each individual word, but different letters for different words. Fill in the letters.

```
_ _ EPSA _ _        _ _ RISCO _ _
_ _ IT _ _          _ _ BL _ _
```

## September 13

Each of the following words contains the letters SEP. There may be other appearances of each letter in the word, but each letter is shown only once. Using the definitions, fill in the words.

Architectural term for a church section:

$$\_ \_ \_ \_ S E P \_$$

A dangerous occupation working on high locations:

$$S \_ E \_ P \_ \_ \_ \_ \_ \_$$

Put apart:         $$S E P \_ \_ \_ \_ \_$$

## September 14

Just by chance, you run into your dead-beat friend. You lent him $88 some time ago, and haven't seen him (or the money) since. He greets you fondly and says, "Well, it just so happens I have six bills in my pocket that total the $88 I owe you. If you can come up with the denominations of the six bills in thirty seconds, I'll pay you back right now." Spurred on by the only hope of ever seeing your money again, you come up with the six different denominations. What are they?

## September 15

Each of the following groups of letters is actually a scrambled word that has had one letter—the same letter for all six words—removed. The remaining letters were then scrambled. Reconstitute the words.

ENCU    RUEC    CATU    RCHA
IOAR    ANVI

## September 16

In the following mathematics example, you can substitute a different number for each letter (that is, A = the same number each time), and come up with a correct math example.

$$
\begin{array}{r}
A\,B\,C\,D\,E\,F\,G\,H\,I \\
\times\ I \\
\hline
+\ A\,J \\
\hline
A\,A\,A\,A\,A\,A\,A\,A\,A\,A
\end{array}
$$

## September 17

A pithy saying has been dropped into the boxes below. Word divisions are indicated and the letters for each of the boxes have been placed, not in their correct order but in alphabetical order, below each column. A dash on the right indicates that a word continues on the next line. Fill in the letters in their proper places in the columns above them to read the statement.

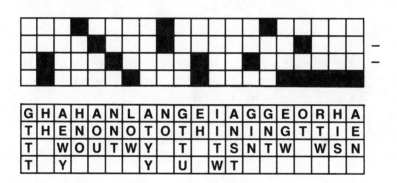

## September 18

Can you go from DIRT to ROAD in only seven steps, changing one letter at a time and making a good English word each time? (Example: CAP to HAT—CAP, CAT, HAT)

```
D   I   R   T
—   —   —   —
—   —   —   —
—   —   —   —
—   —   —   —
—   —   —   —
—   —   —   —
R   O   A   D
```

## September 19

The first word of a word square is given in the diagram below. Fill in the rest, using, in addition to the letters shown, one D, one S, one P, and two each A, E, and T.

```
L I K E
I
K
E
```

## September 20

One three-letter word can be placed in front of each of the following words to make four new words. The same three-letter word must be used in each case.

```
_ _ _ BLED
_ _ _ ROW
_ _ _ GIN
_ _ _ TIN
```

## September 21

This brief old-fashioned verse will give you an appropriate word.

My first is in father but not in dad
My second in lass and also lad
My third is in low but not in we
My last in live but not in be
If in my whole no one believes
For thirteen weeks I'll give you leaves.

## September 22

The professor posted the grades in the seminar exam (coding them by Social Security number). The student who came in two places below the highest score also came in three places above the poor student who found himself at the bottom of the list. How many students were in the seminar?

## September 23

This date marks the birthdate of William McGuffey in 1800. His *Eclectic Readers* sold 122 million copies and taught generations of Americans to read. Can you read this reasonably common word that has been shaped into a square?

N O C
N   R
I V E

## September 24

The following sentences are missing two words of seven letters each. The same seven letters can be rearranged to make the two missing words.

> The young couple was having trouble fixing a wall, and a visitor said, "I could have told you that you would need _ _ _ _ _ _ _ ." "Oh," said the very much of an amateur young husband, "a piece of grasscloth and a _ _ _ _ _ _ _ won't work?"

## September 25

The following multisyllabic pronouncement is a badly garbled proverb. Translate it into common English.

Individuals residing in habitations composed of dried vegetable matter are seriously advised to consider the inadvisability of having seats of power kept for safekeeping in a repository in said domicile.

## September 26

I lost my wallet, and I don't remember how much money I had, but I remember thinking the first time I bought something that it cost 10 percent of what I had. Then I noticed that the second purchase was also exactly 10 percent of what I had left. My sales slips totaled $19. How much was in the wallet when I lost it?

## September 27

We have a slow set of trains here. One train runs from A to B at 19 miles per hour. The other runs from B to A at 21 miles per hour (it's a slightly improved model). One hour before the trains pass each other, how far apart are they?

## September 28

The two youngsters were given different amounts for their allowances. This week, the older received 40¢ plus one-half the total of the younger's allowance. The younger one got 20¢ plus half again as much. The two together received 85¢. How much did each of them have?

## September 29

The youngsters decided to spend their weekly allowance on bubble gum. In addition to their 85¢, they managed to dig up $1.31 from under a sofa cushion. If the pieces of bubble gum had been one cent cheaper each, they would have received three more pieces of bubble gum than they did. How many pieces did they actually get?

## September 30

Using the numbers 0, 4, 8, and 12 in the following square, you can complete it so that all the vertical, horizontal, and long diagonal rows add up to 24. (You may use each number more than once.)

| 0 |  | 12 | 0 |
|---|---|---|---|
|  |  |  |  |
| 4 |  |  |  |
|  |  |  | 12 |

# October

The October Revolution that brought the Bolsheviks to
power in Russia actually took place on November 7, 1917,
according to most history books. This confusion has its roots
in a slight error in Julius Caesar's calculations, which
caused his calendar to fall slowly behind the seasons. By the
time of Pope Gregory XIII, dates were once again confused.
In 1582, Gregory decreed that October 5–14 should be
dropped from that year, and that every fourth year should
be a Leap Year *except* for centenary years that are *not* divisible by 400 (e.g., 1800). Dropping ten days produced considerable dismay in the countries that were affected. Many
people were absolutely convinced that Gregory had chopped
ten days off their life!

The non-Catholic countries of Europe ignored the new
Gregorian calendar until the pressure of being "behind" the
rest of the world grew too great. England and its colonies
finally accepted the new calendar in 1752, skipping September 3–13. Russia maintained the old Julian calendar into
the twentieth century. Only after the Revolution, which occurred on October 26, 1917 (Julian style), did the Russians
"catch up" with the rest of the world.

## October 1

The school faculty is conducting a prize drawing to raise money for Mensa memberships for bright students. You have to pick the tickets out of a box that looks like a dictionary. There are fifteen nonprizewinning slips, ten $1.00 winners, and five slips that are worth $25 each. How much would you have to spend at $1.00 per ticket to be sure of winning one of the $25 prizes?

## October 2

Make as many common English words as you can from the letters ECRTU using each of the letters only once in each word. (Many people found five or more.)

## October 3

Each of the words shown below contains the letters OCT. Definitions are given and the number of letters is shown for each. Fill in the words.

A form of firework: _ _ _ _ O C _ _ T
A form of marine life: O C T _ _ _ _
A soup: _ O C _ T _ _ _ _ _

## October 4

The famous mathematician Dr. Square Root had two sons, exactly a year apart. One day, shortly after they had both turned a year older, he noticed that if you squared their ages and then added the squares the total would be 1105. How old were his sons?

## October 5

One of the marks of creativity is seeing associations. The following list of words should call to mind other words using this word, whether as part of a word, or part of a phrase, or just in a related manner. (Example: TAG—tagalong, tag out, ragtag) Four each will earn you full credit.

WAIST
SPOT
LOVE
CHECK

## October 6

The field shown below belonged to a rancher. Twelve oil wells were drilled on it. The rancher, who had four sons, left them the field, divided into four equal sections, each with three oil wells on it. Divide the land so that each has an identical share, and every plot has square corners.

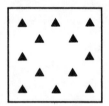

## October 7

The same seven letters, if rearranged into two words, will make sense of the following sentence.

Said the angry husband, "I'm leaving. We are
_ _ _ _ _ _ _ . I cannot put up with your
ceaseless gabble and _ _ _ _ _ _ _ ."

## October 8

We're between fall and winter at the moment, but can you change FALL to COLD in five steps, using a good English word each time? (Example: CAT to DOG—CAT COT COG DOG) Slang words don't count.

F A L L
— — — —
— — — —
— — — —
C O L D

## October 9

Lost in Liars and Truthtellers Town, you are in real trouble. You need to ask directions from a Truthteller, but how can you tell who is a Truthteller? You stop a group of three women and ask if they are Truthtellers. The first says, "Two of us are Truthtellers." The second says, "Only one of us is a Truthteller." And the third one chimes in, "The last woman who spoke is telling the truth." Well, who was or were Truthtellers?

## October 10

It was the middle of the winter in Scandinavia, and the poor boy, sick with a cold, was lying in bed. He woke up in the night, but he knew that the night lasted from 3:00 P.M. to 9:00 A.M. at that time of year. The boy wearily glanced at his clock and, thinking it said 4:42, buried his head back in the pillow. But as he fell asleep he realized he hadn't distinguished the hour hand from the minute hand. If it wasn't 4:42 in the morning, what other time (or times) could it have been?

## October 11

The following visual puzzle has been set up so that each of the signs has a numerical value. The sum of each row and column except one is shown. Figure out the missing number.

| | | | | |
|---|---|---|---|---|
| ⊗R | 🚸 | ⚠ | ☎ | **110** |
| 🚸 | ⊗R | ⚠ | ☎ | **110** |
| 🚸 | ☎ | ⚠ | ⊗R | **110** |
| ⊗R | 🚸 | ☎ | ⚠ | **110** |
| **90** | **105** | **125** | **?** | |

## October 12

If 7 is a prime number, cross out all the A's and E's below; if not, cross out the C's and L's. If the square root of 625 is 25, cross out the I's and R's; if not, cross out the C's and U's. If 0°C and 10°F are the same, cross out the B's, M's, and S's; if not, cross out the X's. What do you have left?

C A O X L E U E M I B R U X S E

## October 13

Since this is the day after Columbus discovered America, here's a Columbus puzzle. Sum the digits of the year in which Columbus reached the New World. Add to that the number of the king whom Mary, Ferdinand and Isabella's daughter, married. Add the number of ships in Columbus's fleet, and divide by 3. What do you have?

## October 14

I met my friend the test pilot, who had just received a lot of publicity for a record round-the-world flight by balloon. With the pilot was a little girl of about two. "What's her name?" I asked my friend, whom I hadn't seen in five or six years and who had married in that time. "Same as her mother." "Hello, Susan," I said. How did I know if I had never seen the wedding announcement?

## October 15

Start with the letter A. Add the letters below in order, making a new word each step, until you make a seven-letter word. Adding an S to make a plural is not allowed; you must rearrange the letters or add a letter to make a completely new word. (Example: I, it, tin, tine)

R E C S S T

## October 16

The weary clothing merchant was cleaning up after his Columbus week coat sale. He had already marked the coats down twice, but he still had one nice coat for sale. It had originally been $300. At the first markdown, he had reduced it to $210. At the second markdown, for Columbus week, he had tagged it at $147. If he marks it down now on the same principle, what will the new price be?

## October 17

What is the four-digit number, no zeros, in which the first number is five times the last, the second is four more than the first and three times the third, and the third is two more than the last and two less than the first?

## October 18

Of the three finalists in the science scholarship contest, John, William, and Sally came in one, two, and three, but not necessarily in that order. The winner was the physicist. The one who was not last or first was the mathematician. The one who came in last had black hair. John had brown hair. Sally had red hair. John did not have any training in physics. Who was first?

## October 19

George Bernard Shaw said that fish could be spelled *ghoti* (*gh* as in rough, *o* as in women, and *ti* as in nation). Can you come up with the longest way of spelling SIGH, following the same idea?

## October 20

People have already started buying Halloween candy, the better to eat before Halloween. Our local candy store was selling large sacks of candy for 25¢ and small sacks for 10¢. The new cashier wasn't up to the job, though; she marked down the number of sacks she sold, but she forgot to record their prices. At the end of the day she found she had sold 385 candy sacks and had $62.65 in her cash register. Before her boss came by, however, she figured out how many of each size of candy sack she had sold. Can you?

## October 21

Palindromes are words, phrases or sentences reading the same backward as forward, like Madam I'm Adam. Here are some palindrome definitions. Fill in the palindromes. (One word is given in each to get you started.)

Some confusion about a vehicle or an animal in sight:

— — —   — —   —   C A R   — —
—   — — —   —   — — — ?

Roy didn't like the big city at all and wouldn't stay.

— — —   — — —   — — — — ,
— — —   WENT   — — .

## October 22

A simple magic square is easy. It's a square in which all the numbers from 1 to 9, placed in a grid as shown below, add up to 15 in each direction. Make an anti-magic square, in which each line total—across, down, and long diagonals—is different.

**Magic Square**

| 4 | 9 | 2 |
|---|---|---|
| 3 | 5 | 7 |
| 8 | 1 | 6 |

**Anti-Magic Square**

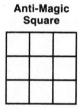

## October 23

It's difficult being called on unexpectedly in class, but Professor Jones decided to do it to wake up his sleeping students. "I don't mind if you know my age," he said. "It's in all the directories, and I can assume the approximate age of one of you. No written homework tonight for the first person who can solve this: If you subtract one age from mine, you'll get 44, but if you multiply them together, you'll get 1280." It took Tom fifteen seconds, because he tried his age in the problem, and it was right. How old were Tom and the professor?

## October 24

The spider web shown below contains eight words. Each section contains four letters which have been jumbled. They all contain one missing letter, which should be placed in the box with the question mark. Figure out the missing letter, and reassemble the eight words.

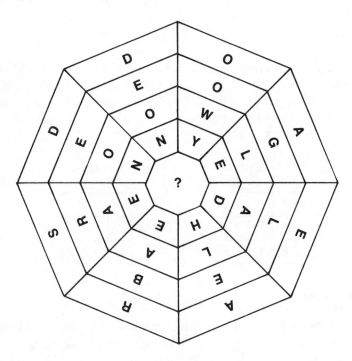

## October 25

Sometimes it helps to be bigger—especially when you're only four or five years old. The children were making candy apples for the Halloween party, eating as they worked. The bigger kids managed to gobble up seven apples apiece (and got stomachaches for their pains), but the little kids got only two apiece. The children managed to eat twenty-four apples among them. How many kids, big and small, were making the candy apples?

## October 26

A rather softhearted antique dealer often paid more than she should and sold for less than she could. This time, she was figuring out her costs and profits. Her sister said, "You sold that dish for only a 5 percent profit. If you had bought it for 10 percent less than you did pay, and sold it at the same price, you would have made a $15 profit." How much did the antique dealer pay for the dish?

## October 27

Sheila, buying favors for a party she was giving, was having difficulty deciding on how many more favors to buy. She started out by planning to give everyone three favors, but when she divided the favors she had by 3, she had one left over; when she divided by 4, she had two left over; by 5, she had three left over; and by 6, she had four left over. Since she was going to have ten guests, this wouldn't work. She counted the favors and realized that, by adding two more, she could divide the favors evenly. What is the smallest number of favors she could already have bought to meet those specifications?

## October 28

Another word to guess letter by letter.

> My first is in water but not in tears
> My second in listen but not in hears
> My third in three but not in she
> My fourth in clear but not in tea
> My last in hang but not in grand
> My whole assembles in a band.

## October 29

A word square is a square in which words read the same across and down.

> Example: C A T
>           A T E
>           T E A

Make up a four-letter-by-four-letter word square in which you use five E's, four N's, two M's, two each, A and D, and one S.

## October 30

This may be an old one, but many people seem not to have heard it. Samantha and Suzy were squabbling over a small cake. Their mother solved the question of which one should cut it, as well as the problem of how to make sure the pieces were even, in a very simple manner. No one could complain. What was her solution?

## October 31

This being Halloween, we will consider the problem of witches and their cats. The whole crowd is out tonight, naturally, and an interested observer, seeing them fly by (yes, witches' cats fly), noticed that the number of legs, all told, was three and a half times the number of heads, and the total of heads and legs was seventy-two. How many cats and witches are out this Halloween?

# November

November starts with All Saints' Day. This holiday dates back to the seventh century, when the Pantheon, which means "all saints," was dedicated by Pope Boniface IV in Rome. In many countries All Saints' remains the traditional day for remembering the dead with visits to the cemetery and the placing of flowers on tombs. In our country, however, this holiday has been overshadowed by All Hallows' Eve, "All Souls' Evening," the night before, when supernatural spirits are supposed to be abroad. We now know October 31 as Halloween.

Since 1941, the fourth Thursday of November has been the date to observe Thanksgiving. This peculiarly American holiday celebrates the survival of the colony at Plymouth, Massachusetts, after many hardships. Turkey, cranberry sauce, and succotash, all strictly North American foods, have become traditional. It is not generally realized that when the Pilgrims landed, they were greeted by an English-speaking native named Squanto. It must have been a shock for the Pilgrims to hear him—and it seems to be a shock for people to hear about him now. Squanto had already been taken to England by whalers and fishermen plying the North American coast.

## November 1

Up north, November is not too early for snow. Fill the square below with the letters SNOW. Each line down, sideways, and along the diagonals must contain each of the four letters, though their order is not important. Three letters have been inserted to give you a start.

|   |   |   |   |
|---|---|---|---|
| S |   |   | N |
|   |   |   |   |
|   |   |   |   |
|   |   | S |   |

## November 2

The following is a simple substitution cryptogram in which a number has been substituted for a letter. The same number stands for the same letter each time.

26    25 18 9 23    18 13    7 19 22
19 26 13 23    18 8    14 22 8 8 2.

## November 3

The poor knight who is madly in love with the beautiful Princess of Puzzleland is ready to elope again. He missed his princess once because of his bad math. This time he has it right. He's figured out exactly how fast he must go to reach the castle exactly at noon when she will slip out. If he goes at 75 miles per hour in his brand-new twelve-elf-powered Magicmobile, and leaves at 7:00 A.M., he'll get there an hour too soon. On the other hand, if he goes at a steady 50 miles per hour, he'll be an hour too late, he finds. How fast must he tell his lead elf to travel to reach his intended bride just on time?

## November 4

The wicked witch of Puzzleland, angered by three Liars from the under-30 set, told each of them how much longer he was going to live. The witch said, "You have a total of 130 years left among you. The oldest has already lived half his life; the second oldest has lived one third; and the youngest, who told me more lies than anyone else, has already lived one third of his life." How old were the Liars?

## November 5

The phrase coiled below is rather unusual and not just because it has (unintended) political overtones. If you start at the correct letter, and move to any letter, up, down, diagonally, or sideways, you can read the phrase.

```
S   A   D   Y   Y   T   S
T   R   E   B   D   A   R
C   O   M   E   M   O   C
```

## November 6

Each of the following words contains the letters NOV. (There may be more than one of each of those letters, but they are not shown.) Using the definitions, fill in the words.

A dispute or argument:

\_ \_ N \_ \_ O V \_ \_ \_ \_

An astronomical feature:

\_ \_ \_ \_ \_ N O V \_

New or original:     \_ \_ N O V \_ \_ \_ \_ \_

## November 7

What is the four-digit number in which the first digit is one-fourth of the last digit, the second digit is 6 times the first digit, and the third digit is the second digit plus 3?

## November 8

Five letters can be rearranged for *each pair* of words below to match the two definitions. A different set of five letters is used for each line.

To toss; the value of
To perch; part of the human body
One who looks; feed on meadow grass, etc.

## November 9

Another palindrome set of definitions—the word or phrase will read the same backward and forward (Example: First man introduces himself—Madam I'm Adam)

The big chiefs are showing grief:

__ __ __ __ __ __   __ __ __

A person who lives in a city in Nevada and tends to be solitary:   __ __ __ __   __ __ __ __ __

## November 10

All the vowels have been removed from the following remark, and the letters have been broken into groups of three. Replace the missing vowels (one null letter at end).

FLS RSH NWH RNG LSF RTT RDX.

## November 11

A solemn holiday like Veterans Day really isn't the subject for a joke or humor, but test your memory of the day. The two interlettered lines below contain names in the first line, and places in the second, relating to World War I and World War II.

PFCEOHRCUSHHRCIHNILGL

BEYALPSARTLEOAMSGENIEN

## November 12

A group of youngsters found a large sum of money on the street and took it to the police. The grateful owner gave each of them a reward. If there had been two more youngsters in the group, they each would have received $1.00 less, with $2.00 left over to be divided into cents. If there had been double the number, each would have received exactly $2.50 less. If there had been three fewer of them, each one would have received $2.00 more and there would have been $1.00 left to split into pennies. This way, each received an exact sum in dollars, with no cents left over. How many youngsters and how large a reward for each?

## November 13

Divide 110 into two parts so that one will be 150 percent of the other. What are the 2 numbers?

## November 14

The following matchsticks make one triangle. Rearrange five of them to make 5 triangles.

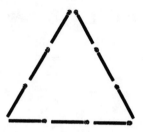

## November 15

As Amy was strolling one day with her baby daughter in her carriage, she met her husband's mother's only daughter-in-law's sister's husband. What relationship was this man to Amy?

## November 16

A word square is composed of four words that read the same across and down. The first word of the square below has been filled in for you. Make up a word square, using this as a start, in which you use, in total, four E's; two each, S, O, L, N, and D; and one each, A and P.

```
S O L E
O
L
E
```

## November 17

Can you go from GLOW to WORM in only seven steps,
changing one letter at a time and making a good English
word at each step?

| G | L | O | W |
|---|---|---|---|
| — | — | — | — |
| — | — | — | — |
| — | — | — | — |
| — | — | — | — |
| — | — | — | — |
| W | O | R | M |

## November 18

Another Victorian-type poem in which the correct letter
from each clue gives you a new word.

> My first is in ocean but not in sea
> My second in milk but not in me
> My third in three but not in throw
> My fourth in vow but not in crow
> My fifth in eight but not in night
> My last in wrong and also right
> My whole is praise for thoughts or men
> Or women, too, or tongue or pen.

## November 19

Your pockets are tearing from the weight of all the coins in
them. After you unload them onto the kitchen table, you discover something surprising. You have exactly the same
number of pennies, nickels, dimes, and quarters, totaling
$6.15. How many of each coin do you have?

## November 20

Sally likes things with certain characteristics. She likes apples but not pears. She likes beets but not turnips. She likes beef but not lamb. Does she like cheese or custard, and why?

## November 21

Gabe was having a terrible time lining up his tin soldiers. He didn't have all that many, fewer than one hundred, but he couldn't seem to arrange them on parade properly. He kept having odd numbers left over. He tried rows of five and there were four left over; he tried rows of six—four left over; rows of 7—one left over. He finally decided to have a very narrow parade and arranged them four abreast. That worked. What's the smallest number of toy soldiers he could have had?

## November 22

Still wandering in Liars and Truthtellers Town, you run into two women, but cannot tell if either tells the truth. You ask the first one, "Is either of you a Truthteller?" After she answers, you know the truth. What did she say?

## November 23

You've almost finished renovating the storage room in the basement, but find you are short two panels and send your young son out to buy one oak panel and one plain. He comes back with the panels and change, so you can tell he spent $65.15, but he's lost the sales slip, and you don't know what each cost. All he can remember is that the oak panel cost $5.45 more than the plain one. What did each panel cost?

## November 24

Today may not be Thanksgiving, but it's an appropriate time for a Thanksgiving puzzle. A pertinent message has been dropped into the boxes below. Word divisions are indicated by black boxes, and the letters for each of the boxes have been placed, not in correct order but in alphabetical order, below each column. Fill in the letters in their proper places in the columns above them to read the message. A dash represents a broken word.

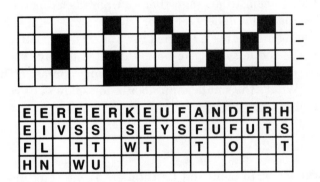

## November 25

If you haven't heard this one before, good. If you have, our apologies, but it's so clever we had to include it. After a heavy Thanksgiving meal, the night watchman went to work. In the morning, he told his boss he had dreamed that a saboteur planted a bomb in the factory and that he felt it was a warning. The boss promptly fired him. Why?

## November 26

You are on your way home for the holidays with the family. You fill the gas tank of your nice new small car, which holds 10 gallons and gives you 25 miles to the gallon. That should get you home easily, as home is 220 miles away. Unfortunately, about 20 miles from home, the car stops, and you discover the tank is dry—obviously a leak, because you can see drops dripping. How many gallons of gasoline have you lost? (And although it is not part of the question, what will you say to the new car dealer who just sold you the car?)

## November 27

The following statement has been coiled. If you start at the right letter and move in any direction, you can come up with a Tom Swifty.

```
W  I  T  C  R  U
C  E  P  H  H  C
A  Y  R  S  E  H
L  R  A  E  R  T
L  C  O  I  U  E
Y  M  T  D  N  D
```

## November 28

What are three single digits whose sum is the same as that of the digits multiplied?

## November 29

The following words contain some unusual letter combinations. Fill in the missing letters.

     _ Y N A _ _      _ W K W _ _ _
           _ Y Z Y _ _

## November 30

The family had missed the plane back home and all its members were very irritated. "Oh well," said the older boy, "if it were six hours later, we'd only have to wait one-fifth as long until midnight, when the plane comes, as we'd have to wait if it were two hours earlier now." Figuring that out helped pass the time. What time was it?

# December

In much of the country, December can be recognized by the Christmas decorations. Lights and ornaments go up immediately after Thanksgiving. (In France, I've seen them up as early as November 12, right after Armistice Day.) Actually, most of these trappings date back to pre-Christian times. The Christmas tree is a relic of ancient tree worship. The custom of decorating such a tree was brought to England from Germany by Queen Victoria's husband, Prince Albert, and it spread to the United States from there. "The Holly and the Ivy" are both Druid symbols.

Even the date of Christmas was not set until sometime in the third century, and it was probably chosen to be near the winter solstice, around December 21. Many people already celebrated a festival on that day to bring back the sun after the longest night of the year. Even now, exchanging gifts on Christmas Day is actually peculiar to the English-speaking world. Other cultures use different dates, the most common being January 6. That would give people a little more time to finish their shopping!

## December 1

Each of the following words contains the letters DEC once, if not twice.

Not sedate or proper:

$\_\ \_$ D E C $\_\ \_\ \_\ \_\ \_$

A statistical term:   D E C $\_\ \_\ \_$

Ornamented, often used for overornamented:

$\_\ \_$ D E C $\_\ \_\ \_$

## December 2

A word square is composed of four words that read the same across as down. The first word of the following square has been filled in for you. Complete the square with the missing three words using five E's; four N's; two each M, A, D; and one S, in total (16 letters for the complete square).

```
M A N E
A
N
E
```

## December 3

You can, if you want to waste a lot of time, count sheep by counting heads and legs and dividing by 5. However, could you figure out how many birds (two-legged) and how many mammals (four-legged) your local zoo had? You counted 78 legs and 35 heads. How many of each were there?

# December 4

It was one of those silly guessing games for a prize. How many Christmas tree balls were in the big bowl in the department store? Surprisingly, there were only five guesses. Jim was five under, Susan was two under, Willy was the winner, Jack was one over, and Alice was six over. The numbers were: 26, 15, 18, 21, and 20. How many ornaments were in the bowl?

# December 5

The old lady who lived in a shoe was having some real trouble buying Christmas presents for her enormous family. Although she bought the least expensive stocking stuffers she could find, the bill was high. Of course, both a 15 percent sales tax and a 5 percent luxury tax were added to the original price. She paid a total of $100. What was the cost of the stuffers before taxes?

# December 6

The farmers were bringing their fowl to market to sell for Christmas dinner, all nicely frozen, of course. Farmer Jones had three plump, nice fowl and had managed to simplify her pricing by getting them all to the identical weight. Farmer Smith had geese, four of them, and he, too, had all of them at the same weight, which was different from that of Farmer Jones's birds. Three fowl from Farmer Jones and four fowl from Farmer Smith weighed 38 pounds. On the other hand, if Farmer Jones had had four fowl and Farmer Smith had had three, the combined weight would have been 39 pounds. How much did each of Farmer Jones's fowl weigh?

## December 7

An illuminating statement has been inserted into the boxes as shown. The letters comprising the statement are below their appropriate location, but in alphabetical order. Dashes indicate word breaks. Put the letters in their proper places to read the message.

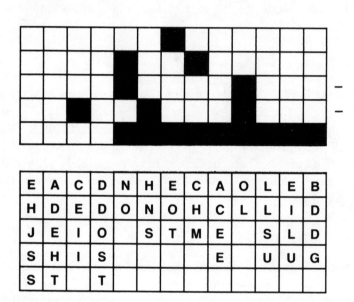

## December 8

The following sentence is missing two words composed of the same six letters. Find the two words composed of the same six letters that will make (reasonable) sense in this puzzle.

The versatile dance team could, in a

— — — — — — , switch from a waltz to a

— — — — — — .

# December 9

A palindrome is a word, phrase, sentence, or line that can be read backward or forward. (Example: First man to first woman, Madam I'm Adam) Here are two palindrome descriptions to figure out. Letter divisions are shown.

Instruction to someone who is afraid, in a gun duel:

_ _ _ _    _    _ _ _ _ _ _

All the inhabitants of ancient Rome were smart, not stupid: _ _    _ _ _ _ _    _

_ _ _ _ _

# December 10

Each of the lines below has a blank space between the two words. Find a letter that can replace the first letter in each pair of words to make two new words and put it on that line. When you have finished, if you do it correctly, you will have a new word, reading down.

| CHOP | _____ | HAVING |
| AIL | _____ | PURSE |
| AVER | _____ | AIL |
| FOUND | _____ | BRIGHT |

# December 11

"Aha," said the math professor to her husband, "it's a very simple problem, but I see that our two sons have now reached interesting ages. The product of their ages is six times the amount you get if you add their ages. On the other hand, if you add the square of each age, the total of the two will be 325." How old were their boys?

## December 12

One letter has been left out of the center of this scrambled words puzzle. If you take each of the letters in the sections reading down toward the center, rearrange them, and add the missing letter from the middle, you will have eight different five-letter words. Fill in the missing letter and unscramble the words.

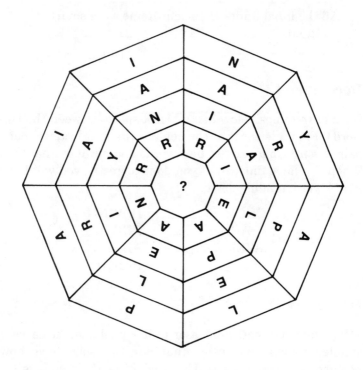

## December 13

The Wantsits were going to buy a used, but serviceable car. Mr. Wantsits was quite upset. He said he had seen one he liked but it was $6950, and they couldn't afford that much. At least, that's what he thought it cost. His wife had been shopping around and was pretty sure that she had seen one for $4575. As it turned out, both of them had faulty memories and were wrong by the identical amount; one was over and one was under. They had been looking at the same car! What did it really cost?

## December 14

Johnny, despite his mother's objections, spent his whole allowance of $2.16 ($2.00, with 16¢ left from last week) on bubble gum. If the pieces of gum had been a penny cheaper, he would have received three more pieces than he did. How many did he actually buy?

## December 15

Find a five-digit number in which the last number is the sum of the first, second, and third; the third is four less than the last; the fourth is two less than the last; and the first and fourth added are one less than the last. The last number is also three times the second.

## December 16

You have an appointment to meet your friend the logic professor during the winter holidays when she is on vacation. Today is Friday. She has told you to meet her two days after the day before the day after tomorrow. What day does she expect you?

## December 17

The combined ages of Jim and his daughter total thirty-one. Jim is exactly thirty years older than his daughter. How old is his daughter?

## December 18

At the Winter Carnival, you see a new ring-toss game on sale. There are five rings, numbered 16, 17, 23, 24, and 39. You can use each ring as many times as you want to reach the score that is picked for each game. While you are watching, the salesman chooses 100, and dares the crowd to pick the smallest combination of ring tosses that will give that score. Naturally, you win. What rings did you pick?

## December 19

By changing one letter at a time, can you go from GRASS to GREEN in seven steps, making a good English word at each step? Fill in the word ladder below.

G   R   A   S   S

—   —   —   —   —

—   —   —   —   —

—   —   —   —   —

—   —   —   —   —

—   —   —   —   —

G   R   E   E   N

## December 20

Santa had hired extra workers for the packing process. He really didn't know quite how many he would need, so he watched his new workers for a while. He found out that six elves could pack eighteen packages in half an hour. How many packages could twelve elves pack in ninety minutes?

## December 21

You're stumbling through the forest at the edge of Liars and Truthtellers Town. In the dark you bump into a man. "Who are you?" you ask wearily. "I'm a Liar," he replies. What have you learned?

**NOTE:** Winter's back, and so are some old favorites. The remaining ten puzzles are special. Each is an "oldie but goody" disguised in a slightly different garb. Some of them will probably be new to you. None is original, but each has been fooling and delighting readers for many years. The percentage of correct responses has been omitted from the answers.

## December 22

The following diagram is one I remember from my high school math class. You must draw one continuous, curving line (in two dimensions) that passes through every single line segment in the diagram at one point, and one point only, not along the line. Can you solve it?

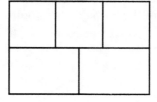

## December 23

My colleague, in addition to being intelligent, witty, and a fine dancer, has long red hair and blue eyes. Everybody in the office except the boss is under thirty; I'm twenty-five. I am young, male, single and unattached, and not particularly shy. I happen to be attracted to women with long red hair and blue eyes, but I have never complimented my colleague or suggested that we go out on a date. Why not?

## December 24

My friend is coming to share Christmas Eve with me. I live on the fifteenth floor. Unfortunately, he arrives without being announced by the doorman, puffing and panting from walking the last five flights. When he leaves, however, he gets into the elevator for the ride down. How can this be?

## December 25

We are going home for Christmas Day. I note that it takes us two and a half hours to get there because of the terrible traffic. The traffic is just as bad on the way home—identical, in fact—but we make it in 150 minutes. How do we manage this trick?

## December 26

Daddy gave his three boys the same present—money. He gave them $17 and, being a bit of a practical joker, said, "The oldest gets one-half the money, the middle one gets one-third of the money, and the baby gets one-ninth. However, it must be in even dollars." How did the boys solve that one?

## December 27

My brother started out from Boston, and I started out from New York, to meet in New Haven for lunch. When we met in New Haven, which of us was farther from Boston?

## December 28

Your aged grandmother tells you she was born on February 29, 1900. How old is she as of the date you are doing this puzzle?

## December 29

How many 9's do you pass when you start at 1 and count up to 100?

## December 30

It's a mistake to hire amateurs, as the archaeologist found to his great distress. One of his new staff came running in one day, all excited. He had just paid a local a great deal of money for an extremely valuable coin. As he said, "I've never seen one like this before, and I've been looking in museums for thirty years. It's a genuine Egyptian coin marked 100 B.C.—solid gold!" The director of the expedition sighed wearily and fired him. Why?

## December 31

Joe said to his friend at a New Year's Eve Party, "Yesterday I was twenty, but next year I will be twenty-two." When is Joe's birthday?

# Answers

## Day 1 of Each Month

**January:** WAS IT A RAT I SAW? and DESSERTS I STRESSED. (79%)

**February:** TEN ANIMALS I SLAM IN A NET; STAR BRATS. Only 20% of the Mensa members found both palindromes, though 95% found the latter.

**March:** The correct answer is (a) 9 1. There are two series, one starting with 10 and going down one number each time, and one starting with 1 and going up one number. (98%)

**April:** You'd call her Sally or Lorraine or Chun-Li or whatever her name was. This is an impossible relationship to figure out. Only 15 percent of the Mensans spotted the April Fools' Day joke. The rest had many names to call *me*.

**May:** SPRING (75%)

**June:** PERMUTATION is the only permutation of the word IMPORTUNATE. (55%)

**July:** Jim (65%)

**August:** CORNELIUS can be anagrammed to RECLUSION; DANIEL to DENIAL (and NAILED); CAMERON to ROMANCE and CREMONA; and BOSWELL TO BELLOWS. Only THOMAS cannot be rearranged. (75%)

**September:** BORROW OR ROB; DEKAYAKED; SEE REFEREES (85%)

**October:** The cost of winning a $25 ticket for certain is $26. Of course, you're certain to win more than $25 with that investment. (85%)

**November:** This was the most common solution. (65%)

| S | O | W | N |
|---|---|---|---|
| N | W | O | S |
| O | S | N | W |
| W | N | S | O |

**December:** INDECOROUS; DECILE; BEDECKED (85%)

## Day 2 of Each Month

**January:** A mango costs 15¢. The "logic" is 3¢ per letter (that's the way stores in Puzzleland operate). (73%)

**February:** A FOOL AND HIS MONEY ARE SOON PARTED. (98%)

**March:** ATTACK AT DAWN MONDAY. The lieutenant read the first letter of each word. (100%)

**April:** NEEDS and DENSE are the missing words. (100%)

**May:** Nineteen hundred eighty pennies are worth one cent more than 1979 pennies, just as ten pennies are worth one cent more than nine pennies. (80%)

**June:** PEDESTRIANS COME IN TWO SORTS: THE QUICK AND THE DEAD. (75%)

**July:** There are four girls and three boys. (70%)

**August:** She will be twenty. (75%)

**September:** (80%)

```
C  O  N  E
O  P  E  N
N  E  E  D
E  N  D  S
```

**October:** CRUET, CURET, CUTER, ERUCT, RECUT, and TRUCE were all found. Ninety-five percent of the Mensa members found four anagrams, and 55 percent found five.

**November:** A BIRD IN THE HAND IS MESSY. Number the alphabet backward from 26. (80%)

**December:** (85%)

```
M  A  N  E
A  M  E  N
N  E  E  D
E  N  D  S
```

## Day 3 of Each Month

**January:** CATASTROPHE; CAT BURGLAR; CATALOGUE (100%)

**February:** IT KEEPS YOUR NECK OFF THE LINE. (95%)

**March:** The solution favored by 60 percent of the Mensans was:

$$|||-|=||$$

Another 30 percent gave:

$$\setminus/\ |-|=\setminus/$$

Give yourself credit for either, or for one of your own.

**April:** CAMEL; ELAND; SEAL (90%)

**May:** RENO; BARRE; BUTTE (90%)

**June:** HAPPINESS IS A STOCK THAT SPLITS THREE FOR ONE THE DAY AFTER YOU BUY IT. This cryptogram could be figured out through word structure and trial and error, or you could simply look at the characters on a typewriter. Each letter was replaced with the one to its right on the standard Qwerty keyboard. (65%)

**July:** (40%)

$$
\begin{array}{r}
396 \\
\underline{45} \\
17820
\end{array}
$$

**August:** Potatoes are 25¢. Eggplants are 75¢. (35%)

**September:** "I THINK I'VE FOUND THE WIRE," SAID TOM SHOCKINGLY. Start at the top left letter. (90%)

**October:** SKYROCKET; OCTOPUS; MOCK TURTLE (95%)

**November:** Sixty miles per hour will do it. (75%)

**December:** Thirty-one birds and four mammals (65%)

## Day 4 of Each Month

**January:** Margot likes unknown writers. She only likes words with a silent letter. (60%)

**February:** The word is HAND. (100%)

**March:** LLOYD for a boy, DOLLY for a girl (98%)

**April:** Women equal 23–15–13–5–14. The numbers represent the position of each letter of the word in the alphabet: i.e., A = 1, B = 2, and so on. (70%)

**May:** TSGSI. This is a substitution cipher which has to be worked letter by letter. (60%)

**June:** Only 40 percent of the Mensans surveyed tried this puzzle, but all those who did got it right.

| 214 | 219 | 254 | 259 |
|-----|-----|-----|-----|
| 659 | 654 | 619 | 614 |
| 873 | 873 | 873 | 873 |

**July:** If you answered every question right, you were left with INDEPENDENCE. (95%)

**August:** PINK, PINE, PONE, POSE, ROSE is one solution. (100%)

**September:** Cube 5 cannot be made from the unfolded one. Only 30 percent of the Mensans got this one right. Three of those confessed they had photocopied the drawing and folded it themselves. That's not cheating—that's using all your resources.

**October:** Twenty-three and twenty-four (60%)

**November:** Their ages were 28, 26, and 25. Only 40% of the Mensans who took it got this one.

**December:** Twenty (95%)

## Day 5 of Each Month

**January:** Twenty hours (96%)

**February:** Nine puzzle makers. Each puzzler can compose one puzzle per day. (75%)

**March:** TIMID, I'M IT. Only 65 percent of the Mensans got this one correct. Several said that either you see palindromes or you don't. Those who do love them.

**April:** The package will cost 5¢. If, as many people assume, the package cost 10¢ and the widget cost $1.00, then their total cost would be more than $1.10. (75%)

**May:** NUPTIALS (95%)

**June:** Ann is four years old now. (80%)

**July:** Your question was, "Would the other person tell me that this apple is all right to eat?" If the person is the Truthteller and the apple is fine, she'll say, "No," because that's what the Liar would say. If the person is the Liar and the apple is fine, she'll say, "No," because that's *not* what the Truthteller would say. Similarly, if the apple will put you to sleep, the person will have to say "Yes." Only 40 percent got this one.

**August:** All that glitters is not gold. (85%)

**September:** "THERE ISN'T A MUSICIAN IN THIS WHOLE PLACE," SAID THE CONDUCTOR TONELESSLY. (65%)

**October:** WAIST appears in SHIRTWAIST, WAISTBAND, WAIST-COAT, WAISTLINE, and other words. SPOT is in SPOT CHECK, SPOT ON, SPOTLIGHT, HOT SPOT, and RUN SPOT RUN. LOVE helps to make up LOVEBIRD, LOVESONG, LOVELIGHT, PUPPY LOVE, TRUE LOVE, and more. CHECK is the root of CHECK-MATE, CHECK OUT, CHECK UP, CHECKBOOK, BED CHECK, and CHECKERED. Give yourself full credit if you found four associations for each word. (40%)

**November:** STAR COMEDY BY DEMOCRATS. You can start either at the upper left or the upper right, since this phrase is a palindrome. (70%)

**December:** $83.33. The taxes are 20 percent of the *selling* price. (65%)

## Day 6 of Each Month

**January:** Cressida is four years old. (64%)

**February:** There were half a dozen different ways to make this move. The most common was POOR, POOL, POLL, POLE, PILE, RILE, RICE, RICH. (100%)

**March:** The presents cost $30, $25, $20, and $40. (85%)

**April:** A minimum of three buses (90%)

**May:** SABER (or SABRE) and BEARS are the missing words. (90%)

**June:** Seven of each coin (84%)

**July:** Start at the upper left corner.

>   HE SPOKE JUST ONCE.
>   "LOOK, HANS, NO MA," HE SAID. (95%)

**August:** ATTENTIVE and TENTATIVE (65%)

**September:** Five (35%)

**October:** (30%)

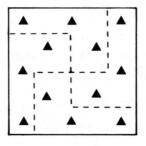

**November:** CONTROVERSY; SUPERNOVA; INNOVATIVE (95%)

**December:** Farmer Jones's fowl weighed 6 pounds each, and Farmer Smith's weighed 5 pounds each. (80%)

## Day 7 of Each Month

**January:** The answer is FRUIT. (92%)

**February:** The correct answer is 4.8, not 5, miles per hour. The answer is obtained by dividing the distance covered by the time elapsed, and *any* distance will do. Take a 12-mile run, for instance. That will take them two hours out and three hours back. It therefore took them five hours to travel 24 miles. (60%)

**March:** CHEESE, FRUIT, and MEAT; APPLES, PEARS, and PLUMS (100%)

**April:** There are 301 tiles. This is the smallest number that will give you a remainder of 1 when divided by 2, 3, 4, 5, and 6, but divided by 7 leaves nothing over. (45%)

**May:** The lid weighs $6\frac{2}{3}$ ounces. (75%)

**June:** Maria was twenty-four. She subtracted one-seventh of her real age. (50%)

**July:** There are thirty-two three-legged animals and nineteen with two legs. (65%)

**August:** BANANA, PINEAPPLE, KIWI FRUIT, and PEACH; PIZZA, SPAGHETTI, and MEATBALLS; CAKE, PUDDING, and CREAM PUFFS (75%)

**September:** CHINA; SWEDEN; SPAIN (98%)

**October:** PARTING and PRATING (75%)

**November:** 1694 (85%)

**December:** EDISON CALLED. SAID HE COULD SHED SOME LIGHT ON THE SUBJECT. (90%)

## Day 8 of Each Month

**January:** BIRDS OF A FEATHER FLOCK TOGETHER. (88%)

**February:** With the right answers you are left with MENSA. (85%)

**March:** AIRMEN, MARINE, and REMAIN. Ninety-five percent of the Mensans responded with all three words.

**April:** HAND (95%)

**May:** MAYONNAISE; AMAZINGLY. One hundred percent of the Mensa members answered this puzzle right, though some had trouble spelling MAYONNAISE.

**June:** D31. The sequence is made up of the initials of the months and the number of days in each month. (94%)

**July:** He saved 65.7 percent on fuel, using 34.3 percent of what he did before. (65%)

**August:** $42 (85%)

**September:** "T" is the missing letter, and the word is ANATHEMA. (75%)

**October:** FALL, HALL, HALE, HOLE, HOLD, COLD (98%)

**November:** THROW and WORTH; ROOST and TORSO; GAZER and GRAZE (98%)

**December:** MINUTE and MINUET will fill out the sentence. (100%)

## Day 9 of Each Month

**January:** GIGGLING; HAMMERMAN; WILLOWWARE. Of Mensans who took this quiz, 92% got all three correct. A few more missed only one word.

**February:** (75%)

$$
\begin{array}{r}
23 \\
23 \\
23 \\
\underline{23} \\
92
\end{array}
$$

**March:** There are fifty-five squares of all sizes in this design. Seventy percent of the Mensa members got this one right. Wrong answers ranged from twenty-six (all the small squares plus the large one) to 166.

**April:** Monday (100%)

**May:** The toys are priced at 7¢ per consonant, so a pinwheel costs 35¢. (45%)

**June:** SPRITE and STRIPE will fill out the sad story. (96%)

**July:** Jack won by one yard. He can run 100 yards while Jill can run 90, so with 10 yards left, the two of them are tied. (60%)

**August:** DOGGED; DOGMA; SEADOG (95%)

**September:** The answer to the problem is 0, once you multiply by the 0 on the telephone dial. Seventy-five percent of the Mensans who tried this puzzle said they did it within thirty seconds.

**October:** None of them could be Truthtellers. (35%)

**November:** BOSSES SOB; RENO LONER (70%)

**December:** DRAW, O COWARD; NO ROMAN A MORON (65%)

## Day 10 of Each Month

**January:** 1349. Several Mensa members said they worked out this answer by logic. If the second number is three times the first, and the last is three times the second, then the last number must be 9. It's easy to work backward from there. (96%)

**February:** ALL THAT GLITTERS IS NOT GOLD. (100%)

**March:** Seven operators (65%)

**April:** Mensaman flew at 666.67 miles per hour over his entire trip. (90%)

**May:** Andy likes Byron. He only likes words whose first two letters make separate words: or, to, be, by. (35%)

**June:** Barbara likes jodhpurs because she only likes foreign words. Forty-five percent got the correct answer and the reason.

**July:** He makes it with more than 5 gallons to spare. (65%)

**August:** (35%)

$$\begin{array}{r} 927 \\ \underline{63} \\ 58401 \end{array}$$

**September:** CAL, BILL (also REA); HATTIE and SALLY; GEORGE and NORA (90%)

**October:** When no distinction is made between the hour and minute hands, the clock would look the same at 8:23 A.M., 4:42 P.M., and 8:23 P.M. (85%)

**November:** FOOLS RUSH IN WHERE ANGELS FEAR TO TREAD. (100%)

**December:** SNOW is the answer. (95%)

## Day 11 of Each Month

**January:** $1.00. Wonkles cost 1¢ each, and winkles cost 2¢. (88%)

**February:** FEBRILE; INDEFENSIBLE; FEEBLE. All the Mensans figured out FEBRILE and FEEBLE, but only 45 percent found INDEFENSIBLE.

**March:** KNITTER (100%)

**April:** SMART (95%)

**May:** April is six, May is nine, and June is twenty. (55%)

**June:** JACK BE NIMBLE, JACK BE QUICK, FOR THE LIGHT JUST CHANGED AND THE ROAD IS SLICK. (65%)

**July:** LAPWING; PLOVER; GREBE; CARDINAL (90%)

**August:** HOW'S YOUR MOM, TOM? WELL, APPARENTLY. Start at the top left. (70%)

**September:** Thirty percent found this square, while 65 percent came up with other solutions, including one which used the word *neve*, a type of granular snow.

$$\begin{array}{cccc} P & I & N & E \\ I & D & E & A \\ N & E & W & S \\ E & A & S & Y \end{array}$$

**October:** The missing number is 120. (70%)

**November:** PERSHING, FOCH, and CHURCHILL; BASTOGNE, YPRES, and EL ALAMEIN (60%)

**December:** Their sons were ten and fifteen. (75%)

## Day 12 of Each Month

**January:** CHEDDAR; ROQUEFORT; and LIMBURGER (100%)

**February:** You have twenty of each coin. (85%)

**March:** A bicycle costs $10.50 at this toy store. The owner charges $1.50 for each letter. (85%)

**April:** (50%)

$$
\begin{array}{r}
715 \\
46 \\
\hline
32890
\end{array}
$$

**May:** The most common word square, turned in by 75 percent of the Mensans, was:

$$
\begin{array}{cccc}
O & G & R & E \\
G & O & A & L \\
R & A & T & S \\
E & L & S & E
\end{array}
$$

**June:** Half a dozen dozen, if you like dimes. That's six dozen, while a dozen and a half is eighteen. It's not just six of one and half a dozen of the other. (96%)

**July:** $51.20. You've marked it down 20 percent each time. One Mensa member told me he'd never buy a TV that was baroque! (75%)

**August:** PARSLEY, SARDINE, SAUSAGE, and BARLEY (75%)

**September:** KEEPSAKE, PERISCOPE, EDITED, and EMBLEM (65%)

**October:** COLUMBUS (70%)

**November:** There are ten youngsters, each received $5.00, and this puzzle contains a great deal of extraneous information. (90%)

**December:** D is the missing letter. The words are DRAIN, NADIR, DINAR, DIARY, DAIRY, PALED, PLEAD, and PEDAL, in no particular order. (65%)

## Day 13 of Each Month

**January:** TEDIOUS and OUTSIDE are the missing words. (84%)

**February:** Jennifer is fifteen, in a system that awards five for each syllable. (75%)

**March:** Because the word *phobia* has Greek roots, you use Greek prefixes with it to make new words. AILUROPHOBIA (from the Greek *ailouros,* cat); XENOPHOBIA (from *xenos,* strange); and AGORAPHOBIA (from *agora,* open marketplace). (85%)

**April:** ACRES, CARES, RACES, and SCARE are the missing anagrams. (100%)

**May:** Eight. There were forty-eight states before Alaska, four winds blowing, forty thieves, and thirty-one days in May. (80%)

**June:** Cubes A and C cannot be made. This is a good test of your structural visualization skills. (75%)

**July:** "I LIKE THESE CHIPS," SAID TOM CRISPLY. Start with the middle letter in the top line. (90%)

**August:** DAWN, DARN, DARK, DIRK, DISK, DUSK is one route. (100%)

**September:** TRANSEPT; STEEPLEJACK; SEPARATE (100%)

**October:** Nine. Columbus sailed in 1492 with three ships in his fleet, and Mary married Henry VIII of England. (90%)

**November:** Sixty-six and forty-four (85%)

**December:** $5762.50 (85%)

## Day 14 of Each Month

**January:** FAIL, PAIL, PALL, PALS, PASS. There were several variations on this pattern, but 100 percent of the Mensa members found one that worked.

**February:** The same hour and forty minutes (90%)

**March:** RAISE and RAZE, which mean "to erect" and "to tear down." There were other suggestions, such as WHOLE and HOLE, but this is the only pair of homonyms we found with exactly opposite meanings. (40%)

**April:** Answer (b), 104 96, fits the two series involved, one starting up from 101, the other starting down from 99. (90%)

**May:** There are two ways you can have fifty coins totalling $1.00: two dimes, forty pennies, and eight nickels; or two dimes, forty-five pennies, two nickels, and one quarter. These arrangements are equally probable, so there is a one-half chance you had a quarter to begin with. The probability that you then dropped that quarter from all the coins in your hand is one fiftieth. Therefore, the total probability that you lost a quarter is one half times one fiftieth, or one one-hundredth. (15%)

**June:** Our ages now are seventy-three and thirty-seven. (75%)

**July:** Pierre started with $64. He spent $34 for the Sauternes (a real bargain), $18 for the foie gras (also cheap), and $10 for the special brioche customarily eaten with this combination of foods. That left $2.00 for the inevitable medication for the liver—Americans have heartburn, but the French have crises of the liver. (90%)

**August:** INAUGURATE; DAUGHTER; HAUGHTY; LAUGHED (95%)

**September:** He has bills worth $50, $20, $10, $5.00, $2.00, and $1.00. Most people forget about the Thomas Jefferson two-dollar bill, but it's still out there. (75%)

**October:** My friend the test pilot was named Susan. (65%)

**November:** (95%)

**December:** Twenty-four pieces of gum (90%)

## Day 15 of Each Month

**January:** The total for the top row of snowflakes is 91. (48%)

**February:** Samantha won. Just make a chart of all the information you have. (90%)

**March:** Seconds in 100 hours, by far: 360,000 seconds as against 3600 inches in 100 yards. (100%)

**April:** AN EFFICIENT BUSINESSWOMAN WHO FOUND A MACHINE THAT WOULD DO HALF HER WORK BOUGHT TWO. (90%)

**May:** "THERE IS NO WATER," SAID TOM DRYLY. (95%)

**June:** That she was lying. A Liar can't admit that he's a Liar, as she said she heard a man doing, because then he would be telling the truth about himself. The woman is either a Liar or, perhaps, an outsider like you. (85%)

**July:** RAIN is the missing word. July 15 is Saint Swithin's Day, and the story goes that if it rains on Saint Swithin's, it will rain for forty days thereafter. Conversely, if Saint Swithin's is dry, it will be fair for forty more days. Meteorological records don't bear out this tradition. (95%)

**August:** This puzzle was included in the belief that you wouldn't want to do anything more intellectually strenuous in August. (100%)

| H | T | E | A |
|---|---|---|---|
| A | E | T | H |
| T | H | A | E |
| E | A | H | T |

**September:** D is the missing letter. The words are DUNCE, CRUDE, DUCAT, CHARD, RADIO or DORIA, and DIVAN or VIAND. (75%)

**October:** There are several ways, but the most common was: A, RA, ARE, CARE, SCARE, CARESS, CASTERS. (90%)

**November:** He was Amy's brother-in-law—and the baby's uncle. (75%)

**December:** 13579 (80%)

### Day 16 of Each Month

**January:** The answer I originally thought up was:

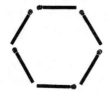

Twenty percent of Mensans replying to this question found that answer. But another 20 percent came up with:

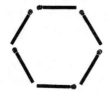

Take your pick.

**February:** KALE, LAKE, and LEAK (100%)

**March:** MADDER; MARKETPLACE; MEAGER (100%)

**April:** $60 (70%)

**May:** SCARE is the oddity. All the other words are anagrams of each other. (90%)

**June:** She lives at number 1640. (20%)

**July:** Sally (35%)

**August:** The knight will arrive at 12:45. The Princess might do better with someone who knows he shouldn't just average speed and distance. (75%)

**September:** A is 1, B is 2, and so on up to J is 0. Then the puzzle works out to $(123456789 \times 9) + 10 = 1111111111$. (45%)

**October:** The new price will be $102.90; the merchant reduced it 30 percent each time. (90%)

**November:** (80%)

```
S  O  L  E
O  P  E  N
L  E  A  D
E  N  D  S
```

**December:** Monday (95%)

## Day 17 of Each Month

**January:** HE WHO IS TOO SHARP SOMETIMES CUTS HIMSELF. The code is the alphabet reversed, so that Z becomes A, Y becomes B, and so on. (84%)

**February:** You made $15. Only 75 percent of the Mensa members got this one. Their most common error was not realizing that you have to treat each transaction separately. Then simply add up all the money laid out and all the money taken in. The fact that you bought the same lamp twice is irrelevant.

**March:**

| E | I | N | R |
|---|---|---|---|
| N | R | E | I |
| R | N | I | E |
| I | E | R | N |

This was the most common solution, though there are at least two more. (90%)

**April:** 26789 (95%)

**May:** WILL POWER: ADMIRABLE IN OURSELVES BUT PLAIN STUBBORNNESS WHEN WE FIND IT ELSEWHERE (55%)

**June:** EVE CALLED. APPLE SEASON OVER. WILL PEACHES BE OK? (65%)

**July:** 16. The middle figure is derived by adding the numbers in the surrounding circles and squaring the result. (80%)

**August:** IT IS MUCH TOO HOT TO DO THESE THINGS RIGHT NOW! The key is one to the left on a Qwerty typewriter. More relief from the August heat. (95%)

**September:** THE ONLY THING WORSE THAN NOT GETTING WHAT YOU WANT IS GETTING WHAT YOU WANT. (85%)

**October:** 5931 (95%)

**November:** GLOW, SLOW, SLOT, SOOT, FOOT, FORT, FORM, WORM. Other solutions used FOOD and FORD. (95%)

**December:** Jim's daughter is only six months old, and Jim is thirty and a half years old. If the baby were one year, Jim would have to be thirty, which is only twenty-nine years older. (75%)

## Day 18 of Each Month

**January:** Only 62 percent of the Mensans got all four examples correct, but 98 percent found two or more.

| 193 | 175 | 195 | 295 |
|-----|-----|-----|-----|
| 275 | 293 | 273 | 173 |
| 468 | 468 | 468 | 468 |

**February:** Mother, Mom, or whatever he called his mother (95%)

**March:** He is your father. (90%)

**April:** The bride was thirty, the groom twenty-seven. (55%)

**May:** He had twenty minutes. (50%)
The puzzles for May 17 and 18 marked a clear division between Mensans who are verbally inclined and those who are mathematically inclined. Those who succeeded with May 17 (55%) tended to get May 18 wrong (50%), and vice versa.

**June:** A plum is worth 4¢. The proprietor values one penny per letter, with any letter in a pair counted twice. (55%)

**July:** Twenty pounds (82%)

**August:** MANE, MEAN, AMEN, and NAME (95%)

**September:** DIRT, DINT, DENT, LENT, LEND, LEAD, LOAD, ROAD is the most common solution. (95%)

**October:** Sally (75%)

**November:** CLEVER (80%)

**December:** Two tosses of the 16-point ring and four tosses of the 17-point ring. Your aim is perfect, of course. (85%)

## Day 19 of Each Month

**January:** BRAID and RABID are the only two commonly accepted anagrams. (96%)

**February:** A COMMITTEE IS A GROUP THAT KEEPS MINUTES BUT WASTES HOURS. (65%)

**March:** FISSURE and FUSSIER; SUPREME and PRESUME; PRESENT, REPENTS, and SERPENT. (90%)

**April:** Twenty people split a $600 bill. (65%)

**May:** $20 (75%)

**June:** If you and your friend each have ten coins totaling 49¢, then they must be four pennies, three dimes, and three nickels. Between you, you have six dimes out of twenty coins. The chance is six out of twenty, or 30 percent. (65%)

**July:** The clock will be five minutes fast at sunset on the twenty-eighth day. Of course, it will lose time and become more correct during the night that follows, so it won't be five minutes fast at sunrise until the thirtieth day. Seventy-five percent of the Mensa members realized that the twenty-eighth day was correct, and one-third of those noted that the thirtieth day was also significant.

**August:** You can form the word COLD in twelve ways, though it won't make you any colder. (55%)

**September:** (90%)

```
L  I  K  E
I  D  E  A
K  E  P  T
E  A  T  S
```

**October:** The cleverest answer seems to be SCHEYE: SCH as in schism, and EYE as in eye. (95%)

**November:** Fifteen of each coin (90%)

**December:** GRASS, CRASS, CRESS, CREES, CREED, GREED, GREEN (95%)

## Day 20 of Each Month

**January:** You can't do it at all. For example, if your run is 6 miles, you would have to do it in one hour to average 6 miles per hour. However, you've already taken an hour to do the first half of the run, thereby using all the available time. (30%)

**February:** LUXEMBOURG, HUNGARY, and ARGENTINA (90%)

**March:** Sheree had $1.80 in play money, and Tyler had $1.40 (75%).

**April:** There were a good many answers that didn't fit the puzzle's criteria, such as PA, PAS, PASS, which uses slang. Only 25 percent of the Mensa members came up with good English words. CARE, CARES, CARESS was one common set; PRINCE, PRINCES, PRINCESS was another; and there are probably more.

**May:** THE ONLY DATA TO PROVE ME RIGHT / ARE THOSE I DID NOT SAVE. Start at the upper left corner. (60%)

**June:** Cristoforo was Isabella's grandfather and Ferdinand's grandfather-in-law. (95%)

**July:** JULIET; JONQUIL; JUBILANT (98%)

**August:** 20 (85%)

**September:** The word is MAR. (70%)

**October:** 161 large and 224 small sacks (70%)

**November:** Sally likes cheese because it has a double letter. (95%)

**December:** 108 (95%)

## Day 21 of Each Month

**January:** Jim was last. Just set up a chart of the runners. (100%)

**February:** The probability is 85 percent. There are only two ways in which fifty coins can total $1.00. One is forty-five pennies, two nickels, two dimes, and a quarter; the other is forty pennies, eight nickels, and two dimes. So there are eighty-five chances out of one hundred that the coin was a penny. (30%)

**March:** Six salesmen can sell sixty stoves in seventy minutes. (65%)

**April:** The missing letter is S. If you spiral clockwise around each square into the center, and then move on to the next square, you spell out THIS PUZZLE IS MADE OF SQUARES. (40%)

**May:** PORTFOLIO; PERSEVERE or PRESERVE (35%)

**June:** METHYLENE; DUNDERHEAD; DISSENSION (44%)

**July:** REPAPER; TUBE DEBUT (75%)

**August:** MONEY TALKS, BUT TO ME IT SAYS GOODBYE. Just substitute letters for their numerical place in the alphabet. (65%)

**September:** FALL (100%)

**October:** WAS IT A CAR OR A CAT I SAW? (75%)
NOT NEW YORK, ROY WENT ON. (65%)

**November:** Sixty-four (75%)

**December:** You have a paradox. No one who lies all the time can say he is a Liar. Therefore the man is not a Liar, though he is lying. You are outside Liars and Truthtellers Town at last. Forty-five percent of the Mensa members spotted the paradox.

## Day 22 of Each Month

**January:** You have twenty-four coins of each kind. (92%)

**February:** ROOSEVELT, TRUMAN, and KENNEDY; JOHNSON, TYLER, and JEFFERSON; TAFT, COOLIDGE, and WASHINGTON (100%)

**March:** Two pounds 4 ounces (or $2\frac{1}{4}$ pounds or 36 ounces). Three-fourths of three-fourths of a pound is 9 ounces, so the fish weighed 9 ounces plus the remaining three-fourths of its weight. Or, 9 ounces is one-quarter of its weight. (55%)

**April:** If you have good geographical knowledge, you found the word CORRECT after crossing out letters. (70%)

**May:** MADAME CURIE CALLED. SAID SHE WAS GETTING GLOWING REPORTS ON HER WORK. The substitution is the alphabet numbered backward. (90%)

**June:** Six of each coin. (95%)

**July:** Thirteen triangles (85%)

**August:** Abe had seven pennies and Lizzy thirteen. (75%)

**September:** There were six students. (90%)

**October:** Seventy-five percent of the Mensa members found at least one anti-magic square. Here's an example:

| 3 | 4 | 5 |
|---|---|---|
| 2 | 1 | 6 |
| 9 | 8 | 7 |

**November:** She said, "No." Furthermore, you know she is a Liar and her companion is a Truthteller. If they were both Liars, both Truthtellers, or she was a Truthteller and her companion a Liar, she would have answered, "Yes"—and you wouldn't have known whether she was lying. (45%)

**December:** No, you can't solve it. For topographical reasons, you will always miss one line segment. But there are some very creative ways to cheat!

## Day 23 of Each Month

**January:** MANILA; SCHUBERT; PASTEUR; NAPLES. VIKING cannot be anagrammed. Eighty-eight percent of the Mensans got this right; the name missed most was SCHUBERT.

**February:** Of the twelve pies, Sally must have brought three, Jane four, and Hector five. Dividing the meal evenly, they ate three pies apiece. That means William paid $3.00. Sally ate the three pies she brought (or their equivalent). Jane, who brought four, got $1.00 for the extra pie she contributed, and Hector, who brought five pies got $2.00. (45%)

**March:** RECIPE and PIERCE (95%)

**April:** CONSIDERATION (90%)

**May:** (65%)

$$
\begin{array}{r}
7142 \\
7142 \\
\underline{7142} \\
21426
\end{array}
$$

**June:** ADJUNCT; JUVENILE; JUNIPER; JOURNAL (95%)

**July:** Sally was short by 6.75 inches. She needed 180 inches, but the owner gave her only 165 plus 5 percent of that. (60%)

**August:** THE ONLY THING WORSE THAN A HUSBAND WHO NEVER NOTICES WHAT YOU COOK OR WHAT YOU WEAR IS A HUSBAND WHO ALWAYS NOTICES WHAT YOU COOK AND WHAT YOU WEAR. (90%)

**September:** CONNIVER (100%)

**October:** Tom was twenty, Professor Jones sixty-four. (65%)

**November:** $35.30 and $29.85 (75%)

**December:** Because my red-haired colleague is male.

## Day 24 of Each Month

**January:** ATE FETA; ELBA TABLE. Sixty percent had both right, and 80 percent had one (usually ELBA TABLE) right.

**February:** ANGEL, ANGLE, and GLEAN (100%)

**March:** BRAIN (75%)

**April:** TOO MANY BOOKS SPOIL THE CLOTH. Start at the upper left corner. (90%)

**May:** CHEER (95%)

**June:** This puzzle caused major problems when two eminent mathematicians came up with alternate answers! One had pairs of weights at 1, 4, 24, and 55 pounds. The other insisted equally vehemently that the weights were 1, 4, 16, and 64 pounds. Who was right? They both are! Only 40 percent of the Mensa members did this puzzle, and they split their votes between the two answers.

**July:** I'd save four hours, not counting recovery time. (90%)

**August:** PORTUGAL; DENMARK; ZAIRE (75%)

**September:** PLASTER and STAPLER (75%)

**October:** "Z" is the missing letter; the words are, clockwise from the top, WOOZY, GLAZE, LAZED, HAZEL, BRAZE, RAZES, DOZEN, and ZONED. (90%)

**November:** FIRST WE STUFF THE TURKEY; AND THEN WE STUFF OURSELVES. (90%)

**December:** My friend is too short to reach the button in the elevator for the fifteenth floor—he can reach only as high as ten. On the way down, the first-floor button is easy for him to reach.

## Day 25 of Each Month

**January:** CHINA; CANADA; PERU (100%)

**February:** DEB ABED; DELIA AND EDNA AILED. (95%)

**March:** It's now 1:00 A.M. (100%)

**April:** (40%)

$$
\begin{array}{r}
757 \\
757 \\
45 \\
\hline
1559
\end{array}
$$

**May:** Six. Each seamstress sews one seam in twenty minutes. (75%)

**June:** WETTISH and WHITEST are the only common English words Mensans could find. (90%)

**July:** ADMIRER and MARRIED (25%)

**August:** COURTS, because all the others are anagrams of each other (90%)

**September:** People who live in grass houses shouldn't stow thrones. (95%)

**October:** There were seven of them. (80%)

**November:** The watchman had been sleeping on the job. Otherwise, he wouldn't have been dreaming. (80%)

**December:** One hundred fifty minutes *is* two and a half hours.

# Day 26 of Each Month

**January:** Each little bag of chocolates cost 3¢. (80%)

**February:** PERMEATE, REHEARSE, TEENAGER, FORESEER (65%)

**March:** CATAMARAN, CALAMARI, and MARCHIONESS (90%)

**April:** The next day, or tomorrow (95%)

**May:** The missing letter is "Y." Clockwise from the top the words are: GUSHY, JOLLY, YAWED, WEARY, OXEYE, and YOUNG. (25%)

**June:** POLAND, CANADA, and INDIA are hidden in these sentences. (95%)

**July:** ABSTEMIOUS(LY), AERONAUTICS, FACETIOUS(LY), NEFARIOUS, PNEUMONIA, and SEQUOIA are the most common. One hundred percent of the Mensans polled thought of at least three, but only 40 percent found six.

**August:** ABSTEMIOUSLY; Sallie Lou likes to have all five vowels in her words. Some of her other favorites are listed in the July 26 answer above. (70%)

**September:** $81, left from an original $100 (75%)

**October:** $100 (90%)

**November:** You've lost 2 gallons, or 50 miles' worth of driving. Seventy percent of the Mensans got this right as far as the math was concerned, and there were some interesting but unprintable suggestions about what they'd say to the dealer who sold them that nice new car.

**December:** The oldest boy asked Daddy for another dollar, making $18. He took $9.00, gave the middle brother $6.00, and gave the baby $2.00. Then he returned the extra dollar to Daddy.

## Day 27 of Each Month

**January:** "THE TIME HAS COME," THE WALRUS SAID, / "TO TALK OF MANY THINGS: / OF SHOES—AND SHIPS—AND SEALING-WAX— / OF CABBAGES—AND KINGS." These immortal lines and many others came from the pen of Charles Dodgson. He achieved worldwide fame as children's author Lewis Carroll, but not as the logician he really was. There is a perhaps apocryphal story that Queen Victoria so enjoyed his *Through the Looking-Glass* that she asked him, as a favor, to send her his next book. Shortly thereafter, she received an abstruse mathematical text. She was not amused. (75%)

**February:** Because $6 = 3 \times 2$, then $6 \times 5 = (3 \times 2) \times 5 = 3 \times (2 \times 5)$. If "twice 5 is 9," according to the conditions of the problem, the answer is $3 \times 9 = 27$. This type of puzzle is often used to introduce students to the idea of base numbers other than 10. (80%)

**March:** PERSISTING is the only word we can find, and only 60 percent of the Mensans found it.

**April:** Dot likes a star. She only likes words that also spell words backward. (90%)

**May:** You had fifteen eggs to begin with. (85%)

**June:** Darlene likes 1600. She only likes perfect squares. (65%)

**July:** Fifty-seven. The forty-nine recycled from the original batch could be recycled themselves, and so on. (44%)

**August:** $16 (75%)

**September:** The trains are 40 miles apart. (85%)

**October:** Sheila had fifty-eight favors and planned to buy two more. (60%)

**November:** "WE'RE UNDER THE CHURCH," SAID TOM CRYPTICALLY. Start at the top left. (75%)

**December:** When we meet, we're the same distance from Boston.

## Day 28 of Each Month

**January:** A ROAD MAP TELLS YOU EVERYTHING EXCEPT HOW TO REFOLD IT. You start at the A in the middle of the array. (84%)

**February:** 2688 (100%)

**March:** COLD, CORD, WORD, WARD, WARM. One hundred percent of the Mensans who did this puzzle found either this solution or one which used WOLD.

**April:** (75%)

```
4  1  4
1     1
4  1  4
```

**May:** Yourself (90%)

**June:** If you want to be absolutely certain, you have to pick out eleven pieces of fruit. Your first ten might be five nectarines and five peaches, unlikely as that is. (95%)

**July:** There were several answers, but the square that 65 percent of the Mensans found was:

```
H  A  B  I  T
A  R  O  S  E
B  O  I  L  S
I  S  L  E  T
T  E  S  T  S
```

**August:** Jack is forty-seven, and John is forty-one. (75%)

**September:** The older one got 55¢, and the younger got 30¢. (95%)

**October:** WITCH (95%)

**November:** 1, 2, and 3 (90%)

**December:** Your aged grandmother is pulling your leg. Nineteen hundred was not a Leap Year under the Gregorian calendar since it was not divisible by 400. But the year 2000 will be.

# Day 29 of Each Month

**January:** SMART (90%)

**February:** Colonel Cholomondely-Snaithworth-Jones was lying, and the explorers knew it. There are no wild tigers at the headwaters of the Nile, or anywhere else in Africa. Liars like the colonel come along only once every four years. (95%)

**March:** The missing letter is A. The words are, reading clockwise from the two on top, AMPLE, MAPLE, AILED, IDEAL, DOGMA, DWARF, DAFFY, and LAXLY. Sixty-five percent of the Mensa members found these words, with LAXLY giving the most trouble.

**April:** APRICOT; CAPTURED; CAPRICORN (95%)

**May:** The correct response is (b), S G. The series are the alphabet forward from A, skipping two letters, and the alphabet backward from Y, skipping two letters. (90%)

**June:** BANALITIES (75%)

**July:** Friday (90%)

**August:** WARD, KEY, LOCK, and MILL are the four words. (95%)

**September:** They chewed twenty-four pieces. (60%)

**October:** Of the 90 percent who did this puzzle correctly, 50 percent came up with this solution.

M A N E
A M E N
N E E D
E N D S

**November:** DYNAMO; AWKWARD; SYZYGY. The most commonly missed word was SYZYGY, an astronomical conjunction. (75%)

**December:** There are twenty 9's, the first in 9 and the last two in 99.

## Day 30 of Each Month

**January:** Boxes A and D cannot be made from the unfolded box. A whopping 96 percent of the Mensa members answered this correctly; perhaps they cut out and folded the box.

**March:** No matter how many socks of a particular color there are, there are four different colors in the drawer. Your brother must take out five socks, or one more than there are colors, before he can be guaranteed a matching pair. (100%)

**April:** Maura started with $20. You work backward on these puzzles, starting with the fact that if half of what she has left plus $1.00 is all that she has, she must have $2.00 left. (65%)

**May:** There is no "E" at all in the paragraph. That's very uncommon, as "E" is the letter most used in English. (75%)

**June:** BOUQUET, BRIDESMAID, and VEIL; GROOM, RING, and HONEYMOON; MOTHER-IN-LAW, FLOWER GIRL, and WEDDING MARCH (95%)

**July:** For exactly 50¢, you can buy seven peanut butter cups and one chocolate bar. If you're a bargain hunter, you can also buy eight peanut butter cups for only 48¢. (50%)

**August:** 12643 (65%)

**September:** (85%)

| 0 | 12 | 12 | 0 |
|---|----|----|---|
| 8 | 4 | 4 | 8 |
| 4 | 8 | 8 | 4 |
| 12 | 0 | 0 | 12 |

**October:** One sister was allowed to cut the cake in two, and the other got first choice of the two pieces. (75%)

**November:** 4:00 P.M. (65%)

**December:** The amateur was swindled. No authentic coins are dated B.C., because no one knew then that the era would eventually be called B.C. In fact, "before" is an English word, and English hadn't been developed.

## Day 31 of Each Month

**January:** JACINTH; JANISSARY; JEFFERSONIAN (85%) (Many missed janissary.)

**March:** Tony likes tomatoes. He only likes words that start with prepositions. (65%)

**May:** MA IS AS SELFLESS AS I AM; RED RUM, SIR, IS MURDER. Ninety percent found the second palindrome, but only 30 percent solved the first.

**July:** (45%)

$$\begin{array}{r} 402 \\ \underline{39} \\ 15678 \end{array}$$

**August:** IT IS VERY HARD TO WIN AN ARGUMENT WHEN THE OTHER SIDE ISN'T BOTHERED BY TELLING UNTRUTHS. (35%)

**October:** There are four witches and twelve cats. (80%)

**December:** Joe was speaking on December 31, his birthday. He was twenty on December 30, turned twenty-one on December 31, and will be twenty-two next year on December 31. This puzzle was tested on a ninety-year-old woman neighbor, who saw it immediately.

# THE MENSA GENIUS
# A-B-C QUIZ BOOK

*Alan Stillson*
*and the Members of American Mensa, Ltd.*

To Gail and our ever-supportive extended family, including Jeff, Debi, Howard, Cedelle, Jill, Gary, Jack, Rose, Sharon, Steven, Helene, Jocelyn, Dave, and Sam

# Foreword

L ittle did the late Marvin Grosswirth and I know what we started when we created the first *Mensa Genius Quiz Book*. The "Match Wits with Mensa" feature fascinated hundreds of thousands of readers, and the book, first published in 1981, is still selling. Another two books followed, and now there is a fourth in the line of "Match Wits with Mensa." Hooray!

Alan Stillson, a member of Mensa and a wonderful puzzle expert, has written a book, similar in concept, but with entirely new puzzles, including several types of verbal puzzles never seen before (at least by me). He has matched Mensa members against his skill.

Mr. Stillson has also continued the tradition and original purpose of the Mensa books. A substantial portion of the royalties from this series goes toward

Mensa scholarships. Mensa scholarships were started in the early 1970s under the direction of Marvin Grosswirth, the organization's chairman at the time. They are unique. They are based, in general, not on financial need, nor academic achievement, nor I.Q. scores. They are based on commitment. Mensa commits its money; the applicants must commit themselves. Applicants at any level from college freshmen to postdoctoral students, working for a degree in an American-accredited institution of higher learning, submit a 550-word essay, which is judged anonymously. This essay must contain a statement of the applicant's life's goals and *what the applicant has done to achieve them*. A student who wants to be a doctor, cure cancer, and save lives won't get an award, but an applicant who has been a candy striper for five years, worked in a medical lab during school vacations, and done a small amount of research with the family doctor will score very high on the rating scale. That applicant has demonstrated a dedication and a purpose and has worked to achieve it. Part of the proceeds of Mr. Stillson's book will help to reward these serious, dedicated scholars.

Now a brief bit about Mensa, for those readers who are encountering this unique society for the first time. *Mensa*, which means "table" in Latin, was founded by Dr. L. L. Ware and the late Roland Berrill when they were at Oxford after World War II. It was originally thought of as a roundtable of equals, for serious intellectual discussions. Of course, the organization being what it is, the official logo is a SQUARE table. That's Mensa for you.

The society grew slowly in Great Britain. Roland Berrill died young, and for a long time, Mensa remained a purely British organization. Then, in 1960, Victor Serebriakoff, a bouncing, energetic go-getter, full of ideas, arrived in New York to start an American chapter. He eventually hired the late Margot Seitelman as executive director, and the American baby soon outgrew its parent. Mensa International also took off, and now there are several dozen recognized Mensas around the world, in Canada, France, Germany, Malaysia, Australia and New Zealand, and many other nations, and even more emerging Mensas, as they are called, in countries that were formerly in closed territory, such as Hungary, Slovakia, the Czech Republic, and more, some of which will be full-fledged operating Mensas by the time this book is published.

In short, the appeal of Mensa crosses all national boundaries, all ethnic and religious lines, and all geographical barriers. The idea is appealing—a worldwide society of equals, held together solely by the glue of intelligence and friendship—with no political agenda, no opinions, and no barriers. Mensa is one of the most democratic societies in the world. It has only one requirement: a score on a standardized, supervised intelligence test (or the equivalent) at or above the 98th percentile. In the United States that translates to a score of 132 on the Stanford-Binet and most school tests, 130 on the various Wechsler Intelligence Scales, and 148 on the Raven's Advanced Progressive Matrices. Mensa does much of its own testing, and, of course, has tests available that have been normed for other than a standard American, English-speaking population.

And just what does Mensa do? I can speak from experience here, having been a member for considerably more than thirty years. It has local chapters that run everything from dinner meetings, to great books discussions, to poker games, to what are called Regional Gatherings (a term taken from the British), where members of several local groups, and often from far away, join for several days of lectures, games, and above all, social interaction. The Annual Gathering can draw up to 1,500 members (and guests) from around the world. It is three or four days of interesting, amusing, informative lectures, games rooms, contests, and awards banquets for the volunteers who run Mensa, which has a paid staff of only a dozen. The volunteers are what makes Mensa so fascinating. They tend to have their own ideas and, being volunteers, feel free to express them. Many of our best and most interesting events have come about because volunteers were willing to work to put on an event they thought would be interesting.

A significant attraction in Mensa is its Special Interest Groups. These range from quilting to wine-making, and everything in between. As a Mensa member, if you don't find a Special Interest Group that matches your special interest, you can go out and start one, subject to the rules governing such groups. The

Special Interest Groups operate basically by mail, publish newsletters, and provide a part of the colorful fabric that makes up the Mensa patchwork.

Finally, there is the Mensa Education and Research Foundation. This separate 501(c)3 entity, known as MERF, awards the scholarships. It also sponsors research grants, gifted-children projects, and other educational and charitable activities, in accordance with its charter, which basically states that it should help to foster intelligence.

In short, whatever you are looking for, if you qualify for Mensa, you'll probably find it somewhere under the Mensa umbrella. With members ranging from truck drivers to nuclear engineers, look and you will find.

Marvin and I had fun writing the first and second books. I had fun doing the third. Readers apparently had fun reading them and matching their wits against those of the Mensas who participated. Now you have a chance to join the group of happy puzzle solvers, match your wits against those of the top 2 percent, and—who knows?—perhaps even decide to join the group.

Happy puzzle solving!

*—Abbie F. Salny*

# Introduction

*Bach, Mozart, and Beethoven are to music*
*as*
*Carroll, Dudeney, and Loyd are to...?*

The answer is "puzzles." Lewis Carroll, Henry Dudeney, and Sam Loyd drew on an art form that had been around for centuries and refined it, creating masterpieces that we recognize as both modern and timeless. They were prolific puzzle makers, and they inspired all of us who followed.

Lewis Carroll, whose real name was Charles Dodgson, was an English mathematics professor who lived from 1832 to 1898. He wrote thousands of original puzzles in and beyond his classic children's books,

477

*Alice in Wonderland* and *Through the Looking-Glass.* Carroll specialized in logic problems, wordplay, and a form he called doublets, which ask us to form a chain from one word to another, changing one letter at a time. Henry Dudeney, another English giant in this field, lived from 1857 to 1930. He wrote *Amusements in Mathematics* and published a wide assortment of mathematics puzzles, chess problems, and word games. Sam Loyd, an American who lived from 1841 to 1911, compiled his many brainteasers into *Sam Loyd's Cyclopedia of 5,000 Puzzles, Tricks and Conundrums.*

One trait that united these modern puzzle masters was their love of language, in all its forms. But all humans love language games to some extent. Wordplay has been around nearly as long as words have. For centuries Japanese poets have composed haiku, a term formed from two Chinese characters that mean "playful phrases." When Julius Caesar reportedly said of Gaul, *"Veni, vidi, vici,"* he was playing on the alliteration of "I came, I saw, I conquered" in Latin. Even the ancient riddle of the Sphinx—"What walks on four feet in the morning, two feet at noon, and three feet in the evening?"—requires us to consider what words can mean metaphorically. Carroll, Dudeney, and Loyd had millennia of wordplay to build on.

That tradition has continued to develop. The twentieth century has seen the invention of the crossword puzzle (designed in quite different forms around the world). In the 1950s and 1960s, more notable creators emerged. Martin Gardner wrote many puzzle books as well as a long-running monthly column for *Scientific American.* Publisher and game-show panelist Bennett Cerf wrote numerous books on riddles and wordplay. Before he became famous for popularizing jogging, Mensa member Jim Fixx wrote *Games for the Superintelligent.* Today such authors as Paul Sloan (*Lateral Thinking*), Helen Nash (*Cryptograms*), Will Shortz (crossword puzzle editor of the *New York Times* and former editor of *Games* magazine), and Abbie Salny (American Mensa's Supervisory Psychologist) carry on this long tradition.

Why have we humans always asked riddles, worked out puns, and wracked our brains over questions we knew would turn out to be tricks? The clinical psychiatrist's answer may be complicated, but the puzzle lover's answer is simple: they're fun.

What a great feeling it is to figure out a riddle, to spot a pun, to find the eight letters that spell out "a large water-loving rodent" (capybara)! Whatever form the puzzles take, the joy of working on them is the joy of figuring something out. And it's especially fun to figure out something about words, those little collections of symbols or sounds that we depend on every day.

In today's busy world, the potential pleasure of solving a time-consuming puzzle is often lost to other demands. That's why this book is designed so that you can enjoy one puzzle at a time, or as many as you want to do. Most of the word games in this book can be completed in less than a minute—either you'll figure one out or you'll figure out that you won't figure it out without some library work. Only a few require writing anything down. Yes, it's possible to experience the joy of puzzles when you want and in as little or as much time as you choose.

When you're ready to look at the answer to a particular puzzle, look for the dark patch on the outside of the page. Match that patch to the corresponding dark patch in the Solutions (riffle the side of the book if you have to). The numbers on the sides of the pages will guide you to the correct answer. Try not to peek at the others!

For further pleasure, this book also gives you an opportunity to "Match Wits with Mensa." Each of these puzzles has been tested by a panel of brave volunteers from American Mensa, Ltd., as the next section explains in detail.

Just as some words have two meanings, some of these puzzles have two or more valid answers, listed in the Solutions. Give yourself full credit if you come up with any of them. When two or more members of the Mensa testing panel suggested the same wrong answer, I mentioned it in the Solutions as well—under "not"! You may not be able to give yourself credit for those answers, but at least you can tell yourself that you're thinking like a Mensa member.

Finally, it's quite possible that you might discover an alternative answer not mentioned in the Solutions. Check your sources to be sure you're right. Then give yourself extra credit!

This is a puzzle book, not a scientific test. If you

want to track your results against the testing panel, go ahead. If you don't want to, don't. Puzzle books are for fun. Doing well doesn't guarantee success in anything else, and doing not so well (whatever that means to you) is no sure sign of trouble where "gray matter" matters. The one conclusion that you can draw is that it takes a hefty combination of word power, imagination, and general knowledge to score at least 55 percent in this puzzle book.

Stumped? Remember that words have many facets. They have shapes, sounds, grammar, meanings, histories, contexts, and ingredients. Here are fifteen hints of where to probe for a breakthrough:

**1.** Look for words or expressions with more than one meaning.

**2.** Count letters, syllables, and so on.

**3.** Consider pronunciation and sounds.

**4.** Check alphabetical order.

**5.** Play with letters: reverse them, add new ones, delete some.

**6.** Look for words within words.

**7.** Spot common or unusual letter combinations.

**8.** Consider key words and phrases.

**9.** Review parts of speech.

**10.** Notice uncommon sentence structure and grammar.

**11.** Beware of simplicity disguised as complexity.

**12.** Don't forget common names, brand names, abbreviations, and colloquialisms.

**13.** Review your knowledge of popular culture, sports, and hobbies.

**14.** Consider your practical, academic, and artistic knowledge.

**15.** Finally, remember that puzzle-makers enjoy sharing imaginative uses of words and phrases.

# The "Match Wits with Mensa" Panel

All of the puzzles in this book were tested by 104 Mensa members selected on the basis of just one quality—their willingness to participate. The panel included students, professors, doctors, lawyers, and retirees. Members' ages ranged from the teens to over seventy. Some testers had published puzzles in magazines, others had served on the testing panels for previous books in this series, and for some English was a second language.

To the panel members I mailed all the puzzles in this book (and a few more). They responded within two weeks, answering as many puzzles as they could in that time. I then calculated the percentage of testers who answered each question correctly, rounding off to the nearest 5 percent. That figure appears in parentheses with the answer to each puzzle. A small percentage—as low as 5 percent—indicates that the puzzle was especially difficult even for Mensa volunteers.

For each section of the book, you'll see the average score of the Mensa testing panel on that set of puzzles. Naturally, that score varies depending on the difficulty of the puzzles and the amount of general knowledge they test. Overall, the Mensa volunteers answered an average of 55 percent of the puzzles in this book correctly. So let that percentage be your benchmark as you "Match Wits with Mensa"!

My first round of thanks goes to the leaders of the Greater Los Angeles Mensa writers' group for inspiration and valuable critiques: Marty Elkort, Jerry Hicks, and Sonny Cooper.

The next round of thanks goes to members of Greater Los Angeles Mensa for preliminary puzzle testing and initial editing: Roy Ball, Jana Bickell, Rhonda Byer, Andy Cohen, Flo Cohen, Joy Gaylord, Barbara Harvey, Victor Huang, Gloria Krauss, Stratton Lindemeyer, Mirk Mirkin, Kathryn Morrison, Ken Rosenchek, and Betty Schneider.

And the last round of thanks goes to 104 additional members of American Mensa for puzzle testing and further editing: Marion Alpern (IN), Damon Antos (FL), Daniel Babcock (MO), Rod Baker (CA),

Stephen H. Bauer (OR), Wendy Bell (TN), Nancy Beringer (NH), Ginni Betts (IL), John H. Bickford (MA), George Blance (MA), David Broome (AZ), Lois Cappellano (MA), Paul Conover (PA), Kimberly A. Cope (MN), Lois Corsello (CA), Karen Darmetko (FL), Maryann Donovan (CA), Nancy Eisenmann (CT), Ted Elzinga (CA), Mary Ensley (AL), Dara Esfandiary (DC), Thomas L. Fagan (PA), Bill Fisher (IN), Rita Foudray (TX), Peter Fuchs (NC), Thomas G. Funk (AL), Barney Gallussio (NJ), Bonita M. Garvey (FL), Esther Gottlieb (NY), David N. Groff (PA), Thomas Gunning III (TX), Kent B. Hake (IL), Charles Hall (IN), Monroe Harden (KY), Megan Heber (OH), John T. Henderson (FL), Maynard J. Hirshon (FL), Amy Holm (AZ), Emily Hsuan (CA), Jane Hsuan (CA), Karl Kabanek (TX), David P. Keeser (WA), Charles Keifer (MA), Amy Kent (PA), Steve Krattiger (CA), Linda Kriegel (NJ), Carol Kuhns (OH), Nancy Laine (OH), Larry Larson (OR), Steve Latterell (IL), Richard A. LeCain (NH), David Leith (TX), David Linko (PA), Richard Loeffler (WI), Susan Macke (KS), Michael W. Maher (MI), Jennifer Martin (CA), Celia Manolesco (CA), Douglas G. May (WA), Mike Mayer (OH), Palmer McCurdy (VA), Alan T. McDonald (VA), John Mochan (FL), James J. Murphy (NY), Kevin Murray (FL), Sastry Nanduri (NJ), Sandra J. Nelson (IA), Dawn Novak (AR), Shane J. Orr (IA), Chuck Osborne (IL), Shawn Otto (MN), Tony Parillo (CA), G. Vaughan Parker (CA), Jeffrey L. Peace (OH), Rena Popna (NH), Thomas W. Reeves (TX), David F. Ries (MA), Bob

Roach (MN), Elizabeth Roberts (WA), Guy Rosenschein (NY), Brad Sanford (TN), Rorianne Schrade (NY), Larry Schwartz (CT), Lisa Schwartz (VA), Harold C. Sebring (VA), Jim Segerson (WI), Jason Sharpe (TX), Wm. Sheehan (MA), Scott Sheldon (NJ), Joseph A. Spadero (CT), Gene Staver (WI), David Steinberg (VA), Steve Story (FL), John Suarez (CA), Steve Swiader (RI), Greg Taylor (OH), Richard Till (IA), Heidi Van Ert (UT), Deborah Vernier (NV), Paul Westley (UK), Chuck Wiese (IA), Jefferson Wolski (TN), Rachel Young (MI), and Matt Zimmermann (KS).

# chapter 1

# No-Pencil Quickies

## LIMERICKS

For those who like puzzles in verse, a limerick may be too terse. Just five lines of clues yield few answers to choose from; only a haiku is worse. Here's one example of a limerick puzzle:

> Penning works that were fit for a king,
> I created the world's longest ring.
> You will need at least four
> Lengthy evenings or more
> If you want to take in the whole thing.

The answer is "Richard Wagner," the composer of *The Ring of the Nibelung,* a cycle of four full-length operas (literally "works").

The answers to the following puzzles can be people, things, places, words, or abstract nouns. Can you name the subject of each of the following limericks?

(The average score of the Mensa testing panel on these poetic puzzles was 65 percent.)

# 1

I'm amazing 'cause I've got the force
To hold down a cow or a horse.
As you've doubtlessly found,
I am always around,
And I'm constantly working, of course.

# 2

I knew who I was long ago,
Though no one today seems to know.
Every year, millions cry
At the grave where I lie,
In the sunshine, the rain, and the snow.

# 3

On the charts, I remain number one;
This position cannot be undone.
If I burn, you may get
Just a little bit wet.
In a zeppelin, I am no fun.

# 4

Though in theory I'm always behind you,
I'm also around to remind you.
But in case it's your way
To give me too much say,
I can hamper or, even worse, blind you.

# 5

I'm a unit of heat generation.
I am prone to great quantification.
There are many aware
Of the numbers I bear—
Some in triumph, and some in frustration.

# 6

A metropolis in the U.S.,
I hold millions of people, no less.
But if you were to be
Just a mile south of me,
Would that put you in Canada? Yes!

# 7

I am just a small letter, you see,
As irrational as I can be.
Though it sounds quite insane,
When I'm cubed, you'll obtain
The negative of little me.

# 8

As a worker, I'm earning my pay.
When I hear what the first people say,
Then I change every word
So the things that are heard
By the others can help make their day.

# 9

There are times I'm a spot or a grade
Or a strike or a spare that was made;
I have also gained fame
As a masculine name
And a person on whom tricks are played.

# FLOWERY MOVIE TITLES

Sometimes people with large vocabularies use unnecessarily flowery language. Sometimes even Mensa members do! For example, the title of not one but two Alfred Hitchcock thrillers could have been "The Male Homo Sapiens with an Overabundance of Accumulated Data." Fortunately, the title he used for both versions of this classic was *The Man Who Knew Too Much.*

What were the original names behind the following florid movie titles?

(The "Match Wits with Mensa" panel scored an average of 65 percent on these puzzles.)

## 1
### GREETINGS, HANDTRUCK

## 2
### TAURUS THROWING A TANTRUM

## 3
### OCCIDENTALLY LOCATED NARRATIVE

# 4
## THE GARGANTUAN FACILE

# 5
## SOLAR SATELLITE OF THE MEMBERS OF THE PONGIDAE FAMILY

# 6
## DISTANCE DIVIDED BY TIME

# 7
## OBLITERATED FROM EXISTENCE IN CONJUNCTION WITH ATMOSPHERIC VAPORS IN MOTION

# 8
## DEPARTING FROM THE MOST POPULOUS METROPOLITAN AREA OF THE SILVER STATE

## STRANGE QUESTIONS

Here's a classic puzzle that ends with an unexpected question:

> A bear walks ten miles due south, ten miles east, and ten miles north, ending up on the spot where it started. What color was the bear?

The answer is white. And the reason is that there are very few places on the globe where one can take that walk and end up in the same place—all of them on or near the North Pole or near the South Pole. Since there are no bears on Antarctica, and the only bears in the Arctic are polar bears, this bear has to be white.

Here are some new puzzles with equally strange questions at the ends.

(The Mensa testers answered 55 percent of these puzzles correctly on average.)

# 1 The Missing Cards

Eight cards were missing from a standard poker deck with no jokers, making it impossible to get a straight flush. Which cards were missing?

## 2 The Basketball Team

Avery, Jones, Robinson, Kucic, and Himmel-farb are the starting players on the college basketball team. Avery, who wears jersey number 30, told number 45, Jones, that Robinson was the mean one. Kucic, who wears number 35, told Himmelfarb that Avery was absolutely right. But Robinson, number 40, is even-tempered and kind to everybody. What number is on Himmel-farb's jersey?

## 3 The Emergency Call

Halfway through the season, Kucic the bas-ketball player was hurried into the largest hospital in Lexington, Kentucky. The admit-ting nurse called Dr. Masterson's emergency beeper. In five minutes Dr. Masterson called back. The nurse explained the emergency and asked, "Where are you?"

"We're in the middle of Gary, Indiana," she heard the doctor say.

"How long will it take you to get here?"

"Two minutes."

What was Dr. Masterson doing when she received the emergency call?

## 4 The Cause of Hospitalization

Kucic's mother received a call from the college basketball coach. "I'm sorry, Mrs. Kucic," the coach said, "but during our Kentucky game your son had to be taken to the hospital. Don't worry, I understand it's the largest—"

"What's wrong?" Mrs. Kucic wailed.

The coach's reply echoed in her mind: "I'm afraid the booze got to him.... I'm afraid the booze got to him." Mrs. Kucic was too shocked to hear anything else. Her son had never drunk alcohol before going to college. And the coach had assured her that the campus had strict rules against underage drinking.

In fact, Kucic was not drunk and was not injured. What had caused his hospitalization?

## 5 The Violin Lesson

During Santiago's violin lesson, Professor Arion suddenly said, "You really should play piano."

Santiago kept on playing the violin.

Finally, Professor Arion clapped his hands and said, "Good!"

What change had Santiago made in his violin playing?

## 6 The Football Game

Andy and Mike, who live in the bay area, had a busy Sunday. They drove 20 miles west and went to the 49ers game in the afternoon. Then they drove about 120 miles nearly due east to their favorite seafood restaurant and had dinner overlooking the ocean. Whom did the 49ers play?

## 7 The Jumpy Pilot

The airline pilot Captain King has stopped going to the employees' lounge at the airport. Whenever he entered, his colleagues would call out informal greetings, naturally upsetting everyone else in the room. It didn't matter whether they called to him with just his first name or his full name—he was still causing too many scares. What is Captain King's first name?

## 8 The Transfer Student

After Elspeth Peters's family moved from Leeds to Phoenix, she had to take a placement exam for her new high school. Her best subject, she knew, was chemistry. And, indeed, her science teacher congratulated her on scoring 99 percent.

"How can that be?" Elspeth asked. "The test asked me to identify elements from their chemical symbols. There were only ten questions!"

"And you did very well," said the science teacher, "but I had to take off one point for spelling."

What element had tripped up this exemplary chemistry student?

## 9 The Active Activist

After two years, Tom Antonucci was stepping down from being the secretary of a group of animal rights activists. To show him a good time, some of the members took him out one sunny day. Tom shot an eagle, and everyone congratulated him. Where had they gone?

## 10 The Repeat Customer

John Travis was a man of habits, even when he was traveling. From January to December 1997, no matter what American city he was in, he made the same $3.84 purchase with a $5.00 bill and received back the same four coins. What did he buy?

# ABBREVIATIONS

Every field must have its own abbreviations. For instance, Mensa is full of SIGs (Special Interest Groups). On the back of this book you'll find its ISBN (International Standard Book Number).

Abbreviations can become complicated when several are used together. For example, a trucker going from Los Angeles to Phoenix, Tucson, El Paso, and San Antonio might note her route as LA/PHX/TUC/EP/SA. A baseball coach might use P, C, 1B, 2B, 3B, SS, LF, CF, RF for the fielding positions of pitcher, catcher, first base, second base, third base, shortstop, left field, center field, and right field.

What do the following lists of abbreviations mean?

(The "Match Wits with Mensa" panel scored 65 percent on this section. Like them, for your answer you can identify most of the abbreviated items, state the underlying reasoning, or both.)

# 1

## ARI, ALG, GEO, TRI, PRO, STA, CAL

## 2

COM, DRA, ADV, ACT, SPO, MUS, HOR, SCI

## 3

VLN, VLA, CEL, BA, TRU, TRO, FH

## 4

SON, SAM, MIT, GOL, TOS, PAN, ZEN, QUA

## 5

CEL, KNI, BUL, ROC, CAV, JAZ, LAK

## 6

LGA, LAX, SFO, DAL, SEA, MIA, DET

## 7

YOS, YEL, OLY, GLA, CAR, MAM, EVE, SHE

## 8

FIR, GDY, DUN, GDR, MIC, KEL, UNI

## FLOWERY SONG TITLES

In theory, flowery language is just right for songs. When Fats Waller sang, "Your pedal extremities are colossal," didn't that sound better than that song's synonymous title: "Your Feet's Too Big"? Unfortunately, extraneous verbiage can be burdensome to articulate. Try crooning "Planet Satellite Riparian Entity" instead of "Moon River."

What were the original names of the following flowery song titles? (Hint: each came from, or is strongly associated with, a movie.)

(The Mensa puzzle testers correctly transposed 65 percent of these songs.)

# 1

*Individual components of liquid precipitation are relentlessly descending upon this individual's cranium*

# 2

*Elevated aspirations*

# 3

*The moment within the continuum of time in which you relate a personal desire to the center of a group of planets*

# 4

*Coincident with the passage of the ratio of distance to velocity*

# 5

*A 1,440-minute interval exists in which my monarch's male offspring will arrive*

# 6

*Exhale with an audible sound of controllable pitch in the process of performing labor*

# 7

*Above the natural spectrum following liquid precipitation*

# 8

*Permit us to exit to aviate a quadrilateral all of whose sides are equal to one adjacent side and unequal to another and with perpendicular diagonals*

# 9

*Homo sapiens preceded with commercially acceptable mixtures typically consisting of sucrose, pectin, and numerous combinations of edible stimulants*

# 10

*The universal set of humans is verbalizing*

# THREEESQUES

As of this writing, there are no English words in the dictionary containing consecutive triple letters. But we could make up some. If an ornament using classical Arabic motifs is an "arabesque," then a word using a triple motif could be a "threeesque." If something easy to loathe is "loathsome," something easy to iron could be "presssome." And what would a male calf be? If a baby pig is a "piglet," a baby bull would be a "bulllet." Who knows? One day these threeesques might be in the dictionary.

Using similar reasoning and lots of imagination, what words with consecutive triple letters could you make up to fit the following definitions?

(Members of the Mensa testing panel averaged 55 percent on these threeesques. But between them they found at least two new words for every definition below. For full credit, all you have to find is one.)

## 1

**THE OWNER OF A PASSAGEWAY IN A BUILDING**

## 2

**A CHART OF CHICKEN PRODUCTIVITY**

# 3

## A FAIRY-TALE EXPERT

# 4

## A SERIOUS CLIMBER OF LOW HILLS

# 5

## THE STUDY OF THE LARGEST MARSUPIALS

# 6

## A PLACE TO MAKE MISTAKES

# 7

## THE LONGEVITY OF A LIGHT BULB

# 8

## AN ECCENTRIC GAUGE

# chapter
# 2

# Commoner Puzzles

Commoner puzzles are made up of two columns with
five things (words, names, and places) in each. The goal
is to find what all the things in Column A have in common that none of the things in Column B shares as
well. Here are two examples:

| COLUMN A | COLUMN B |
|----------|----------|
| Allegiance | Practical |
| Flag | Yard |
| Of | Drum |
| Republic | Patriotic |
| Stand | Sit |

*Solution:* All the words in Column A are in the "Pledge
of Allegiance."

| COLUMN A | COLUMN B |
|----------|----------|
| Hammer | Porter |
| Soothe | Hardly |
| Spleen | Kidney |
| Attend | Cleric |
| Stress | Murmur |

*Solution:* All the words in Column A have a consecutive double letter.

# MISCELLANY

(The Mensa panel solved 45 percent of these commoner puzzles on average.)

## 1

| COLUMN A | COLUMN B |
| --- | --- |
| Mud | Flour |
| Lemonade | Glass |
| Cement | Steel |
| Tea | Onyx |
| Coffee | Oxygen |

## 2

| COLUMN A | COLUMN B |
| --- | --- |
| Lime | Pear |
| Apple | Plum |
| Pineapple | Lemon |
| Cantaloupe | Honeydew |
| Orange | Fig |

# 3

| COLUMN A | COLUMN B |
| --- | --- |
| Lung | Pillow |
| Cast | Drip |
| Horse | Oat |
| Maiden | Jump |
| Grid | Loud |

# 4

| COLUMN A | COLUMN B |
| --- | --- |
| Birds | Salesmen |
| Rings | Lions |
| Lords | Carpenters |
| Maids | Skunks |
| Hens | Surfers |

# 5

| COLUMN A | COLUMN B |
| --- | --- |
| Bear | Lion |
| Grouse | Alligator |
| Carp | Moth |
| Fly | Dolphin |
| Duck | Cougar |

# 6

| COLUMN A | COLUMN B |
|----------|----------|
| Mercury | Aluminum |
| Gold | Magnesium |
| Iron | Phosphorus |
| Potassium | Sulphur |
| Lead | Chromium |

# 7

| COLUMN A | COLUMN B |
|----------|----------|
| Friend | Club |
| Hard | Barn |
| Owner | Please |
| Steam | Circle |
| Court | Enough |

# 8

| COLUMN A | COLUMN B |
|----------|----------|
| Dialogue | Borderline |
| Education | Oxygen |
| Facetious | Biological |
| Outpatient | Questionable |
| Regulation | Chop |

# 9

| COLUMN A | COLUMN B |
|----------|----------|
| Gifts | Plane |
| Down | Oak |
| Resemblance | Sure |
| Pain | Shy |
| Grudge | Blue |

# 10

| COLUMN A | COLUMN B |
|----------|----------|
| Kangaroo | Deer |
| Chimpanzee | Orangutan |
| Boa | Crocodile |
| Flea | Elephant |
| Caribou | Flamingo |

# 11

| COLUMN A | COLUMN B |
|----------|----------|
| Junk | Peck |
| Blank | Speak |
| Cask | Flank |
| Sock | Work |
| Mark | Truck |

# 12

| COLUMN A | COLUMN B |
|----------|----------|
| Fig | Crane |
| Case | Sprig |
| Ease | Oar |
| Pig | Vase |
| Base | Blind |

# 13

| COLUMN A | COLUMN B |
|----------|----------|
| Unique | Placid |
| Piccolo | Chart |
| Shock | Indict |
| Kindle | Moderate |
| Because | Cipher |

# 14

| COLUMN A | COLUMN B |
|----------|----------|
| Astronomical | Lack |
| Raze | Portable |
| Ape | Rocket |
| Loom | Usual |
| Listening | Atom |

# 15

| COLUMN A | COLUMN B |
|----------|----------|
| Facts | Trump |
| Boiled | Read |
| Ware | Yard |
| Knocks | And |
| Pressed | Breadth |

# SAME-SIZE WORDS

In these commoner puzzles, every word in both columns is the same length—but what do the words in Column A share that the words in Column B lack?

(The "Match Wits with Mensa" panel managed to answer only 30 percent of these commoners.)

## 1

| COLUMN A | COLUMN B |
| --- | --- |
| Elite | Earth |
| Tempt | Tutor |
| Civic | Puppy |
| Label | Style |
| Hatch | Melts |

## 2

| COLUMN A | COLUMN B |
| --- | --- |
| Banana | Babble |
| Needed | Chimes |
| Horror | Tatter |
| Inning | Sorrow |
| Pepper | Murmur |

# 3

| COLUMN A | COLUMN B |
|----------|----------|
| Men | Fly |
| Ban | Son |
| Ice | The |
| War | Map |
| See | Oar |

# 4

| COLUMN A | COLUMN B |
|----------|----------|
| Pea | Wee |
| Why | Say |
| Cue | Toy |
| Sea | New |
| Owe | Cow |

# 5

| COLUMN A | COLUMN B |
|----------|----------|
| Bold | Flaw |
| Able | Gulf |
| Warm | They |
| Cold | Hike |
| Full | When |

# 6

| COLUMN A | COLUMN B |
|---|---|
| Emit | Lamp |
| Garb | Idea |
| Loop | Cool |
| Trap | Grow |
| Draw | Them |

# 7

| COLUMN A | COLUMN B |
|---|---|
| Cute | Fool |
| Side | Wide |
| Wash | Bond |
| Mass | Clap |
| Corn | Stun |

# 8

| COLUMN A | COLUMN B |
|---|---|
| Are | Act |
| Lay | Big |
| Hop | Urn |
| One | Leg |
| Ape | Sew |

# 9

| COLUMN A | COLUMN B |
| --- | --- |
| Gavel | Label |
| Petty | Blown |
| Diver | Pesky |
| Fight | Alone |
| Towel | Magic |

# 10

| COLUMN A | COLUMN B |
| --- | --- |
| Arch | Page |
| Care | Itch |
| Peal | Very |
| Many | Star |
| Kite | Brim |

# 11

| COLUMN A | COLUMN B |
| --- | --- |
| Hot | Era |
| Air | Get |
| Dip | Toy |
| Pry | Red |
| For | Arm |

## 12

| COLUMN A | COLUMN B |
|----------|----------|
| Proven | Gather |
| Loathe | Quiver |
| Stripe | Misery |
| Sacred | Octave |
| Fringe | Rounds |

## 13

| COLUMN A | COLUMN B |
|----------|----------|
| Cape | Claw |
| Chew | Curb |
| Crow | Fold |
| Teem | Used |
| Says | Mild |

## 14

| COLUMN A | COLUMN B |
|----------|----------|
| Flue | Mole |
| Flea | Feel |
| Coat | Evil |
| Crud | Sort |
| Flap | Nose |

# 15

| COLUMN A | COLUMN B |
|----------|----------|
| Real | Gold |
| Hare | Blue |
| Char | Port |
| Spas | Idol |
| Mode | Cats |

## NAMES AND PLACES

These commoner puzzles use the names of specific people, places, brands, and breeds. As you look for what the things in Column A share, look not just at spelling and pronunciation but also at the specifics of those people, places, brands, and breeds.

(The Mensa puzzle testers pulled in an average score of 40 percent on this section.)

# 1

| COLUMN A | COLUMN B |
| --- | --- |
| Empire State Building | Disneyland |
| Baseball Hall of Fame | White House |
| Central Park | Everglades |
| Niagara Falls | Alamo |
| Statue of Liberty | Yellowstone Park |

# 2

| COLUMN A | COLUMN B |
| --- | --- |
| Mercedes-Benz | Chevrolet |
| Volvo | Toyota |
| Renault | Hyundai |
| Volkswagen | Plymouth |
| Rolls-Royce | Subaru |

# 3

| COLUMN A | COLUMN B |
|---|---|
| German shepherd | Greyhound |
| Golden retriever | Bloodhound |
| Norwegian elkhound | Chihuahua |
| Toy poodle | Husky |
| Irish setter | Pug |

# 4

| COLUMN A | COLUMN B |
|---|---|
| The Beatles | The Supremes |
| The Monkees | The Rolling Stones |
| The Shirelles | The Beach Boys |
| Creedence Clearwater Revival | The Platters |
| The Doors | Peter, Paul, and Mary |

# 5

| COLUMN A | COLUMN B |
|---|---|
| "Some Enchanted Evening" | "If Ever I Would Leave You" |
| "Oklahoma" | "Hey There" |
| "Do-Re-Mi" | "Maria" |
| "If I Loved You" | "What I Did for Love" |
| "Shall We Dance" | "Old Man River" |

# 6

**COLUMN A**
"I Walk the Line"
"Rocky Mountain
  High"
"Imagine"
"Chances Are"
"Battle of New
  Orleans"

**COLUMN B**
"Strangers in the Night"
"I Left My Heart in San
  Francisco"
"The Twist"
"Love Me Tender"
"The Gambler"

# 7

**COLUMN A**
Swedish
Hebrew
Japanese
Tagalog
Hungarian

**COLUMN B**
French
Arabic
Portuguese
English
Spanish

# 8

**COLUMN A**
"Que Sera Sera"
"I'm Sorry"
"Walk on By"
"People"
"Where the Boys Are"

**COLUMN B**
"Johnny B. Goode"
"Diana"
"Blue Velvet"
"Welcome to My
  World"
"Mona Lisa"

## 9

| COLUMN A | COLUMN B |
|---|---|
| Cubs | Twins |
| Red Sox | Panthers |
| Red Wings | Patriots |
| Trail Blazers | Jazz |
| Cowboys | Pacers |

## 10

| COLUMN A | COLUMN B |
|---|---|
| Taylor | Truman |
| Wilson | Lincoln |
| Nixon | Adams |
| Taft | Monroe |
| Pierce | Eisenhower |

## 11

| COLUMN A | COLUMN B |
|---|---|
| Columbia | Yale |
| Princeton | Stanford |
| Syracuse | Harvard |
| Brown | Michigan State |
| Duke | Southern Methodist |

# 12

**COLUMN A**
*Vertigo*
*Flower Drum Song*
*Dirty Harry*
*Bullitt*
*The Woman in Red*

**COLUMN B**
*Splendor in the Grass*
*Gone with the Wind*
*Marty*
*Alfie*
*Down and Out in
    Beverly Hills*

# 13

**COLUMN A**
*Breakfast at Tiffany's*
*The Joker Is Wild*
*The Sandpiper*
*The Lion King*
*High Noon*

**COLUMN B**
*Dirty Harry*
*The Odd Couple*
*Ghandi*
*A Streetcar Named
    Desire*
*From Russia with Love*

# 14

**COLUMN A**
Alexander Hamilton
George Washington
Andrew Jackson
John F. Kennedy
Franklin D. Roosevelt

**COLUMN B**
John Adams
John C. Calhoun
Theodore Roosevelt
Earl Warren
John Hancock

# 15

| COLUMN A | COLUMN B |
|----------|----------|
| Brazil | Canada |
| Switzerland | Mexico |
| Zaire | Iraq |
| Mozambique | Portugal |
| Belize | Japan |

# CIRCLE WORDS

A circle word is one that comes back around to where it started, ending with the same letter that it began with. A common circle word is *that*. As another example, how about *example?*

Circle words can be written in a circle, with the first and last letter sharing one space. That's how the puzzles in this section are laid out. For each you will see a single letter that begins and ends the answer, with blanks equal to the number of letters you have to fill in. Thus if you see the letter *s* and seven blanks, you know you're looking for a nine-letter word that starts and ends with *s*, such as *seventies.*

(The Mensa puzzle testers scored 40 percent on these circle words. For all but the last, the group came up with at least two answers.)

**1**

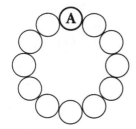

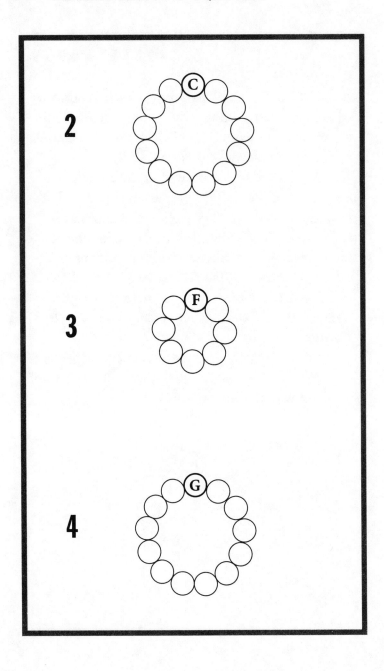

**5**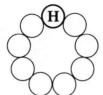

**6**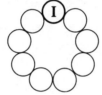

**7**

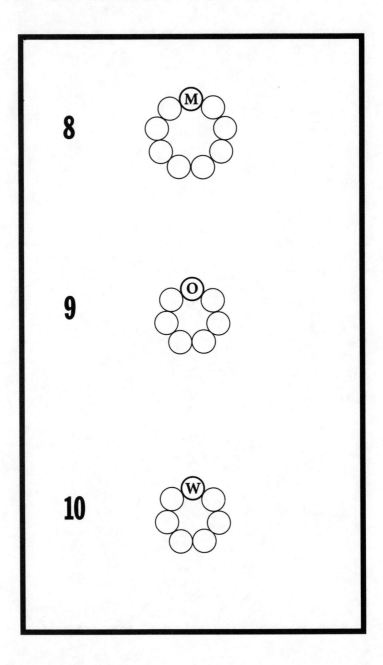

**11**

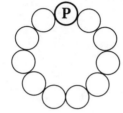

**12**

# chapter
# 3

# Jargon

Jargon is specialized vocabulary used in a particular profession, whether it's bee-keeping or bookkeeping. A punster might find a clever way to use jargon in a sentence, but puzzle solvers do things the hard way: they start with the incomplete sentence and try to figure out a word or name from the particular jargon that completes the sentence in a meaningful way.

Here are some examples using jargon from the world of art:

**1.** Can a man's _____ much about his future?
*Solution:* pastel (past tell)

**2.** The salesman was asked to _____ the neighborhood.
*Solution:* canvas

532 • THE MENSA GENIUS A•B•C QUIZ BOOK

**3.** My father watched _____ the boat ashore.
*Solution:* Miro (me row)

**4.** The defense attorney said that a mobster
tried to _____ his client.
*Solution:* frame ("Erase" could also work, but
not "rub out," because that's two words.)

As you see, the solutions both are a single word or
name from the given field *and* create a sensible sentence (grammatical, but taking some stylistic liberties).
In solving these puzzles it sometimes helps to say the
jargon word quickly. For an answer to be correct, it
must avoid mispronunciations such as "model" for
"muddle" or "sienna" for "seen a," for instance.

In each jargon category that follows, complete the
sentence with an appropriate word. Then you can show
your best *palette* is *hue* who is master of jargon.

## MATH

The sentence "I can't believe I _____ the whole thing" can be completed with a word from the world of mathematics: *eight*. The sentence "Noah built an _____" can be completed with another bit of math jargon: *arc*. The sentence "Did Attilla the _____ the cold weather?" can be completed with *hundred*.

Find the right math jargon to make these sentences *add* up.

(The "Match Wits with Mensa" panel scored 75 percent on these questions.)

**1** He came to the beach a pale man, but went home as a _____.

**2** Even in good weather, a trouble-free crossing of the North _____ be guaranteed.

**3** They had a handsome kitten and _____ puppy.

**4** She turned down the _____ on the radio.

**5** The horse placed, but never _____.

**6** Because he had little credit, his parents had to _____ his car loan.

**7** The most difficult part about being a good judge is deciding if sworn testimony is _____ fiction.

**8** Doctor grandma always told us that good nutrition comes from eating three _____ meals each day.

**9** Inflexible people have a _____ way of doing things.

**10** The _____ an enemy carrier and torpe-doed it.

## LAW

The sentence "I'll pick a _____ there's enough cotton" can be completed with a legal term: *bailiff*. The sentence "As he got older, Beethoven's _____ got progressively worse" can be completed with *hearing*. The sentence "Ghengis _____ down many enemies" can be completed with *contract*.

Use your *judgment* to complete the following *sentences*.

(The puzzle testers from Mensa were able to find correct answers 55 percent of the time.)

**1** Every citrus fruit has _____.

**2** The witness with the Cockney accent said, "When 'e made _____ 'it the other bloke's motorcar."

**3** There is copper _____ coin.

**4** At the Celtics game, the fans kept yelling "_____!"

**5** You _____ me with those chocolates, but you can't make me eat them.

**6** She enjoyed a Viennese _____ with her coffee.

**7** The best speeches are _____.

**8** A _____ of beer usually costs a little less than four six-packs.

**9** If the owners and the players'll stop bashing each other, the commissioner of the _____ try to get the parties to settle their differences.

**10** After he uses a _____ for six months, the orthodontic work will be completed.

## BUSINESS

The sentence "Dracula was _____" can be completed with business term: *account*. The sentence "She had a complete set of James _____ movies" can be completed with *bond*. The sentence "Once you cover your head with your red baseball _____ mean that you're part of the team" can be completed with *capital*.

See how many business jargon solutions you can *manufacture*.

(The Mensa volunteers scored 55 percent in this section.)

**1** He tried to move a heavy sofa, but he couldn't _____.

**2** The captain of the _____ to sail at 5:00 A.M., but he overslept.

**3** Elijah was her favorite _____.

**4** Take all the Frito _____ the top shelf and put it on the bottom.

**5** After checking the progress of my healing broken arm, the doctor made an appointment _____ removal in two weeks.

**6** The world traveler needs to know if tipping is a _____ not.

**7** These _____ were designed to stand up to ninety-knot gusts of wind.

**8** If you don't get a _____ means the most you can bowl is 90.

**9** You can't _____ and uncles for the misdeeds of their nieces and nephews.

**10** She loved old horror movies starring actors like Lugosi, Cushing, and _____.

## CHEMISTRY

The sentence "I hope the carpenter will _____ this nail into the wall" can be completed with a word from the language of chemistry: *compound*. The sentence "The wrestler had one _____ the mat" can be completed with that elementary word *neon*. The sentence "On *I Love Lucy*, the Ricardos' neighbors were Fred and _____ Mertz" can be completed with *ethyl*.

Keep your *ion* these puzzles in chemistry jargon as they stir up in your brain.

(Our Mensa members completed 45 percent of these sentences correctly on average.)

**1** The days of the past _____ forever.

**2** The horse _____ until the final furlong.

**3** The rancher compiled a _____.

**4** Why has the _____ in the repair shop for three days?

**5** The English restaurant had roasted _____ the menu.

**6** At a Stephen King movie, when ya hear _____ scream.

**7** In this parking garage, you're only charged the _____ if you enter after 6:00 P.M.

**8** _____ Williams was a great swimmer.

**9** The fighter said, "Let me _____."

**10** Although they were unsuccessful with Gerry in 1976, the Republicans were able to _____ in 1980.

## MEDICINE

The sentence "My high _____ his low diamond" can be completed with a word from medical jargon: *heartbeat*. The sentence "You can't _____ if you're over ten" can be completed with *benign*. And "The robins all _____ south for the winter," can be completed with *flu*.

Find a word in medical jargon to complete each of these *prescribed* sentences.

(At these medical mind benders the Mensa members' median measured 50 percent.)

**1** If you get dandruff, your _____ itch.

**2** Carly sang, "You're So _____."

**3** One would find _____ a list of fuels.

**4** He packed a _____ toothbrush, and a shaver.

**5** When Angela asked him for something sweet, he gave _____ cracker.

**6** He was great in thinkin' up new gizmos, but poor _____ 'em to see if they really worked.

**7** When I was a _____ bends and sit-ups were much easier to do.

**8** How _____ Lancelot be as important a part as King Arthur?

**9** The tackle was _____ forward as the half-back was runnin' to his right.

**10** Seeing little Suzy with an after-dinner _____ she had eaten all her vegetables.

## MUSIC

The sentence "The toothpaste factory donated a _____ day to a local charity" can be completed with a word from the vocabulary of music: *tuba*. The sentence "The gift box had a _____ on it" can be completed with *bow*. The sentence "The frying pan had a wooden _____" can be completed with the name of the composer *Handel.*

Find a word or a name in musical jargon to *conduct* these sentences to their completion.

(The "Match Wits with Mensa" panel scored 55 percent on these puzzles.)

**1** Mr. Capone's prison guards tried to make Big _____ the line.

**2** Thy castles art filthy and thy _____ slimy.

**3** If an individual _____ corporation, the names of the directors must be found.

**4** _____ make it too dangerous for truckers to drive through the canyon?

**5** If Nurse Barton were living today, chances are a business agent would be helping _____ substantial income for her hospital foundation.

**6** Mrs. Long wrote her will _____ penny of her fortune would go into the wrong hands.

**7** The children were trying to _____ the closet.

**8** The sheriff looked at the ruffians, spat, and drawled, "Git feathers and _____."

**9** She bought a _____ of wood.

**10** In shuffleboard, a _____ an eight is a good score.

# GEOGRAPHY

Countries may not share common languages, but they do make up a common jargon we can use in puzzles. The sentence "When I play Scrabble, _____ up as many points as possible" can be completed with the name of a country: *Iraq*. The sentence, "When a chanteuse is paid to _____ performance is unacceptable" can be completed with *Singapore*. And "First I walked, then I jogged, then _____" can be completed with *Iran*.

You'll ooh and ah and get one credit *Peru* as you correctly complete each of the following sentences with the name of a country.

(The Mensa puzzle testers answered 65 percent of these puzzles correctly.)

**1** When he walked into his _____ Spitz could see all his swimming medals.

**2** Never _____ friend into making a quick decision.

**3** Though some people can't, others _____ column of numbers very quickly.

**4** If you _____ number that ends in 3, the result ends in 7.

**5** Pants should never be excessively tight _____ too loose.

**6** Verification means making sure a statement _____.

**7** When it comes to great Cardinal hitters, many think that the leader of the _____ Musial.

**8** John and Olivia starred in _____.

**9** The head plotter whispered, "Before you begin the _____ for my signal."

**10** Her favorite jazz musician was Chick _____.

## ZOOLOGY

An animal can make sense of this sentence: "The waiter gave the _____ bag and a cup of boiling water." That animal is a *manatee*. Similarly, the sentence "If Johann Sebastian were arrested, one of his sons would have paid the bail to _____ from jail" can be completed with *springbok*. And "There's a big fine to pay if your car's _____ away" can be completed with *toad*.

*Bear* down and unleash an animal into each of the following sentences to create a sentence that can stand on its own four legs.

(The "Match Wits with Mensa" puzzle testers soared to a 60 percent score on these jargon puzzles.)

**1** The patient would often rant and _____ his padded cell.

**2** Some automobile engineers think that a well-designed overhead _____ provide more horsepower.

**3** The accused holdup man said he had to _____ order to eat.

**4** The candidate's voice became _____ after the sixth speech.

**5** It's easier to _____ guitar than a piano.

**6** Her favorite song was "Let It _____."

**7** Her parents watched her uncle and _____ and get married in Las Vegas.

**8** Riviera, Torrey Pines, and Pebble Beach are among the best _____ on the West Coast.

**9** When playing chemin de _____ is good to be dealt a four and a five.

**10** Ike told Dick, "Be careful or _____ win the election."

# POLITICS

For a field that relies on communication to the public, politics has developed a substantial jargon all its own. The sentence "It would take fifty kids to _____ Brown shoe store" can be completed with a term from that jargon: *filibuster*. The sentence "They found the weakest _____ the chain" can be completed with a highly regarded name in politics: *Lincoln*. The sentence "Would you prefer a Dirt Devil, a _____, or a Eureka?" can be completed with another presidential name: *Hoover*.

*Elect* a word or a name in American political jargon to complete these fine, upstanding sentences.

(Our Mensa members scored 65 percent on this quiz.)

**1** If you invite more guests, you'll have to _____ glasses with champagne.

**2** When I went to summer _____ Rand's book *The Fountainhead* was popular.

**3** If you lie 20 percent of the time, you're _____ times out of ten.

**4** He used an old razor and got several _____ his face.

**5** Did Rock Hudson ever help Sandra _____ a hook?

**6** If tomorrow is a hot day, she _____ herself at the beach.

**7** When you return a _____ sure not to hit it into the net.

**8** Barbie gave _____ in individuality and an A in popularity.

**9** If Muppets had a senior _____ Piggy would go with Kermit.

**10** Is that a tall _____ the truth?

## CLOTHING

Clothes don't really make the person, but the right words from garment jargon make these sentences complete. For instance, "We _____ a circle around the campfire" can be completed with the word *satin*. The sentence "He enjoyed _____ and Vietnamese food" can be completed with another word from the jargon of garments: *tie*. And "If a ship flies the Union _____ means that it's English" can be completed with *jacket*.

*Outfit* the following sentences with the right word from the rag trade.

(The "Match Wits with Mensa" panel of puzzlers racked up 65 percent on these problems.)

**1** It's difficult to _____ large car in a small space.

**2** There were two small beds and a _____ the cabin.

**3** If you want to make a traditional baseball _____ is not the wood to use.

**4** The lead male role in *The Prince of Tides* went _____ Nolte.

**5** They used to listen to Bob and _____ the radio.

**6** It's annoying to find a cigarette _____ a no-smoking area.

**7** The retired catcher kept his first _____ his den.

**8** Would the ability to make a two-foot-high _____ the coach as the minimum standard for making the basketball team?

**9** If Steve Martin made a detergent commercial for _____ Moranis could be a pitchman for Tide.

**10** Pennsylvania is known for its _____ fly pie.

# WHAT'S NEXT?

You can challenge your math skills with number sequences such as, "1, 4, 9, 16, 25, ___." (The next number is 36, the next perfect square.) But this is an A-B-C quiz book, so we have *non-number* sequences to challenge your other thinking skills. For example:

O, T, T, F, F, S, S, E, ___
*Solution:* N (This sequence is made up of the first letters in "one, two, three, . . . ")

fly, spider, bird, cat, dog, _____
*Solution:* horse (This is the next thing the "old lady" swallowed in the children's song.)

Johnson, Humphrey, Agnew, Ford, Rockefeller, Mondale, _____
*Solution:* Bush (This is a sequence of U.S. vice presidents since Lyndon Johnson.)

Complete these "What's Next?" puzzles by identifying the next item in the sequence, stating the underlying reasoning, or both.

(Our panel of Mensa puzzle testers scored 50 percent on this section.)

**1** Hillary, Barbara, Nancy, Rosalynn, Betty, Patricia, _____

**2** M, V, E, M, J, S, U, N, _____

**3** H, He, Li, Be, B, C, _____

**4** Kefauver, Lodge, Miller, Muskie, Shriver, _____

**5** A, K, Q, J, _____

**6** Argentina, Bolivia, Brazil, Chile, Colombia, _____

**7** Skies, grain, majesties, _____

**8** Deer, drop, name, long, needle, note, _____

**9** Athens, Paris, St. Louis, Athens, London, Stockholm, Antwerp, Paris, Amsterdam, Los Angeles, _____

**10** Infant, toddler, child, adolescent, _____

**11** Calgary, Vancouver, Winnipeg, Saint John, St. John's, Yellowknife, _____

**12** Badgers, Boilermakers, Buckeyes, Fighting Illini, Gophers, _____

**13** A, T, G, C, L, V, L, S, S, C, A, _____

**14** Patterson, Johannsen, Patterson, Liston, _____

**15** George, Ronald, Gerald, Richard, Dwight, _____

# chapter 4

# Pencil-Optional Puzzles

## MISSING-LETTER SCRAMBLES

Anagrams are one of the oldest and most popular forms of word games. They involve mixing the letters of a word up to spell a new word, as in turning *names* into *Mensa,* or unscrambling a group of letters into a word. Missing-letter scrambles take anagrams one step further by removing two or more of the mixed-up letters and then challenging you to solve them. For example, to each of the following groups of letters restore just two letters to make an anagram from which to form a word.

## H P Y Z

*Solution:* Add *e* and *r* to make the makings of *zephyr.*

# B J N

*Solution:* Add *o* and *a* and unscramble *banjo.*

For each puzzle below, identify the *two* missing letters and then unscramble all the letters to form a word.

(The "Match Wits with Mensa" panel answered 60 percent of these puzzles accurately.)

1     **U U V**

2     **J R R U Y**

3     **N Q U U**

4     **A B C U V**

5     **R T U Z**

6     **A A A T T**

7     **F M M O U**

8     **N N N O U**

9     **A L U U U**

10     **D F J**

11     **A B I R W**

12     **A K Q T U**

13     **B Q R U U**

These last two puzzles each have *three* missing letters. Find them and unscramble the letters to form a word.

14      **G K K L U**

15      **A I I I N N**

## LETTER SEQUENCES

Some common words contain uncommon letter sequences. For example, *vodka* has the sequence *dka*. As another example, *skiing* has the sequence *kiin*.

Try to fill out the English words that contain the listed sequence of consecutive letters.

(Our puzzle testers from Mensa successfully identified 50 percent of the words, on average.)

1      **XYG**

2      **OPSOI**

3      **UPTC**

4      **NKYA**

5     **URTSH**

6     **AKFA**

7     **NNERM**

8     **RDAMO**

9     **UEBI**

10     **NDTHR**

11     **EZVO**

12     **ALFUN**

**13**        **SQUERA**

**14**        **AELST**

**15**        **XSW**

## VANITY TELEPHONE NUMBERS

On a standard late-twentieth century telephone, the buttons are set up like this:

| | | |
|:---:|:---:|:---:|
| **1** | **2**<br>**ABC** | **3**<br>**DEF** |
| **4**<br>**GHI** | **5**<br>**JKL** | **6**<br>**MNO** |
| **7**<br>**PRS** | **8**<br>**TUV** | **9**<br>**WXY** |
| **\*** | **0** | **#** |

Some people and businesses use vanity telephone numbers, which can be dialed using letters related to what that person or business does. For example, a dog trainer may want 748-7829, which can be reached by dialing "SIT-STAY." A bodybuilding gymnasium may want 466-3227, which can be reached by dialing "GOOD-ABS."

What word or words would each of these people or businesses give out as a vanity telephone number?

(This section may have increased the vanity of our Mensa panel as they averaged 85 percent on these puzzles.)

# 1

A deli at **742-5537**

# 2

An attorney at **529-7848**

# 3

A butcher shop at **747-5646**

# 4

A classical music radio station at **332-8779**

# 5

A private detective agency at **486-7463**

## 6

A pizzeria at **262-4689**

## 7

A tavern at **268-7266**

## 8

A consumer advocacy group at **729-3325**

## 9

A cheese company at **243-3327**

## 10

A farmer at **427-8378**

## 11

A French language school at **266-5687**

## 12

A credit card company at **752-7842**

## 13

A poison control hotline at **277-3642**

## 14

A sports announcer at **465-9269**

## 15

Funk & Wagnalls at **539-4266**

# WORD MAKERS

This is one of the simplest forms of word puzzles, found in many puzzle books for young children:

> How many new words can you make from the letters in Mensa?

*Solution:* Names, means, amens, seam, same, sane, mane, mesa, mean, men, man, . . .

The puzzles in this section follow the same pattern, except that your goal is to create a word of a certain length—a fairly long length, at that—from the letters of a famous movie title.

For instance, *The Last Picture Show* contains one *a,* one *c,* two *es,* two *hs,* one *i,* one *l,* one *o,* one *p,* one *r,* two *ss,* three *ts,* one *u,* and one *w.* From that assortment one can form the twelve-letter word *therapeutics.*

For each of the following movie titles, form at least one word of the specified length.

(Between them the "Match Wits with Mensa" testers managed to find at least two words of sufficient length for each of these movie titles, except for the last. Individually, however, they averaged just 30 percent on this section.)

# 1

An eleven-letter word in
*From Russia with Love*

# 2

A seven-letter word in
*On the Beach*

# 3

A twelve-letter word in
*Down and Out in Beverly Hills*

# 4

A ten-letter word in
*Raiders of the Lost Ark*

**5**

An eight-letter word in
*Lilies of the Field*

**6**

A nine-letter word in
*You Only Live Twice*

**7**

An eleven-letter word in
*James and the Giant Peach*

**8**

An eleven-letter word in
*The Philadelphia Story*

# 9

An eight-letter word in
*A Fish Called Wanda*

# 10

A seven-letter word in
*Cape Fear*

# chapter
# 5

# Grab Bag

Now that you've learned how to do all the puzzles in this book, it's time to do them all again.

## 1 Who am I?

In rush-hour traffic, I claim,
The signature of my last name
Appears in large size
To the road-weary eyes—
Of the thousands who say I'm to blame.

Identify the following movie titles:

# 2

## DEPRIVED OF DREAMS WHILE OVERLOOKING PUGET SOUND

# 3

## THE MANNER IN WHICH YOU AND I HERETOFORE EXISTED

# 4

Abraham Jefferson Roosevelt Polk, the Hollywood producer, loved American holidays. To get into the proper mood, he had a habit of spending the evening before each holiday listening to an appropriate speech from history. He listened to a reading of the Declaration of Independence on the evening before July 4. He listened to a recital of the Gettysburg Address before Presidents' Day. One evening in 1994, Polk listened to one such speech and went to bed. Early the next morning, through no fault of his own or anyone else's, Polk found his CD player was badly damaged. Whose speeches had Polk played the night before?

Identify the following series of abbreviations:

# 5
**VANF, NEAP, ROCR, CHEV, CHOC, TINR**

# 6
**EUC, FIC, MAP, RED, SEQ, JAC, POP, MAG**

# 7

Identify the real title of this florid song (also the title of a movie):

*A trio of metallic tender located in the generator of continuous parabolic bursts of water*

# 8

Invent a threeesque that means

**RIGHT OUT OF THE DRYER**

Commoner puzzles: What do the words in the first column share that the words in the second column do not?

# 9

| COLUMN A | COLUMN B |
|----------|----------|
| Football | Tennis |
| Basketball | Volleyball |
| Hockey | Baseball |
| Lacrosse | Bowling |
| Soccer | Golf |

# 10

| COLUMN A | COLUMN B |
|----------|----------|
| Mail | Plan |
| Pairs | Grapes |
| Quoit | Pledge |
| Louse | Party |
| More | Exit |

# 11

| COLUMN A | COLUMN B |
|----------|----------|
| Grove | Part |
| Date | North |
| Handle | Pile |
| Age | Dairy |
| Or | Item |

# 12

| COLUMN A | COLUMN B |
|----------|----------|
| Thirsty | Hungry |
| Unopposed | Force |
| Defined | Yacht |
| Weighing | Impolite |
| Student | Outlasted |

# 13

| COLUMN A | COLUMN B |
|----------|----------|
| Grouch | Bag |
| Page | Gift |
| Graft | Fang |
| Zing | Brought |
| Gone | Gnaw |

# 14

| COLUMN A | COLUMN B |
|----------|----------|
| New York City | Phoenix |
| | Miami |
| Cincinnati | Atlantic City |
| St. Louis | Los Angeles |
| Philadelphia | Denver |
| Memphis | |

# 15

Complete this sentence with a term from chemistry jargon:

When an athlete turns _____ becomes part of the job.

# 16

Complete this sentence with the name of a country:

She used to stand at the piano and sing "_____ Malone."

# 17

Complete this sentence using a word from zoology:

> For the armorer to make a powerful _____ long, strong piece of wood must be cut and prepared.

# 18

Complete this sentence with a term from clothing jargon:

> When we entered the pub, we saw many old _____ at the bar.

# 19

What comes next in this sequence?

P, N, B, R, ___

# 20

What comes next in this sequence?

E, A, D, G, B, ___

## 21

Add two letters to the following assortment and arrange all the letters into a new word:

**A A C C U**

## 22

Add *three* letters to the following assortment and arrange all the letters into a new word:

**M T Y Y**

## 23

Add three letters to the following assortment and arrange them into a new word:

**H H Y**

Identify the standard English words that contain the following letter sequences (with no hyphens between the letters):

## 24
## ALDEH

## 25
## VERSM

## 26
## CKSK

## 27
## ANHO

# 28

Anita Lo, D.D.S., obtained this vanity phone number:

**345-5464**

What word or phrase does Dr. Lo tell her patients to dial in order to make an appointment?

# 29

Form an eight- or, better yet, a nine-letter word
from the letters of this movie:

*Some Like It Hot*

# Solutions

The percentages in parentheses are the "Match Wits with Mensa" results for individual puzzles.

## CHAPTER 1: NO-PENCIL QUICKIES

### LIMERICKS

1. Gravity (90%)

2. The unknown soldier (65%)

3. Hydrogen (85%)

4. The past (40%)

5. Calorie (65%)

6. Detroit (70%). Windsor, Ontario, is immediately south of downtown Detroit.

7. $i$ (55%). $i$ is the mathematical symbol for the square root of $-1$.

8. A translator or interpreter (55%)

9. Mark (55%)

## FLOWERY MOVIE TITLES

1. *Hello, Dolly* (85%)

2. *Raging Bull* (60%)

3. *West Side Story* (55%)

4. *The Big Easy* (80%)

5. *Planet of the Apes* (60%)

6. *Speed* (70%)

7. *Gone with the Wind* (60%)

8. *Leaving Las Vegas* (85%)

## STRANGE QUESTIONS

1. The 5s and the 10s (75%). A straight flush requires five consecutive cards of the same suit. Removing the 5s and 10s will allow consecutive card sequences of A–K–Q–J, 9–8–7–6, or 4–3–2–A only. This eliminates all possible straights and straight flushes.

2. 50 (50%). The word *mean* signifies the average of a group of numbers. Therefore, the missing number—along with 30, 35, 45, and 40—must average 40. This can be solved using algebra or

more quickly with the "over and under" method. Thirty is 10 under the average and 35 is 5 under the average, so the "unders" are 15 below the average. 45 is 5 over the average and the "overs" need to be 15 above the average to make up for the "unders." So the missing number has to be 10 over the average, or 50.

3. Dr. Masterson was watching or perhaps even performing in *The Music Man* (50%). "Gary, Indiana" is a song from that show by Meredith Wilson. Dr. Masterson could also have been operating on a patient named Gary Indiana somewhere else in the hospital.

4. Kucic was oversensitive to booing fans (65%). In the telephone conversation, the words *boos* and *booze* were indistinguishable.

5. Santiago played softly (70%). The musical term *piano* means "low in volume." The original word for the large musical instrument with black-and-white keys was *pianoforte* because it could be played softly or loudly.

6. The Tampa Bay Buccaneers (30%). There are numerous "bay areas," but only two have NFL football teams: San Francisco/Oakland and Tampa Bay. Driving 120 miles east of San Francisco would get you to Sacramento, but driving 120 miles east of Tampa would get you to the Atlantic Ocean. The 49ers were the visiting team.

7. Jack (55%). Pilots get upset when they hear *hijack* or *hijacking.*

8. Aluminum (40%). In England this element is spelled "aluminium" and pronounced with the accent on the third syllable. Not sulfur vs. sulphur. Both these spellings are used by Americans.

9. Golf course (95%). In golf, "shooting an eagle" means scoring two under par.

10. Postage stamps (30%). In 1997, first-class postage stamps were 32 cents each, and buying twelve stamps from a standard stamp machine with a five-dollar bill would bring back four coins: a Susan B. Anthony dollar, a dime, a nickel, and a penny.

**ABBREVIATIONS**

1. Mathematics courses: arithmetic, algebra, geometry, trigonometry, probability, statistics, calculus (90%).

2. Movie/video types: comedy, drama, adventure, action, sports, musicals, horror, science fiction (80%).

3. Orchestral instruments: violin, viola, cello, bass, trumpet, trombone, french horn (60%).

4. Television/electronics brand names: Sony,

Samsung, Mitsubishi, Goldstar, Toshiba, Panasonic, Zenith, Quasar (20%).

5. NBA basketball teams: Celtics, Knicks, Bulls, Rockets, Cavaliers, Jazz, Lakers (80%).

6. U.S. airports: New York–La Guardia Airport, Los Angeles International Airport, San Francisco International Airport, Dallas–Love Field, Seattle–Tacoma Airport, Miami International Airport, Detroit Municipal Airport (80%).

7. U.S. national parks: Yosemite, Yellowstone, Olympia, Glacier, Carlsbad Caverns, Mammoth Caves, Everglades, Shenandoah (80%).

8. Tire brand names: Firestone, Goodyear, Dunlop, Goodrich, Michelin, Kelly, Uniroyal (25%).

## FLOWERY SONG TITLES

1. "Raindrops Keep Fallin' on My Head" from *Butch Cassidy and the Sundance Kid* (95%)

2. "High Hopes" from *A Hole in the Head* (90%)

3. "When You Wish upon a Star" from *Pinocchio* (50%)

4. "As Time Goes By" from *Casablanca* (40%)

5. "Someday My Prince Will Come" from *Snow White and the Seven Dwarfs* (75%)

6. "Whistle While You Work" from *Snow White and the Seven Dwarfs* (85%)

7. "Over the Rainbow" from *The Wizard of Oz* (80%)

8. "Let's Go Fly a Kite" from *Mary Poppins* (45%)

9. "Candy Man" from *Willie Wonka and the Chocolate Factory* (40%)

10. "Everybody's Talkin'" from *Midnight Cowboy* (45%)

## THREEESQUES

1. Halllord, halllessor, halllandlord, and hallleaser (65%). If a person who owns land is a landlord, one who owns a hall would be a *halllord*.

2. Egggraph, egggram, and egggauge (75%). If a chart of pictures is a pictograph, a chart of egg production would be an *egggraph*.

3. Grimmmaster, Grimmmaven, Grimmman, and faultlessstoryteller (40%). If a chess expert can be a chessmaster, a fairy-tale expert would be a *Grimmmaster*.

4. Daleeer, hilllover, knolllover, knollloper, blufffanatic, foothilllover, hillloper, knollleaper, and knolllegger (25%). If a serious mountain climber is a mountaineer, a climber of dales would be a *daleeer*.

5. Kangarooology, Rooology, and Kangarooobservations (70%). If the study of society is sociology, the study of kangaroos would be *kangarooology*.

6. Errroom, errregion, errrealm, errrange, errrink, and missspot (55%). If a place to dance is a ballroom, a place to err would be an *errroom*.

7. Watttime, watttenure, wattterm, and stilllit (50%). If the amount of time that something is not in use is downtime, the amount of time

that a bulb's watttage is in use would be *watt-time.*

8. Odddial, or odddetector (45%). If a fellow who is odd may be an Oddfellow, a dial that is odd could be an *odddial.*

## CHAPTER 2: COMMONER PUZZLES

### MISCELLANY

1. All the things in Column A contain water (65%). They are not simply mixtures (steel in Column B is an alloy of different metals).

2. All the fruits listed in Column A end in *e*. (65%).

3. All the words in Column A can be used before or after the word *iron:* iron lung, cast iron, iron horse, iron maiden, and gridiron (70%).

4. All the items listed in Column A are gifts mentioned in "The Twelve Days of Christmas" (75%).

5. All words listed in Column A are animal names that can also serve as common verbs (45%).

6. All the elements in Column A have chemical symbols that start with a different letter: mercury is Hg, gold is Au, iron is Fe, potassium is K, and lead is Pb (35%).

7. Each word in Column A can form a new word if *ship* is added at the end (45%).

8. All the words in Column A have exactly one of each vowel (40%).

9. All the words in Column A represent things or ways one can "bear" (25%).

10. All the animal names listed in Column A end in two vowels (30%).

11. Each word in Column A can form another word if *et* is added at the end: junket, blanket, casket, socket, and market (45%).

12. Each word in Column A can form a new word if *ment* is added at the end: figment, casement, easement, pigment, and basement (30%).

13. All the words listed in Column A have a *k* sound (30%).

14. Each word in Column A can form a new word if *g* is added at the beginning: gastro-nomical, graze, gape, gloom, and glistening (30%).

15. Each word in Column A can form a new word or common expression by preceding it with the word *hard:* hard facts, hard-boiled, hardware, hard knocks, and hard pressed (40%).

### SAME-SIZE WORDS

1. All the five-letter words in Column A begin and end with the same letter (65%).

2. All the six-letter words in Column A have three of one letter *and* two of another (30%).

3. Each three-letter word in Column A can form another word with *d* added at the end: mend, bend, iced, ward, and seed (25%).

4. The three-letter words in Column A are homonyms of a letter of the alphabet: P, Y, Q, C, and O (55%).

5. The four-letter words in Column A are adjectives (30%).

6. Each of the four-letter words in Column A can form another word if its letters are reversed: time, brag, pool, part, and ward (30%).

7. Each of the four-letter words in Column A can form a new word if *a* is added at the beginning: acute, aside, awash, amass, and acorn (30%).

8. Each of the three-letter words in Column A can form a new word if *c* is added at the beginning: care, clay, chop, cone, and cape (40%).

9. Each of the five-letter words in Column A can form a new word if *r* is added after the first letter: gravel, pretty, driver, fright, and trowel (40%).

10. Each of the four-letter words in Column A can form a new word if you delete the last letter: arc, car, pea, man, and kit (25%).

11. The letters in all the three-letters words in Column A are in alphabetical order (10%).

12. Each of the six-letter words in Column A can form another word if the first and last letters are deleted: rove, oath, trip, acre, and ring (25%).

13. Each of the four-letter words in Column A can form another word if *es* is added at the beginning: escape, eschew, escrow, esteem, and essays (35%).

14. Each of the four-letter words in Column A can form another word if the last letter is changed to *x*: flux, flex, coax, crux, and flax (5%).

15. Each of the four-letter words in Column A can form a new word if *m* is added at the end: realm, harem, charm, spasm, and modem (35%).

### NAMES AND PLACES

1. All the attractions listed in Column A are in the state of New York (95%).

2. All the cars listed in Column A are European, not simply foreign (70%).

3. The dog breeds listed in Column A consist of two words (80%).

4. At the height of their chart success, the musical groups listed in Column A had four members (25%).

5. The show songs listed in Column A were written by Rodgers and Hammerstein (30%).

6. The songs listed in Column A were originally sung by a John or a Johnny: Cash, Denver, Lennon, Mathis, and Horton (30%).

7. The languages listed in Column A are official languages of one country only (15%).

8. The songs listed in Column A were originally sung by women: Doris Day, Brenda Lee, Dionne Warwick, Barbra Streisand, and Connie Francis (40%).

9. The sports teams listed in Column A represent a specific city (Chicago, Boston, Detroit, Portland, and Dallas) as opposed to a region (Minnesota, Carolina, New England, Utah, and Indiana) (25%). Of course, pro sports being how they are, this solution is good only as of the date of publication!

10. The commonly used first name of each of the presidents listed in Column A is longer than his surname: Zachary Taylor, Woodrow Wilson, Richard Nixon, William Taft, and Franklin Pierce (5%).

11. The universities listed in Column A are in

states with two-word names: New York, New Jersey, New York, Rhode Island, and North Carolina (10%).

12. The movies listed in Column A were set primarily in San Francisco (15%).

13. The movies listed in Column A won an Academy Award for best song: "Moon River," "All the Way," "The Shadow of Your Smile," "Can You Feel the Love Tonight?" and "High Noon (Do Not Forsake Me, Oh My Darlin')" (15%).

14. The famous Americans listed in Column A have had their faces depicted on money (35%).

15. The countries listed in Column A contain the letter *z* (60%).

# CIRCLE WORDS

1. Arachnophobia, anisometropia (30%)

2. Characteristic, claustrophobic, chromatophoric (55%)

3. Fisticuff, fireproof, foodstuff (40%)

4. Gerrymandering, grandfathering, groundbreaking (40%)

5. Henceforth, heliograph, hallelujah, hieroglyph, heathenish, horselaugh, hydrograph (40%)

6. Intermezzi, illuminati (25%)

7. Kickback, kinsfolk, kerplunk, knapsack (60%)

8. Moratorium, molybdenum, memorandum, mainstream, militarism, myocardium, metabolism, monarchism (50%)

9. Oratorio, ocotillo, ostinato (50%)

10. Withdraw or withdrew, williwaw, windflaw (50%)

11. Partisanship or partizanship (15%)

12. Yesterday (60%)

## CHAPTER 3: JARGON

### MATH

1. Tangent (80%)

2. Secant (65%)

3. Acute (70%)

4. Volume or power (90%); not hypotenuse— that's not close enough to "hyped-up news."

5. One (95%)

6. Cosine (85%)

7. Factor (70%), also part and pure

8. Square or solid (95%)

9. Set, solid, linear, and straight (60%).

10. Subtract (45%)

### LAW

1. Appeal, cedes, and sections (60%)

2. Attorney (60%)

3. Innocent (35%)

4. Defense (20%)

5. Contempt, bribe, and present (70%)

6. Tort (35%)

7. Brief (50%)

8. Case (90%)

9. Legal (40%)

10. Retainer or mouthpiece (65%)

## BUSINESS

1. Budget or manage (85%)

2. Shipment (55%)

3. Profit (80%)

4. Layoff (60%)

5. Forecast (85%)

6. Customer (55%)

7. Sales (60%)

8. Market (but not strike) (25%)

9. Finance (15%), not blamants or defendants (legal terms)

10. Price (35%)

## CHEMISTRY

1. Argon (90%)

2. Lead (55%)

3. Catalyst, table, and volume (20%)

4. Carbon (90%)

5. Boron (40%)

6. Ammonia (10%)

7. Nitrate (20%)

8. Ester (55%)

9. Atom (60%)

10. Electron (30%)

**MEDICINE**

1. Scalpel (95%)

2. Vein (80%)

3. Colon (45%)

4. Coma (30%)

5. Angiogram (25%)

6. Intestine (55%)

7. Kidney (50%)

8. Cancer (80%)

9. Surgeon or tendon (15%), also blocking and cutting

10. Treatment (40%)

**MUSIC**

1. Alto (80%)

2. Mozart (60%)

3. Sousa (50%)

4. Woodwind or woodwinds (25%)

5. Clarinet (45%), also score

6. Sonata (65%)

7. Haydn (55%)

8. Guitar (35%)

9. Chord, staff, and Bloch (85%)

10. Tenor (40%)

**GEOGRAPHY**

1. Denmark (85%)

2. Russia (50%)

3. Canada (80%)

4. Cuba (35%)

5. Norway (50%)

6. Israel (65%)

7. Pakistan (80%)

8. Greece (75%)

9. Kuwait (70%)

10. Korea (50%)

## ZOOLOGY

1. Raven (90%), also lion (but just *"bearly"*)
2. Camel (60%)
3. Robin (75%), not lion
4. Horse or husky (90%)
5. Tuna (50%), also paca
6. Bee (85%)
7. Antelope (45%), not ant
8. Lynx (30%)
9. Ferret (55%)
10. Jackal (35%), not eel

## POLITICS

1. Fillmore (80%)
2. Campaign (70%), not Camp David
3. Candidate (10%)
4. Nixon (90%)
5. Debate (55%)
6. Wilson (70%)
7. Lobby (30%)
8. Kennedy (75%)
9. Promise (75%)
10. Taylor (90%)

**CLOTHING**

1. Parka (90%)
2. Cotton (65%)
3. Batik (40%)
4. Tunic (85%)
5. Rayon (70%)
6. Button (75%)
7. Mitten (85%)
8. Jumpsuit (30%)
9. Fabric (20%)
10. Shoe (80%)

## WHAT'S NEXT?

1. Lady Bird (65%). This is a sequence of first names of first ladies, going back from Hillary Clinton. You get extra credit if you knew Lady Bird Johnson's real name was Claudia.

2. P (75%). This is a sequence of the first letters of the planets, and Pluto is last.

3. N (60%). This is a sequence of elements on the periodic table, and nitrogen is next.

4. Dole (15%). This is a sequence of losing vice presidential nominees, starting with Kefauver in 1956.

5. 10 or T (80%). This is a sequence of card values in poker.

6. Ecuador (65%). This is a listing of South American countries in alphabetical order.

7. Plain (80%). These are the last words in the lines of "America the Beautiful."

8. Drink (35%). This a sequence of words following the notes of the scale in Rodgers and Hammerstein's "Do-Re-Mi": "Doe, a deer... Ray, a drop... Me, a name... Far, a long... Sew, a needle... La, a note... Tea, a drink..."

9. Berlin (20%). This is a chronological sequence of cities that hosted the modern summer Olympics, starting in 1896.

10. Adult (60%). This is a sequence of growth stages.

11. Halifax (20%). To arrive at this answer, arrange the Canadian provinces alphabetically and then list the city with the largest population in each of the provinces.

12. Hawkeyes (30%). Big Ten team names in alphabetical order.

13. P (10%). These are the first letters of the astrological signs in columnist Sydney Omarr's order, and Pisces is next.

14. Ali or Clay (50%). This is a sequence of world heavyweight boxing champions.

15. Herbert (45%). This is a sequence of first names of Republican presidents, going back from Bush.

## CHAPTER 4: PENCIL-OPTIONAL PUZZLES

### MISSING-LETTER SCRAMBLES

1. Uvula (75%)
2. Perjury or juryrig (50%)
3. Unique (40%)
4. Bivouac (35%)
5. Quartz (25%)
6. Cantata or ratatat (30%)
7. Flummox (20%)
8. Unknown (30%)
9. Unusual (35%)
10. Fjord (40%)
11. Rainbow (15%)
12. Kumquat (25%)
13. Brusque (35%)
14. Skulking (20%)
15. Initiation or initialing (30%)

### LETTER SEQUENCES

1. Oxygen (70%)
2. Topsoil (80%)
3. Bankruptcy (40%)

4. Junkyard (45%)

5. Courtship (55%)

6. Breakfast (50%)

7. Innermost (55%)

8. Cardamom (25%)

9. Bluebird (30%)

10. Spendthrift (25%)

11. Rendezvous (50%)

12. Malfunction (40%)

13. Masquerade (70%)

14. Maelstrom (65%)

15. Coxswain (30%)

## VANITY TELEPHONE NUMBERS

1. Pickles (85%)

2. Lawsuit (90%)

3. Sirloin (90%)

4. Debussy (80%)

5. Gumshoe (90%)

6. Anchovy (90%)

7. Bourbon (70%)

8. Raw deal (85%)

9. Cheddar (90%)

10. Harvest (90%)

11. Bonjour (80%)

12. Plastic (90%)

13. Arsenic (85%)

14. Holy cow (75%)

15. Lexicon (85%)

## WORD MAKERS

1. Formalities, formulators, isothermals, silversmith, meritorious, liverwursts (15%)

2. Heathen, beneath, acetone, cheetah (45%)

3. Outlandishly, evolutionary, deliberation, unshovelable (25%)

4. Fortressed, fatherless, tetrahedra, rehearsals, falsehoods, terrorists (20%)

5. Filleted, hilliest, hillside (25%)

6. Violently, convolute, cotillion, evolution (30%)

7. Decapitates, emancipated, antecedents, eighteenths, detainments (15%)

8. Philatelist, diphtherial, editorially, peridotites, hospitality (25%)

9. Flinched, windfall, alliance, sandwich, swindled, hacienda, dwindles, chainsaw (35%)

10. Preface (70%)

## CHAPTER 5: GRAB BAG

1. Henry Ford, who popularized the automobile in America and whose signature is the logo on millions of Ford vehicles (25%)

2. *Sleepless in Seattle* (95%)

3. *The Way We Were* (95%)

4. Polk had played a recording of Martin Luther King Jr. Early on Martin Luther King Day in 1994 there was a powerful earthquake in southern California, which damaged Polk's CD player. (20%)

5. Flavors of ice cream: vanilla fudge, Neapolitan, rocky road, cherry vanilla, chocolate, tin roof (55%)

6. Types of trees: eucalyptus, ficus, maple, redwood, sequoia, jacaranda, poplar, magnolia (50%)

7. *Three Coins in the Fountain* (90%)

8. If being filled with care is careful, then being filled with fluff from the dryer could be *fluffful* (25%).

9. The sports in Column A are all timed games in which players can score goals (25%).

10. All the words in Column A are anagrams of world capitals: Lima, Paris, Quito, Seoul, and Rome (10%).

11. If you add *man* before all the words in Column A, they form new words: mangrove, mandate, manhandle, manage, manor (20%).

12. In each of the words in Column A there is a series of three letters as they appear in alphabetical order: *rst* in thirsty, for instance (10%).

13. All the words in Column A can form new words if their *g* is replaced by a *c:* crouch, pace, craft, zinc, cone (10%).

14. All the cities in Column A border another American state (5%).

15. Propane (10%)

16. Mali (25%)

17. Boa (5%)

18. Chaps, soles, or loafers (10%)

19. Q (5%). This sequence lists the official symbols of chess pieces in order of strength; a knight is designated as N.

20. E (15%). This is the sequence of guitar strings from lowest to highest pitch.

21. Accrual, accusal (25%)

22. Mystery, mystify, mythify (35%)

23. Highly, hyphen, rhythm (50%)

24. Formaldehyde, aldehyde (50%)

25. Silversmith (30%)

26. Buckskin (35%)

27. Manhole, manhood, womanhood (50%); not man-hour, since that requires a hyphen

28. Dr. Lo's vanity phone number is Filling (95%).

29. Eight letters: milkiest, smoothie, toilsome, homilies, homelike;
nine letters: mistletoe and homeliest (35%)

# How to Join Mensa

**M**ensa has a triple meaning in Latin: it means "mind," "table," and "month," which suggests a monthly meeting of great minds around a table. The society was founded in Great Britain in 1946 by two barristers, Roland Berrill and Dr. Lionel Ware. American Mensa was started in 1960 at the Brooklyn home of Peter and Ines Sturgeon; there were seven members at that meeting, but within three years the roll had grown to over a thousand across North America. In 1967 Mensa Canada became a separate society. As of 1997, there are more than 45,000 members of American Mensa and 3,000 members of Mensa Canada. Worldwide more than 100,000 Mensans represent over a hundred countries.

The only qualification for membership in Mensa is a score in the top 2 percent of the general population on a standardized intelligence test. American Mensa accepts over two hundred tests for membership. It also offers a battery of culturally fair, nonlanguage intelligence tests (for applicants over the age of fourteen), supervised by a certified Mensa proctor. An applicant who scores at or above the 98th percentile in any one of these exams qualifies for membership. Here are the qualifying scores on some common tests:

**COLLEGE SAT (MATH AND VERBAL COMBINED)**

| | |
|---|---|
| prior to 9/30/77 | 1300 |
| 10/1/77 to 1/31/94 | 1250 |
| after 2/1/94 | not accepted |

**GRE**

| | |
|---|---|
| prior to 6/30/94 (math and verbal combined) | 1250 |
| after 6/30/94 (verbal, quantitative, and analytical) | 1875 |

**CALIFORNIA TEST OF MENTAL MATURITY**

IQ 132

**MILLER ANALOGIES TEST**

(raw score) 66

**STANFORD-BINET INTELLIGENCE SCALE (ANY FORM)**

IQ 132

### WECHSLER ADULT INTELLIGENCE SCALE AND WECHSLER INTELLIGENCE SCALE FOR CHILDREN (ANY FORM)

IQ 132

The onetime processing fee for submitting scores from a prior test is $20. To take a supervised Mensa admission test, the fee is $25. Mensa Canada's fees for the equivalent are $25 and $40, respectively.

After an applicant's score has been accepted, he or she is invited to join a local chapter of Mensa. There are 140 chapters of American Mensa in the fifty states, Puerto Rico, and the Virgin Islands. These groups gather at least once a month, with most meeting weekly. There are also more than 150 Special Interest Groups (SIGs) that communicate regularly through newsletters and other media. The interests run the gamut from arts and crafts through chocolate, Monty Python, and skiing to zydeco music. Each year American Mensa has a national convention hosted by one local chapter. Current dues for membership in American Mensa are $45 per year. The annual dues for Mensa Canada are $55.50.

For more information please contact

American Mensa, Ltd.
201 Main Street, Suite 1101
Fort Worth, TX 76102
(800) 66-MENSA, ext. 9710
AmericanMensa@compuserve.com
http://www.us.mensa.org

Mensa Canada
329 March Road
Suite 232, Box 11
Kanata, ON   K2K 2E1
(613) 599-5897
mensa@canadamail.com
http://www.canada.mensa.org/

International Mensa (for information on other national branches of the society)

http://www.mensa.org

**MARVIN GROSSWIRTH** was a journalist and author who specialized in science, technology, and medicine.

**DR. ABBIE F. SALNY** is the Supervisory Psychologist of American Mensa.

**ALAN STILLSON** is puzzle editor for the Los Angeles chapter of American Mensa, Ltd.